Dr Jay Ludowyke holds qualifications in writing, history, and library and information services. She has taught writing at the University of the Sunshine Coast and previously worked in local government and public libraries. She has published works in literary and academic journals and is the recipient of an Australian Postgraduate Award. Of Sri Lankan and Australian heritage, she lives on the Sunshine Coast, Queensland.

CARPATHIA

JAY LUDOWYKE

THE EXTRAORDINARY STORY OF THE SHIP
THAT RESCUED THE SURVIVORS OF
THE *TITANIC*

hachette
AUSTRALIA

Published in Australia and New Zealand in 2018
by Hachette Australia
(an imprint of Hachette Australia Pty Limited)
Level 17, 207 Kent Street, Sydney NSW 2000
www.hachette.com.au

10 9 8 7 6 5 4 3 2 1

NATIONAL
LIBRARY
OF AUSTRALIA
A catalogue record for this
book is available from the
National Library of Australia

ISBN 978 0 7336 4067 4

Cover design by Luke Causby/Blue Cork
Cover image of RMS *Carpathia*, painting by Edward D. Walker, courtesy Susan Walker
Map by MAPgraphics
Author photo: Giselle Peters (Photography)
Typeset in 12/18.2 pt Sabon LT Pro by Bookhouse, Sydney
Printed and bound in Australia by McPherson's Printing Group

MIX
Paper from
responsible sources
FSC
www.fsc.org
FSC® C001695
The paper this book is printed on is certified against the
Forest Stewardship Council® Standards. McPherson's Printing
Group holds FSC® chain of custody certification SA-COC-005379.
FSC® promotes environmentally responsible, socially beneficial
and economically viable management of the world's forests.

For my parents

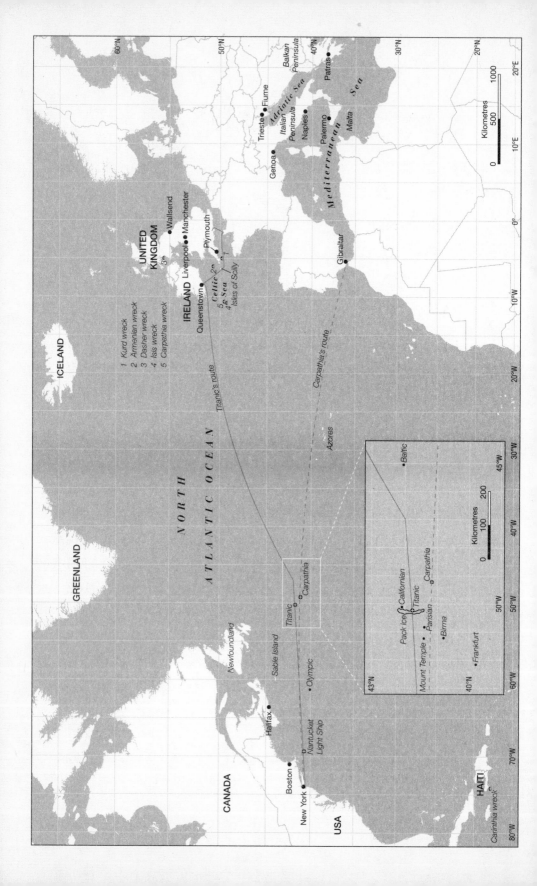

CONTENTS

TO THE READER

THIS IS A TRUE STORY. IT IS ABOUT A SHIP WITH AN EXTRA-ordinary history. In 1912, RMS *Carpathia* sailed full speed through the dark night into iceberg territory, to answer the distress call of the sinking *Titanic*. It was a brave and perilous rescue mission that has been overshadowed by the events of that tragedy, until now. Woven into this story are other facets of *Carpathia*'s history: her service in World War I, when she was sunk by a German U-boat while leading a convoy out of Liverpool; the modern search for her wreck by the National Underwater Marine Agency; and two dangerous expeditions to dive *Carpathia*, which lies at the limits of human reach.

The people and events in this book are all real, and I have endeavoured to depict *Carpathia*, and those whose lives have intersected with hers, with honesty and integrity. While writing this book, I conducted extensive historical and archival research that spans several continents and numerous archives, museums, universities, libraries, historical societies and heritage sites. Wherever possible, I have relied upon primary source material. I have also consulted maritime historians, archaeologists, technical divers and *Titanic* experts.

I constructed the historical figures in this work from the records they left behind, including memoirs, letters, periodicals, official testimonies and photographs. The dialogue attributed to these characters is either quoted or deduced from these sources, and is sometimes edited for clarity and brevity.

The contemporary portions borrow primarily from Richard 'Ric' Waring's experiences and impressions diving *Carpathia*. All of the men who dived her wreck – Zaid Al-obaidi, Helmuth Biechl, Andrea Bolzoni, Tim Cashman, Jeff Cornish, Bruce Dunton, Duncan Keates, Mark Elliott, Edoardo Pavia, Carl Spencer and Richard Stevenson – have valuable stories to tell. I chose to focus on Ric because he is one of only two men who participated in both the 2001 and 2007 dive expeditions, and he led the larger second expedition. Ric allowed me to stay in his home and interview him extensively, and in many places I use his words and thoughts.

Because this is *Carpathia*'s story I have presented the ship in a way intended to enliven her historical significance. For practical reasons, I could not cover many facets of her history, so please forgive any omissions. Writing *Carpathia*'s story has been a challenge, but it has also been an honour, and I hope it will stay with you the way it stays with me.

PREFACE

1903

ON THE BANKS OF THE RIVER TYNE THE AIR SOUNDS WITH the relentless clang of hammers striking steel. From sun-up to sundown, a metallic echo drifts up from the Swan & Hunter shipyard and rounds the small borough of Wallsend until it fades into the shadows of everyday life. The slow *thud-thud-thud* as long steel beams heated pliable in the furnace are sledgehammered into curves, then pinned to cast-iron slabs until cool. The quick *one-two-one-two* as riveters alternately strike white-hot bolts flat against hull plates, before they glow red and harden.

The North Eastern Railway follows an embankment along the shipyard's northern boundary. From behind the windows of passing trains the cacophony is dampened, as though underwater. The passengers have a choice between two views. The first, on the riverside, sees the grass sloping down from the track, down to where a crowd of navvies, capped heads bent, cut away the bank to level a new section of yard. A small company of men cluster, unsure, around something they've unearthed. Beyond them is an industrial landscape of belching smokestacks, towering cranes and wooden gantries sheltering the metal skeletons of ships under construction. In the curve of the Tyne the passengers see the black and red livery of a Cunard steamship fitting out.

The view through the opposite window is less diverting. Rows of tepid brick houses with peaked roofs and chimney stacks slip past, the homes of the men who work the yard. Most of them possess blood memories of a time long gone, which seems to have no real meaning for their lives now. A vague remembrance of what their homes are built upon.

Almost two millennia ago this place was a Roman fort on the empire's frontier. *Segedunum*: Strong Fort. Sheer stone ramparts with towers and gateways enclosed infrastructure that supported a garrison of soldiers. From its western gate ran a great stone wall that extended beyond the horizon, built to separate *Britannia* from *Caledonia*, the Romans from the barbarians. There are still remnants of The Roman Wall scattered across the breadth of England, but all that remains here is the town's name: Wallsend. Because, from *Segedunum* to the coast, the River Tyne succeeded the wall as the barrier that separated the two worlds.

Mostly.

As the men cut away the bank they encounter a line of waterlogged rubble that runs down to the river. For the first ten days they clear it with the rest of the dirt and clay, but when the rubble takes form they begin to take care as they pare back the earth. About two hundred feet from where stood the south-east tower of *Segedunum* they expose ashlar stonework and realise they've discovered ancient Roman relics of the wall.

Work stops. The lyrical tones of Geordie weave through the shipyard as the men try to make sense of the discovery. The wall runs east–west, but this section runs south. Yet, even in ruins, it is unmistakable. Six and a half feet wide, both wall faces have horizontal courses of neatly cut stone blocks. These facing stones are relatively uniform in size, ten inches high by twelve inches wide by at least sixteen inches deep, and flank an exposed core of charcoal-flecked mortar and familiar rubble.

The find evinces great interest amongst local antiquaries, and Swan & Hunter soon realise the significance of what they have uncovered. This is the literal wall's end. While the main Curtain Wall finished at *Segedunum*'s western gate, this short Branch Wall extended from the south-east tower down into the Tyne below the low-tide mark, joining wall to river.

It is a significant discovery, but the demands of the ship-yard take precedence. Before long, the wall that has existed for almost two thousand years is torn down, stone by stone. The rubble and earth from the foot of the bank are used to level the yard, rewriting history. Some of the facing stones are taken away as curiosities, some used to permanently mark the site where they were found, along with a bronze tablet that reads: *These stones were taken from the Roman Wall's End and mark the position of the wall and its course, from the camp of Segedunum to the River Tyne. May 1903.* Most of the stones are removed to a local park and re-erected in a pretty facsimile of how the wall looked when it was first built.

But that is not all. One or two pieces are placed in a glass case aboard the little Cunard ship anchored in the Tyne. The ship's name is *Carpathia*, but on these pages she is Thia.

Stone and steel. Past and present. The Roman Wall. Thia.

One is already remarkable. The other destined to be.

PART
ONE

THE BOAT RIDE

2007

THE MANCHESTER FIREFIGHTER RELAXING IN A RICKETY camp chair on *Ocean Dancer*'s deck blithely ignores the weather, intent on his magazine. Faded jeans and a British green weatherproof keep him warm and dry. Behind *Dancer*, whitecaps and foam trail like breadcrumbs before they're swallowed by the grey sea. The wash leads back to Plymouth Sound, and yesterday.

Swells splash up *Dancer*'s hull and through the open bulwark doorway. They surge across her already wet wood deck, sloshing between the side of the boat and her superstructure before spilling back the way they entered. An endless incursion and retreat.

A small group of men also reclining in camp chairs or leaning against convenient surfaces pretend they're not silently measuring the sky. In the ashy light, the orange skin of the rhib stowed at the bow seems muted. Only the yellow of *Dancer*'s inner hull and the neat rows of scuba tanks and rebreathers, in the same shade of canary, are bright against the grey. Too bright.

'He's brought his *Land Rover* magazine,' Tim Cashman says, looking at the glossy pages the firefighter's holding. His tone implies there is something amusing about Richard Waring and his reverence for Land Rovers. Some inside joke that binds them in a friendship that began with a shared interest in diving, but is now one of old camaraderie.

Ric grins good-naturedly, lets the dig slide and instead says in his gravelly Mancunian accent, 'It's a bit ravin' rough,' as the boat rocks on the swells and tilts his chair first to one side then the other, until he teeters and goes over. The copy of *Land Rover* flicks around when he tries to counterbalance, but he tips into Duncan Keates beside him, who reaches out a hand and shoves him upright while the others all snicker.

When they're not laughing at each other they talk about the things men talk about when they're alone. Privileged conversations. But they're also divers. Some of the best in the world. So they tell those stories too. Anything to distract from the possibility that bad weather will send them scurrying back to port.

Or perhaps not.

These are the kind of men who know that a ship in the harbour is safe, but that is not what ships are made for.

Once, men like them believed that somewhere out there mythical beauties lured sailors to their doom, but here is the truth: the deep blue is the siren. What tempts is its beguiling expanse of glittering waves, the salty wind and the promise of what lies beyond. Or below.

The weather in the Celtic Sea, where it meets the tempestuous North Atlantic, was always going to be their first challenge. Not the most significant or most dangerous one they're facing on this voyage, but one that will determine whether the £30000 they've risked in chartering *Dancer* will pay off, or be the most expensive gamble they have ever lost. When it comes to money, that is.

The other thing they're gambling with is their lives. Technical diving is a dangerous pastime. At the depths they're going – more than five times the depth limit of mainstream recreational diving – it's probably more dangerous than Ric's regular job fighting fires. There, merciful days are spent installing smoke alarms for the elderly and letting kids sit in fire engines.

Most people don't have a profession, much less an avocation, that entertains death on intimate terms. Ask any technical diver and they'll probably play down the risks. Cite thorough preparation and due care as allies. But it's all too telling that they never tell their wives about their close calls. When something goes wrong hundreds of feet below, that's when divers find out whether they really believe in God.

Amongst the men aboard *Dancer* is the Northern Gas Team, who use special gas mixes for deep wreck diving. They've been joined by other divers from the United Kingdom, Italy and Germany. Some of them have been diving for decades. Ric got his start when he was a Boy Scout. It was in a local swimming pool with an aqua lung. Says he flippin' loved it. That it didn't matter how cold it was or that there was no way he could afford the gear, he knew that this was something he wanted.

When he was a stupid kid he tried potholing. He and some friends bought a guide book and used it to find caves to explore. They'd clamber down rope ladders, no equipment, no experience, thinking they could see the bottom when really they were a hundred feet in the air. Eventually, one of those friends offered to sell Ric his old diving kit cheap, if Ric promised to sign up for lessons. There'd been a few too many close calls in the caves.

Ric agreed. He bought the gear second hand and joined the Worsley Sub Aqua Club. His first sea dive was at St Abbs, off Scotland. That first time defined his life. Who he was: Boy Scout. Dry caver. Who he became: Wreck diver. Firefighter. Union man. From that day, in the way of the things that are most important, diving became the mould around which everything else fitted.

It's what brings him here. Now.

Aboard *Dancer*.

Leading this expedition.

Expedition. The word conjures images of Shackleton and Hillary, and challenges that have already been conquered. Of a world where there's nothing new under the sun. Maybe that's because it's under the deep blue that the world's mysteries take shelter. Beyond the willowy incandescence where sunlight fades and blue becomes black. Amidst living fossils, sea monsters, all things imagined and all things sent there. Or that the sea takes for its own.

Over the course of history this has included millions of ships. Most fade into obscurity and rot until they're one more sand dune in a wet desert of dunes. Some few we find, even seek, before they are gone forever.

On deck, the lads are still at it. One of the Italians, Edoardo Pavia, does a credible impression of the Godfather when he rasps, 'I like to say hello to you. I just brought,' he gestures to his heart, 'the head of a horse for you. So I like you to behave as a brave man. You do understand me. We'll make a propose to you that you won't refuse. *I guarantee.*' This sets them all laughing again. They can't help themselves: at the nonsense he's uttering and the pained earnestness on his face as he strains to perfect his imitation of the Sicilian Mafioso.

But it's true. They're all brave men. Behaving as brave men do. Entertaining possibilities. Testing limits. Attempting something extraordinary. They talk quietly as they check their gear, place camera equipment in pressure-resistant housings, configure dive watches and inspect drysuits – at more than 500 feet down, wetsuits won't do. They set their weight belts, check their strobe lights, verify the nitrox mixes in their rebreathers and test their regulators. Test their emergency air tanks.

Time passes until the yellow of those tanks doesn't seem so artificially bright. Until the colour is at ease against the backdrop of water finally gone blue again. Three dolphins break the surface, arcing low and racing *Dancer*. After 36 hours and a respectable start on the crates of beer that accompanied them aboard, the team reach the waters above Thia.

NEW YORK

1912

CAPTAIN ARTHUR ROSTRON'S BLUE EYES CRINKLE AGAINST the sun as he surveys the Hudson River framed by Pier 54, where Thia's docked, and Pier 55. The bow of RMS *Olympic* is slowly eclipsing the river tableau, throwing a shadow across Thia's stern until the view is replaced by a hulking starboard profile that seems to go on forever.

When *Olympic* finally berths, the black tips of her four yellow funnels rise high above the passenger terminal that encloses Pier 59. The cavernous building hides her black-and-white hull from Thia, a quarter-mile away at the foot of West Fourteenth Street.

Arthur can't help but notice the largest ocean liner in the world. The riverbed here had to be deepened to accommodate her draught and the slip lengthened to protect her stern, and, word has it, it takes her purser nine miles to complete his daily inspection. She's a far cry from *Conway*, the tired wooden frigate in the Mersey where he spent two years learning to sail, or his first appointment on *Cedric the Saxon*, a majestic, full-rigged clipper. Yet those days weren't so very long ago. Two decades, perhaps.

When he first came to New York this shoreline was an eyesore of ramshackle waterfront structures. Then the same architects working on Grand Central Terminal flexed their protractors and gave New York the Chelsea Piers, a stately row of pretty pink granite buildings that are identical save the wrought-iron numbers lining their façade. Each pier's entrance is a grand affair. Gabled pediments rest above over-sized arches with windowpanes at the top and doorways at the bottom, sided by ornamental pilasters. Running along-side West Street and bridging the span between the scores of magnificent arches are flat-roofed corridors, though *corridor* implies less grandeur than is present, each with six separate, smaller entrances and eighteen square windows, all with a sense of perfect alignment and geometry.

Outside the blushing granite, the street teems with dockside commerce. Wagon wheels and horse hooves over cobblestones, delivering sugar and flour. Pearl barley and potatoes. Linen and soap and a thousand things needed to restock the docked ocean liners. West Street is wide, bisected by two sets of tram tracks, and it seems as though there are more carts than people.

Thia's been in port more than ten days, discharging and loading cargo, and is due to depart at noon tomorrow. There is only a small window of overlap while both she and *Olympic* are in New York and more than a few of Thia's crew weave along the hectic dockside to marvel at the superliner.

Human nature is one that makes comparisons. It's the method by which judgements are made. As her captain, how can Arthur not compare Thia to *Olympic*? The other ship is colossal. Her bridge is a hundred feet from port to starboard wing. She has a French à la carte restaurant, Turkish and electric baths, a swimming pool, a gymnasium, an atrium with palm trees, like in the most prestigious hotels.

Thia has ... Thia has none of these things.

She's only a decade old but it may as well be a century. Even *Olympic*, not yet a year in service, is about to be outclassed by a larger sister ship. Every year, bigger, faster, more luxurious liners join the world's merchant armada. The race to control the North Atlantic, as though it's a domain to be annexed, is fearsome. But Arthur knows it's wasted endeavour. The only thing more powerful than the sea is God.

—

The Hudson courses a straight line from north to south as though it was designed by man for his convenience. The river is a demarcation of territory, as so many rivers are, but between much easier places than those that lie aside the

Jordan and the Acheron. White sails snap in the breeze and smokestacks emanate from the hundreds of ships churning through its water, rivalling the stacks along its shores. So many that there is no part of the lower Hudson that can be looked upon without the sight of a half-dozen vessels, the spaces between full of fading ripples of wake.

It's a familiar sight for Arthur, a man who has lived his life at sea. He misses the feeling of a windjammer riding high, but there is no denying that the relative ease of serving as a steamship officer has allowed him to weather those years well. He's middle-aged and of average height, but attractively stern-featured. Not an easy accomplishment. Sometimes, he has a way of tilting his shoulders that draws the attention of others. It's unstudied. Enigmatic.

He was five years old when he declared his intention of going to sea to his parents, and, though they tried to dissuade him, even as a boy he was constant. It's not surprising he became Thia's captain, and before Thia, he served on her sisters, *Ivernia* and *Saxonia*. When he first came to Thia then, only a few months ago, he was not so much the stranger that he might otherwise have been. But he is the best kind of man to command her. A man who, if he must, commands with care.

———

The night passes quietly and the next morning Thia embarks 125 first-class, 65 second-class and 550 steerage passengers.

Amongst them are the Ogdens, Louis and Augusta, who are no strangers to Thia, nor to her captain, whom they've befriended during their travels. Augusta is a New York socialite. Though past the first blush, she still smiles like a young girl. Louis is a member of the Tuxedo Park elite. Fabulously wealthy, he likes to travel to distant reaches. A decade ago it was Spain, Portugal, Brazil, Uruguay and the Argentine with Augusta. After that he travelled 500 miles by mule along the slopes of the Andes in Bolivia. For this world tour, through Algiers, the Sahara, Spain, the Mediterranean and Europe, he's purchased a new camera. In the not too distant future, Louis and Augusta will become godparents to Arthur and his wife Minnie's only daughter.

As he does before every voyage, Arthur takes a few moments of privacy in his cabin. He kneels on the Brussels carpet and removes his cap. Cunard issue and worn by all the officers, the cap is dark blue with a gold emblem of a crown and a rampant lion surrounded by a laurel wreath. As he is captain, there are oak leaves embroidered around its brim. Arthur bows his head and prays for a safe voyage. He lives his life close to nature, and it makes him feel keenly that there is a Higher Command. This belief brings him strength and comfort.

From the pier the mooring lines are cast off, like clasped hands releasing. Thick and sinewy, the ropes are coiled on Thia's capstans. She pulls cautiously away from Pier 54 into the Hudson's slim stretch, the place also called the North River. Other ships and boats press so close to her hull that passengers can call tidings across the way. So close that they need hardly raise their voices and the chatter drifts clearly across the river's surface. Some vessels travel upstream, destination in sight. Others, like Thia, have just embarked.

The distinction between the banks is never so clear when standing upon one, looking towards the other; the contrast between the Jersey Shore and the tall buildings of Lower Manhattan never so unadulterated as it is from the river. Hoboken, Jersey City and Bayonne lie in fifteen miles of unbroken cityscape, the people as dolls amongst rows of poor-girl dollhouses, square and beige and dirty.

None of the passengers milling about Thia's decks notices the dirt as they look on the last land they will see until the Rock of Gibraltar. It does not seem to be dirt, more a veneer of indefinable brownness. The hundreds in steerage know that brownness intimately: it is the colour of their tenements.

Then Thia passes Liberty. It is a strange thing, the feelings those pretty verdigris shades evoke. The unique experience – for my happiness is not your happiness – that accompanies each voyager who stands on the deck of a ship and follows the curve of her arm, open and aloft, and bearing light. What Liberty means to those travelling upstream is evident. For those travelling downstream it is not always so clear. For them she marks the start, not the end, of a journey.

She is a marker of many things. Her diadem is an emblem of the seven seas and, like her torch, a symbol of enlightenment. Perhaps this means that when men sail the deep blue they invariably change the world. But then, change and enlightenment are often indifferent. One thing she marks is a message. To all who look upon her. From all who've looked upon her: Make of me what you will. Through me, you.

Thia can also be thought of as a marker. But her message is different. It's difficult to divine, but she will tell it to Arthur. He is not afraid to carry the truth.

1907

Five years ago, when Arthur was serving as chief officer aboard *Campania*, he saw something.

'Keep clear of the snag right ahead,' he said, Lancashire accent strong.

Harry – H. C. Birnie – junior officer, Scotsman and reverend's son, altered course a point. He was the only other person on the bridge. As *Campania* drew nearer, Arthur and Harry became puzzled. What on earth was it? The size, the shape became more distinct, but no more logical as they watched.

Here is one of those facts that just is: a thing in the water is gone too soon. A boat, flotsam – you cannot make them stand still so you can stare. You cannot run back for a second look. You have only the approach and that moment of passing to gape. And the moment was not long enough for Arthur or Harry.

'It's alive!' So startled was Arthur by the realisation that those words were unconsciously exclaimed. The thing's neck was a full foot thick, supporting a head that rose nine feet out of the water, and it was no more than fifty feet from *Campania* when she passed. *Ah, but for a camera.* He had never wanted one so badly before, nor was he likely to again, but, thinking quickly, he began to sketch on a nearby surface before it passed from view.

As they watched, the thing looked about, turning its head for all the world as a bird will on a lawn between its pecks. He could not make out its features, but surely those were bulges where the eyes would be, and tiny ears angling out of its head.

And then it was gone.

When *Campania*'s captain returned to the bridge that evening, the first question he asked Arthur was, 'Have you seen anything?' He expected a reply about Galley Head, for they were off the coast of Ireland and his last order had been to keep watch for it.

'Yes, sir.' And then this followed: 'A sea serpent.'

This earned a look from the captain. 'What did you drink for dinner?'

Deliberately, airily, Arthur replied, 'Not had my dinner yet, sir.'

'Then what did you take in your cabin after I left the bridge?'

'Haven't left the bridge since you saw me, sir.'

Then he showed the captain his sketch.

Arthur was not likely a man who enjoyed the impressionists. The straight lines with which he drew the thing appear as though they were executed with a ruler. No hesitation. No exploratory strokes. It is almost childish in its simplicity: a vertical neck rising true out of the water, perfectly uniform in thickness and topped by a flawless oval head. But it is unlikely a child could manage such elegant simplicity. Such functional accuracy.

On the sketch the small ears, if that's what they are, protrude, antennae-like. About them there is an endearing quality – the life in an otherwise inanimate image, more technical in nature than fantastical.

'I saw it, too, sir.' With Harry to corroborate, their account was hard to refute, and the captain continued to ask them, interestedly, about the thing in the water. But doubt will always accompany such tales.

Only two years prior, Rudyard Kipling had been aboard *Armadale Castle* when it struck and dragged a thing, for fifteen minutes, that was over fifty feet long, and which its passengers could not agree to be fish, whale or shark. There was some suggestion that whatever it was be called *Piscis Rudyardensis*, as though to suggest it was as real as Mowgli or Shere Khan, just a thing from one of Kipling's books.

That Arthur and Harry's thing inhabited their captain's mind well past that night is clear. One might wonder if, were it possible, he would have wished himself upon the bridge. If, given the choice, he would have chosen to be present so he could believe, or absent so he did not have to.

The Friday following the encounter Arthur answered a knock upon his cabin with an invitation to enter.

The captain stepped across the threshold. 'Did you see it, Rostron?' he asked simply.

'Yes, sir.'

1912

In the wake of the contemptuous incredulity displayed by landsmen ignorant of the fathomless potential of the deep blue, there is a secret tradition amongst seafaring men who, but for a brave few, decline to communicate the existence of things in the sea. But, there are sufficient instances on record that make a formidable body of testimony.

Arthur Rostron has never, will never, be afraid to testify.

He is true, like the Hudson, no deviations, flowing to the Atlantic. That is not to say either is easy to divine. No man or thing ever is. For example, the place where the Upper Hudson becomes the Lower Hudson is called the Narrows. But can the place where one becomes the other be pinpointed so easily? This place is only a mark on a map, or it is two opposing shores, but it cannot be the water. If a man called Frank stood on the banks of Brooklyn and looked at the water that lay between him and Staten Island and said, *This water is the Narrows*, it would be true. And if the next day Frank stood on the banks of Brooklyn and looked at the water that lay between him and Staten Island and said, *This water is the Narrows*, it would be true. But it is not the same river and he's not the same man.

Thia, too, is like the Narrows. The place where one thing becomes another. Swan & Hunter gave her quadruple expansion engines and twin screws, but they could not foreswear masts and sails; they still cling to the wind. And when she passes through the Narrows, it is like *one thing becoming another* meeting *another thing becoming another.* And they may commiserate, understanding that no others but those similarly cast can comprehend what it is to be caught in the place of the in-between. Of having the shared fate of being forever stuck in that place with no chance to become unstuck.

But what is on either side of Thia's threshold?

The past and the future.

She is the first day of an industrial evolution.

And when Thia emerges from the Narrows she is in the Lower Bay, and then the Atlantic, eastbound, a thousand souls in her care.

BELLS

2007

IN EVERY SCHOOLYARD THERE IS A PRIME LOCATION. THE tyre fort that provides cover from adult eyes. The shady spot under the trees by the water fountain. The bleachers beside the football field that balance exposure and convenience in one tidy equation. When *Dancer* arrives at Thia's location, someone is in her spot.

Meet *Janus II*. Not just a boat, but an oceanographic survey and subsea intervention vessel. A 30-metre catamaran equipped with a system that, in spite of sea movement, current and wind, can maintain a stationary position over set coordinates. *Janus* achieves this through a combination of computer-controlled propellers and thrusters. Azimuth thrusters are pod-like and can rotate to any horizontal angle, like a rudder, while side thrusters on the bow enable

Janus to move port or starboard independent of the main propulsion system. This allows the ship to turn without moving forward. *Janus* is a technological marvel controlled with a joystick.

She's also French.

While the team aboard *Dancer* are British, Italian and German, *Dancer* herself is Dutch-built and flies under Panama's flag of convenience. International law requires that every ship be registered to a country. In Panama, ship owners can register online, are allowed to employ cheap foreign labour and pay no income tax, though Panama makes half a billion dollars in associated revenue. Panama also has jurisdiction over the vessel and is the only authority to which owners are obligated when it comes to safety and crew conditions. This much latitude is why tiny Panama has the largest shipping fleet in the world.

While *Janus* is a product of the technological age, *Dancer* was built in the sixties as a beam trawler. Amidships she used to have outrigger booms to drag nets across the seabed, which is why her deckhouse is aft. Her function has changed but not her décor. She has a green hull with a thin yellow stripe and a hint of red above the waterline. There are four bunk berths to each of the cabins, with ensuite showers. Dunc Keates and Ric Waring share because they both snore like mad. Carpet below decks, wood trim on the fixtures. In the mess, drab brown bench seats surround fixed tables, like diner booths.

Despite the dated décor, she's more luxurious than the boats the lads normally dive off. Larger, too. At 33 metres, *Dancer*'s bigger than most of the liveaboards in the United Kingdom. She's just a touch longer than *Janus*, who is the flagship of Comex, the ocean research company commissioned by Thia's salvors, RMS Titanic Inc., to survey her and recover artefacts from her wreck.

Where *Dancer* is long and sleek, *Janus* is heavy. A pronounced superstructure sits well forward, leaving room aft for survey equipment and underwater rovers. Her hull is a white canvas, save two wraparound stripes: one azure, the other navy. *Janus*'s decks stack over multiple levels, like mezzanines, with open aluminium safety railings to maximise visibility.

Ric stands beside the other lads and looks over the distance that separates them from the gleaming white cat, named for the Roman god of time. They're asking questions for which he has no answers.

'They're sat right over the wreck. What if they won't move? Props on a boat like that, they're not normal screws. It'll be like diving under a blender.' That's a problem. It's not the only one.

'What if they've already got the bell?'

'If *we* get the bell, will we have to give it to them?'

'Or anything else we bring up?'

On the bridge, *Dancer*'s skipper John Mayo Evans picks up the radio handset. '*Janus, Janus, Janus*, this is *Ocean*

Dancer. Come back, please. Over.' Yorkshiremen tend to pronounce *over* like *ower*.

The French like *ovair*. 'Ocean *Dancer*, this is *Janus*, go a'ead. Over.'

'We've got divers aboard wantin' to dive the wreck below y'. Over.'

'We are engaged in surveying the wreck. Over.'

It becomes clear that a meet is required. On *Dancer*, a derrick lifts the rhib while several of the lads guide it over the gunwale. Another half-dozen men hover, ready for action. Eager for it.

When *Dancer*'s rhib ties up alongside *Janus*, five men climb onto her deck. 'Welcome aboard. Paul-Henry Nargeolet.' The man waiting for them extends his hand. 'I'm leading this survey operation.'

'Nigelly?' The name is familiar and theirs is a small world. 'From the *Titanic* expeditions?'

'Yes.'

Once, Paul-Henry was a commander in the French Navy, a minesweeper. Now he is an explorer of the only realm on Earth that defies delineation. One of *Titanic*'s most frequent callers, he has searched her out dozens of times over the past decades, often in a submersible named *Nautile*. Many of these expeditions were on behalf of *Titanic*'s owners, RMS Titanic Inc. He was recently appointed as the director of their underwater research program. Since they also have salvage rights over Thia, Paul-Henry is the natural choice to lead the team aboard *Janus*.

That team consists of recovery and conservation technician Donald Angel, consulting underwater archaeologist Kenneth Vrana, registrar and archivist Rebecca Parker, education specialist Cheryl Mure, and consulting materials conservator David Galusha, all working for Titanic Inc. There are also independent contractors involved: the Center for Maritime and Underwater Resource Management, Conservation Solutions, Nautilus Marine Group, Maritime Heritage Consulting, and Comex. Given the many different stakeholders, the lads from *Dancer* soon come to refer to them all simply as Comex, since that's who owns and crews *Janus*.

'You plan to dive the wreck?' Paul-Henry asks them. 'Have you . . . dived this deep before?' Those aboard *Janus* have trouble believing the divers can make good their intentions – that even the attempt isn't foolhardy.

The men talk about the issues raised by two ships, on different missions, wanting the same spot on the playground.

'Thing is,' the lads say, 'you're sat right over the wreck. Makes it hard for us. We're concerned about comin' up under you. Your props are a bit of a hazard.'

'What do you want us to do?' Paul-Henry asks.

'We were hopin' that you might move to the stern and leave the bow clear for us to put our line down.' The lads wait. *Janus* was on site first. They can choose to share Thia or make things very difficult, and certainly more dangerous.

Paul-Henry considers the request. His team has already had a week or so with the wreck. He understands the desire to uncover the ocean's secrets. It is a desire they all share, but these men explore the deep blue without a submersible to keep them safe. His reply is measured. 'We have survey work to perform, but we do not wish to impede your diving. We can work from the stern.'

The lads are relieved. But that's only the first round. 'We need to make sure you're okay with operatin' around our shot line. It'd be a bad thing for us if you got fouled with it, especially while we're down. It's got our deco stations and emergency gas.'

The shot line is how divers find their way safely home. They tie it in to the wreck and it runs back up to the surface. After they descend along the line they attach strobe lights at the bottom so they can find it again. Secured along the way are decompression stations with emergency air tanks. Given the potentially fatal repercussions if these men cannot access their backup oxygen during the long hours of decompression, *Janus* has a moral obligation not to endanger them. The two groups continue discussing practicalities. Both are . . . *curious* . . . about the other. So they share a little. Their intentions, sometimes their hopes.

'And artefacts?' the lads ask. How upfront should they be? Certainly they want to recover artefacts. Most wreck divers do. They want the usual: ceramics, telegraphs, portholes, lanterns – anything brass or copper – silverware, glassware. And those are just the rote items of a shipwreck. Oh, the things that lie at the bottom of the sea.

On Thia, both teams hope to find the silver loving cup that belonged to her Captain Rostron. Other than that, there is no expectation of treasure. Not the fanciful kind, like the gold found in 1998 aboard the ninth-century Belitung shipwreck discovered in the Gelasa Strait. She yielded the largest Tang Dynasty gold chalice ever found. How Chinese treasure came to be aboard an Arabian ship wrecked off the Indonesian coast is still a mystery. Or like the half a billion dollars in silver and gold coins found earlier in 2007 at a site dubbed 'Black Swan', that came from the Spanish frigate *Nuestra Senora de las Mercedes*. Or like the quarter of a billion dollars of diamonds – just diamonds – that were lost with *Titanic*.

Of the millions of ships the deep blue has claimed, it is still hiding most of them. Finding lost treasure is not something from centuries ago. It is something with no end in sight. The British SS *Gairsoppa* was lost only recently, in World War II. Somewhere below, her holds are full of water and seven million ounces of silver. There are infinite cargo holds still secure in the deepest reaches. Well beyond the grasp of a group of technical wreck divers.

The treasure on Thia that would please the lads most?

'Have you found her bell?'

———

The first bell Ric ever got was off a liner owned by the Hain Steamship Company. Ric was diving a wreck off Anglesey when he found it. Even now, years later, it remains the biggest bell he has ever found. But more than that, it still does its job and strikes a chord.

For a wreck diver, finding a ship's bell is like the high of the win, the fix, the pearl. They'd give their eyeteeth to become a member of that elite club. It begs the question, why are bells so special? They're beautiful, certainly, patinaed by the deep blue or polished back to gleaming. One of the most beautiful things that can be recovered from a wreck. But that's not why. At least, not alone.

Every ship has a name, as though she is *vivit apparatus*, living machine. Her bell carries her name. It's engraved or cast on the waist. When a ship passes hands she's often give a new name, but the original is always retained on her bell. And a name is everything. It eclipses culture, has meaning and carries power. Names are conferred, earned, sacred, secret. They are legal, religious, magical. Naming is the first act of identity, and bells are name bearers, which means that no other artefact is as unassailable a means of identification as is a ship's bell.

Ric doesn't know much about the Hain shipping line, so after finding that first bell he plays detective. Researches the history of the line and finds out that there is another wreck off Scotland, in an area he knows well. A sheltered spot in the Outer Hebrides. This new wreck is over 260 feet down so he's pretty sure that no one's dived it. He calls around and gets a group together. They hire a boat and head up for a week of diving.

The first time they go down they find Hain's crockery, so they know they're on the right wreck. But no bell. They dive some more, but still no bell. Finally, they move on. Wrecks off the British Isles are not needles in haystacks. There are plenty of others around to try their luck, but they can't resist and before the week's up, they come back for one more try.

Ric cannot think why, but for some reason he is the last in the water on this dive – the last down. He's so intent on his search that when he finally takes his bearings, he realises that he's lost. He tries to find the shot line but all the strobes have gone off it, removed when the others made their ascents. Only his is left and he is struggling to find it. *Right. Sit down. Look around.* Even though it's the shot he's after, he sees a hull plate. It's right there, *so what the hell* . . . He lifts it. And there's the bell, sat under the plate.

The story ends with him finding the line.

Another time he remembers well is on the wreck of SS *Armenian*. Fourteen hundred mules destined for the Western Front sank with her when she became another war casualty. They call her the Bone Wreck. The History Channel made a documentary about the search for her resting place, the kind with beguiling underwater cinematography that makes people wish they were braver. Though the documentary crew find *Armenian*, they never find her bell. Someone scores her numbers so the lads go and dive her.

While he is down there Ric searches the bow, same as the film crew before him, but does no better. As he is swimming back to the line he sees the mast to one side. He checks his watch, but he's already been down awhile and there is no time to search the mast's fall. He goes back to the shot line, which is secured to the *Armenian*'s bridge, and pokes around under some hull plates. It's worked for him before.

It works this time, too, and he finds the little bridge bell. Ships have bells on both their masts and bridges, but the mast bell is the most coveted because it's the largest. Ric's still keen for a try at the *Armenian*'s mast bell, and a few weeks later he finagles a place with another group going off to dive her.

As they're sailing out, the skipper, who at some time in the past lost one of his toes to a conga eel, says he doesn't want to see any of them using GPS since no one else has the *Armenian*'s numbers. A ship's numbers are precious. Trade secrets.

'Chris,' Ric says, 'we dived this the other week. This is how it lies.' He sketches an imaginary diagram. 'I got the bell off the bridge. Bridge is here. I think the main bell will be on the mast on the seabed, here.' He indicates, then glances at the others. They're not the men he usually dives with and are staring at him like he's . . . he can't figure it . . . like he's a lunatic. Like they think he's spouting off and doesn't know jack.

It stings a little. He could have kept silent, but that's not who he is.

When they shoot the wreck the line goes down near the stern, so it's a long swim to the bow. One of the divers finds a telegraph trapped on the bridge. Ric sees him trying to loosen it off, but doesn't stop to help. He locates the mast and swims down the fall and sure enough, there's the bell, sat on the seabed. Two bells off the famous Bone Wreck. *Flippin' great*. He bags it and sends it to the surface while he finishes his dive.

When he gets topside the story has changed. Turns out the lunatic is actually the hero. That's flippin' great too.

———

On *Janus*, the wait for Paul-Henry to answer their question seems interminable. Even if they can't keep the bell, just to be able to say they found it would be enough. But if Comex already beat them . . .

'No. We haven't found it.'

The divers summon their best poker faces. Pretend the answer hasn't made their bloody day. Thia's bell is still down there.

MAURETANIA, LUSITANIA, CARPATHIA

c. 1900

IN AN OFFICE IN NEW YORK, A MAN IN HIS FIFTIES TAKES
a blank cream card from his desk drawer and scribbles *Feb
23* in black ink above the printed red seal of The Liverpool
and London and Globe Insurance Company. Then, lower:
*Dear Commodore, I cannot find Caronia or Carmania in
either the* Enc. Britannica *or the* Enc. Americana. *The others
I give you as opposite. Yours faithfully, Charles H. Marshall.*
He flicks to the inside leaf and heads the page *Lusitania*
before beginning a new line. *A district of ancient Hispania
(Spain). The country of the Lusitano.* Here he refers to a
breed of horse from the Iberian Peninsula, closely related
to the Andalusian, the Spanish warhorse. Underneath, he
writes a new heading. *Mauretania. An ancient kingdom of
Africa inhabited by a people called the Mauri.* Latin for

Moors. *Bounded on the north by the Mediterranean and on the W. by the Atlantic Ocean.* His hand slides across the fine texture of the linen stock to the blank page opposite, where he writes one final heading: *Carpathia.* He considers what he gleaned from the *Britannica,* whose entry was far more informative than the few words recorded in the *Americana. The country of the Carpathian Mountains – a great central European chain 800 miles long enclosing Transylvania and Hungary – Heights from 200 to 9000 feet. Main water shed* – a watershed is a drainage divide created by high land that separates basins, as in a dividing range – *between the Northern Seas and the Black Sea* – He ends in a dash, as though he has more to say, as though the Carpathian Range sparks his interest more so than the district of Lusitania or the kingdom of Mauretania, but there he stills. Everything from the untidily scrawled lines that slant upwards, the scribbled ampersands and the stark, uncrossed t's indicate his haste. It will have to do. Before he can change his mind, he folds the note closed and sets it aside to be delivered to Cunard.

A VIOLENT SIROCCO

1912

THREE HOURS AFTER THIA LEAVES NEW YORK THE SHORE is replaced by a blue horizon that extends in every direction. Above, a seabird spirals on the cold air currents while below, the continental margin gently descends to the abyssal plain. A plume of dirty white smoke pumps out of Thia's distinctive funnel, unfurling behind her like a banner in the breeze.

The salt air is invigorating. Thia's crew are at ease, her passengers even more so. For the former it's one more voyage in a long line of voyages, but for the latter there is a sense of collective anticipation. A sense of setting off.

Most of the steerage passengers are visiting their countries of birth, the people and places they left behind when seeking a better life. Those in saloon class – first and second class – are embarking on an adventure, or so they hope. One that holds the promise of sun-drenched Mediterranean landscapes and a life less ordinary.

It was the desire for that kind of life, one of roaming, which prompted the young Arthur to run away and try to join the crew of a sailing ship. He'd been heartily disappointed when they took one look at him and sent him home.

Growing up in the heartland of the industrialised northeast he could easily have worked in the Bolton cotton mills, like his father and grandfathers, or in any of the machine or chemical works, foundries or collieries, like his brothers. He'd staunchly refused. His father had finally compromised and sent him to a merchant marine school, the best one on the Mersey, which promised to turn the sons of gentlemen into officers – though Arthur is no son of a gentleman. Just the son of a man who worked hard and wanted the best for his children.

Arthur has children of his own now. Three boys, the youngest not yet five. So he understands more readily why his father resisted him going to sea.

In 1892, Arthur almost died on a sailing ship. It was on the barque *Redgauntlet*. He was only 22, and it was his second voyage as a mate. After leaving Liverpool they'd rounded the Cape of Good Hope, been blown too far south and spent three days amongst icebergs. While sailing for Adelaide, off South Australia they were confronted by the most fearsome electrical storm Arthur had ever seen. For six hours the flashes were so blinding they defied description.

But it was neither the icebergs nor the lightning that did them in.

One pitch-black night while Arthur was on the first watch and *Redgauntlet* was passing below New Zealand, the wind freshened until it became dangerous. He ordered the royals lowered. When the first mate relieved him at midnight, Arthur told him about taking in the sails. He was not pleased to hear the other officer give the order to loose them a few minutes later.

Outranked, there was little Arthur could do.

A half-hour later, a vicious southerly gust knocked *Redgauntlet* sideways. The sound of her cargo of coal shifting was like an artillery barrage. The next burst of wind sent her sails aback, ripping them from the yards. Huge swells pushed her onto her beam ends, her lee rail and lower yardarms dipping into the ocean.

Arthur joined the crew, clambering up the slanting masts as waves swept over them and the gale hounded them. As he desperately tried to furl the tattered sails, swells ripped out the bolt ropes, flinging them about like cracking whips, and the wind shrieked through the rigging like a million raging demons.

With every moment Arthur expected to be swamped. As he clambered down from *Redgauntlet*'s mast he found the deck underwater up to her hatches, and that the waves had washed away the submerged railing. He took half the watch down into the hold and they worked to trim the ship so she could right herself, shovelling coal until they were wet with sweat and covered in black dust. As long as *Redgauntlet* remained on her beam ends they remained in mortal danger.

Finally, the wind eased. It took three days to shovel the coal even, clear the deck wreckage and repair the sails. Two decades later he vividly remembers that brush with death. But it wasn't enough to sour him on sailing ships. The boy he was always imagined discovering the world on a windjammer. He'd even sworn never to go into steam. But all boys worth their salt become men, the kind who make sacrifices to provide for their families.

After *Redgauntlet* reached port he still needed six more weeks afloat to qualify for his master's ticket, and another sail voyage would take the better part of a year. So instead he signed on to a steamer, a bug-infested old tub called *River Avon*, and saw the Mediterranean for the first time. After that, as billets in sail became harder to find, he took a job with Cunard, which eventually led him to Thia.

She's not a bad old boat, and by now he's quite reconciled to being a steamship captain. For one thing, he enjoys the social aspect. People change aboard ship, or so Arthur's always thought. Men thaw, throwing aside the cloaks they wear on shore and allowing the spirit of possibility to take hold. They are more themselves or, perhaps, the best part of themselves. The men who share his table at dinner often come to his cabin and talk until the early hours. Nothing of great note – just, as the walrus said, of cabbages and kings.

Carlos and Katherine Hurd examine their cabin on the shelter deck. Katherine is a beautiful woman, fair-skinned with long, golden brown hair. Her blue eyes light up as she inspects the whitewashed walls and polished hardwood fittings. The berths have spring mattresses. There is a handsome washbasin, a large mirror and an electric light.

Carlos relaxes in the sofa seat, upholstered in hair and velvet, and watches his wife. 'Happy?'

She smiles and nods.

They'd originally intended to book their European tour on a new German liner, SS *Berlin*, but when she was signed over to a charter group they were forced to change their plans. Thia was their second choice, and, although she's smaller and slower, they have no complaints with her appointments.

As his wife settles in, Carlos's attention is caught by several broadsheets lying on a shelf in the cabin: morning editions of the New York papers. He picks up a copy of *The World*, the sister paper to the *St Louis Post-Dispatch* where he's worked for the past twelve years, and begins to riffle through the pages.

He'd visited the paper's headquarters on Tuesday. It had been first on his list of places to see, though last on Katherine's. Per her request, he'd left her in bed sleeping after more than a day and a half of train travel. They'd departed Union Station in St Louis on Easter Sunday and upon arriving in New York had been overwhelmed by the reality of a city of five million, with an endless flow of people, streetcars, and buildings whose size was beyond anything they'd ever imagined.

The *New York World* building was no exception. Standing on Newspaper Row – officially Park Row – alongside other skyscrapers belonging to the city's papers, the structure was twenty storeys of ornate Renaissance revival, crowned by a golden cupola. Upon arriving he paid his respects to Charles Chapin, one of the greatest city editors who has ever lived. Chapin could only spare a few minutes to chat. After that, Carlos inspected the giant pressroom – the paper has the biggest circulation in the country – then rejoined Katherine for sightseeing more to her taste.

In their stateroom, a headline on page seven catches Carlos's attention: '*Titanic* Tears the *New York* From Dock'. They'd seen *Titanic*'s sister ship *Olympic* in port today and her sheer size is mindboggling. The news is a day old, a special cable dispatch from Southampton. He scans the article: *The new White Star liner* Titanic *started on her maiden voyage from this port to-day . . . she had a great send-off, crowds coming from London to examine the luxurious accommodation . . . biggest vessel afloat . . . can carry 3,500 passengers and has a crew of 800 . . . is under command of Capt. E. J. Smith.*

The article describes a near miss with the American Line steamer *New York*, dragged from her mooring by the suction of *Titanic*'s triple screws, and concludes by naming some of her high society passengers. As Carlos reads the names, he notes the list is one of unusual distinction. *Col. John Jacob Astor and Mrs. Astor, who embarked at Cherbourg on their return from their honeymoon trip . . . Mr. and Mrs. Isidor Straus, Mr. and Mrs. Washington Dodge . . . Benjamin Guggenheim . . . Mrs. E. D. Appleton, Major Archibald W. Butt . . . Col. Archibald Gracie . . . Mr. and Mrs. Frederick Spedden . . . the Countess of Rothes.* It's a veritable who's who of the rich and famous.

After finishing with the paper Carlos folds it neatly and returns it to the shelf, then he and Katherine head out to better acquaint themselves with Thia. They spend their days making other new acquaintances, relaxing on deck, playing shuffleboard, ring toss and other deck games.

———

On Saturday, Louis Ogden brings out his new camera. Arthur is keenly interested in it. They spend a few minutes posing for snapshots on the boat deck. While Louis takes the photograph, Augusta perches on the steps that lead up to the bridge, one of Thia's white ring buoys gently resting against her knees. Arthur stands beside her, one arm wrapped around the steel balustrade. Next, Louis and Arthur stand, like hunters, one foot on the deck and one on the bottom step, the white buoy that reads 'S.S. Carpathia' propped against their bent knees. Arthur is glad for the company of his friends and pleased that the outbound voyage is already proving to be far superior to their previous voyage – the one that brought them to New York – where Thia had been bedevilled by unwelcome guests.

———

When steward Robert Vaughan serves dinner one evening during that troublesome March 1912 crossing, his attention is snared by a dissatisfied comment from one of the men at table.

'We'll soon be on a big ship and away from this lousy food.'

Robert follows the gaze of the man speaking – one of the ship's musicians – to the object of his scorn. The food atop the blue-and-white china plate is hardly lousy. Plainer than the dish it's served upon, which is to say plainer than some might prefer, but generous and hearty.

As their steward, it is hardly Robert's place to quibble with any of the small group of men dining in the second-class smoking room. In the absence of second cabin passengers, they are using the room as a mess hall for those aboard whose jobs don't fit easily within the traditional roles of a ship's crew. Primary amongst them are Thia's three bandsmen, two of whom are departing for greener pastures when she makes New York. They've been offered positions aboard a new ship. There is also the baggage master, ship inspector, and Harold Cottam, ship's telegraphist. Robert is the youngest man there, if seventeen can be considered a man.

The electric lamps glow softly against the hardwood panelling as he sets out serving dishes. The two departing musicians, French cellist Roger Bricoux and pianist William Theodore Brailey, happily inform their companions about their new appointment.

They have all been dining together for a month. When Thia left Liverpool in February after her annual maintenance, it was on a special cruise carrying English tourists to the Mediterranean. She was already due there to pick up immigrants for transport to America. The tourists transferred to a different Cunarder to return home while Thia continued to New York in March, and without any saloon passengers the smoking room was free to use as a mess hall.

The trouble began after Thia left Palermo.

'Did you hear what happened?' one of the men asks.

Robert looks up at the question, which sobers those present. Though the crew try to keep the news from Thia's passengers, it passes from seaman to steward to engineer to trimmer, as easily and rapidly as gossip is wont to travel amongst a crew at sea. Those more senior, and in this room he is the least senior, always have the most accurate information. Closer to the horse's mouth, as it were. The mess halls are forever ripe with these kinds of conversations. Perhaps because the ritual of mealtime, with the camaraderie it entails, binds a crew together.

'Electric Spark's not pleased,' one of the men says.

That's what Cunard's employees call Arthur, an appellation his officers use when engaging in a bit of friendly ribbing, the crew when they curse him. He's a captain with high expectations and endless energy.

Indeed, when the Electric Spark first heard about it, he was determined to continue as though nothing was amiss. As though below decks, in steerage, a symbol had not appeared. A black hand, on Thia's pristine white bulkheads.

Thia's steerage, consisting entirely of Italian and Sicilian immigrants, has been transformed into a little Italy, redolent with the melodic tones and pungent smells of home. To service the passengers there are Italian cooks, stewards and stewardesses, and an Italian doctor and purser. There's even a complement of Italian ship's police, and, not least, Italian Mafiosi – because the bad comes across the Atlantic just as easily as the good.

In Italy, in the wake of unification, the *Carbonari* – charcoal burners – evolved, or devolved, one could say, into *La Mano Nera* – The Black Hand – a sect within the Mafia. What was once a society devoted to revolution, that had inspired Serbia's Black Hand, and that was peopled first by nobles and scholars who met in the wilds of the Apennines around smoking coal pits, fuelled by the fire of patriotism to unify the states of Italy into a single kingdom, has fallen far from grace. Their symbol, the charcoal handprint, has been corrupted into an emblem of extortion.

These criminals come off the liners that trade in immigration as easily as any of the other hundreds of thousands of Italians who come to America in the transoceanic flood. It is not the first time they have ever been aboard Thia, assigned to the Mediterranean as she is, but this is the time they most make their presence felt, and Arthur is not happy about it. 'Clear it off with turpentine, Mr Elson,' he orders the bosun who reports the vandalism. 'Then whitewash the wall.'

But it's to no avail. The next morning *La Mano Nera* appears again.

Then again.

And again.

Black stains in Thia's alleyways, executed with an insidious defiance that indicates an organised presence. One that eludes the vigilance of her police and crew, though this is unsurprising. Painting the emblem surely takes little time compared to the removal process that follows. But then, destruction usually requires far fewer dues than restoration. The balance is unequal. Things tainted, whether they be corporeal or intangible, such as one's sense of safety, can never regain the same state of grace. Restoration is an illusion. The cracks are still there. The stains below the surface.

There is always a cost.

Cost is something the Mano understand well. As masters of extortion, they advise a reluctant constituency of what price must be paid for the simple pleasure of ensuring their lives continue unchanged. Such a business model can only be sustained if clients receive value for their purchase. Therefore, the Mano deliver letters, signed only with a black hand: *Pay Mano not to bomb your shop. Pay Mano to let you live. Pay Mano to return your child.* Letters that, perhaps even now, circulate in steerage. But this is not Thia's first encounter with the Hand.

1909

When American Consul William Henry Bishop guides his wife, Sheba, up Thia's gangplank in April, they struggle against a swarm of steerage passengers surging from the tender boat. The 'console' was ostentatiously called to come first, but with the true lack of restraint he has come to expect from the Italians during his six years in their country, they do not wait for him to comply.

The two Sicilian men who escort the Bishops scan the crowd warily.

In the distance, Mount Pellegrino towers above the ancient port city of Palermo. For millennia this promontory has provided a clear panorama out past the natural harbour into the Tyrrhenian Sea. First for the Phoenicians, then later the Carthaginians, Romans, Byzantines, Normans and so forth. A few streets away the *Cattedrale di Palermo* is a mosaic and marble tapestry of these civilisations, beginning life as a Byzantine basilica then a Saracen mosque before being reconsecrated as a Norman church. Romanesque architecture, in addition to Catalonian Gothic, Renaissance and Baroque influences carve their way across the cathedral's façades, testament to ages of transfiguration. A ring of mountains, called Palermo's mounts, fortify the basin where the city lies, formed by the ancient rivers Papireto, Kemonia and Oreto.

The city is the glorious product of its occupations, a natural stronghold, encircled by the deep blue and the towering ranges. It is little wonder that it is the home of the Sicilian Mafia – the *Cosa Nostra*, as they call themselves – who hold the city as surely as any who occupied it before them.

Sailboats fleck the harbour, small and white compared to Thia's bulk, as the Bishops stand on her deck taking one last look at the city that has been their home. Thin spectacles perch high on William's nose above a sedate white walrus moustache, the corners stirring in the hot wind.

The two Sicilian detectives who accompany the Bishops are vigilant, as they and their brethren have been for weeks. They were assigned to protect the consul when William received the letters, signed only with a black hand.

The price asked of him? That he do nothing.

It seems such a simple request. In order for your life to go on just as it is, do nothing. But then, no request from *La Mano Nera* is ever simple. It began three months ago, in New York.

———

It's January, 1909. The man who calls himself Simone Velletri, an Italian-Jewish merchant, is careful to keep his gaze casual as he glances around the bustling afternoon dock before boarding *Duca di Genova*, en route for Genoa, though his final destination is Palermo. He calls himself Velletri because every Black Hander on both sides of the Atlantic knows his real name: Lieutenant Joseph Petrosino, the first Italian appointed to the New York Police Department and commander of the Italian Squad.

More than three decades ago Petrosino was a young immigrant at a time when fewer than twenty thousand Italians had voyaged to New York. But now, more than half a million populate the city and amongst them the Black Hand are a transoceanic pandemic, perpetrating crimes on a scale unmatched by any other criminal element.

At first the Mano prey only upon their own people, but increasingly they turn to English-speaking residents. Neighbourhoods like Little Italy and Italian Harlem have no respite. The Mano take advantage of the way Italian victims are reluctant to cooperate with an Irish police force that does not understand them – not their language or their ways. Not *omerta*, a code of silence which decrees that honourable men are not informers.

Petrosino's appointment to the police force marks the beginning of a change. As an Italian American he understands both the victims and the criminals, the long history of the Mano. He establishes himself as an incorruptible cop, trusted by Italians. He is not a perfect man. Not averse to using violence when the law can do nothing.

Still, the Mano's power grows until, in the space of only a few years, they are suspected of more than 300 murders nationwide. When the police uncover more than fifty bodies buried at the New York offices of the *Unione Siciliana*, the city is shrouded in horrified disbelief. The association was once a charitable organisation formed to help new Sicilians in America, but the Mano corrupted it as surely as doubt corrupts faith. They turned it into a slaughterhouse.

Finally, unremitting bombings across New York City prompt the formation of the Italian Squad: Italian-speaking detectives who, under Petrosino's leadership, finally begin to claim back power from the Mano. The officers pioneer new techniques, donning disguises, pretending to be ordinary Italians, infiltrating the Mano and gathering evidence against suspected members. They cultivate informers and develop methods to handle explosives, the Mano being fond of dynamite. The five-man squad sends over five hundred Black Handers to prison. A new police commissioner enlarges the team to include 25 men whose identities are kept from the public. To combat a secret society, they create a secret service: the Italian Legion.

Throughout this war it becomes clear to Petrosino that while some of the Mano are poor, uneducated and unskilled Italians who turn to crime in order to survive, there are hundreds, if not thousands of Black Handers who have criminal records in Italy. Men they could deport.

The possibility tantalises him and he requests to undertake a covert assignment. He asks the police commissioner to send him to Italy to compare the names of suspected Black Handers against Italian *polizia* records. If successful, he may fundamentally change the criminal milieu of New York forever. Change the city's destiny.

As he boards the boat to Italy, Petrosino wants to put the monsters back in the box. But they have tasted the new world and will not go.

———

The letters the Black Hand sent to William Bishop say that if he does not stop his investigations, he will be punished even more severely than Lieutenant Petrosino – and punish the lieutenant they did. Petrosino was murdered.

If William were asked why he is aboard Thia, leaving Palermo, he would say that he is simply taking an annual leave of absence from his post. But people who intend to return do not sell all of their furniture and pack what remains into 21 steamer trunks, then vacate their premises for their replacement. William is glad to be going. He is sick of this place. It has made him weary. But would he admit aloud his feelings of relief at leaving Sicily, where the Mano, whose grip is centuries old, are so much bolder? Where they did not hesitate to assassinate Joseph Petrosino in a darkened piazza in Palermo?

Even in New York the consul will be conscious of the danger in a way he could not seem to make the police officer feel in the two weeks he knew him. As consul, William represents the interests of Americans in Sicily, so Petrosino had sought his assistance when he first arrived. They met almost daily. So many conversations where William tried to make the man understand that New York and Sicily are very different beasts. That the ocean separating them is more than simply geographic.

'Have the Black Hand agents never tried to kill you in New York?' William had asked.

'I have been threatened many times but I am not afraid,' Petrosino replied.

'But the danger is much greater here, in Sicily,' William persisted.

Nothing seemed to penetrate. The man took far too few precautions for William's peace of mind. Petrosino was not attempting some simple feat: the Mano would not leave their new territory willingly. And they were aware of Petrosino's presence in Sicily from newspaper accounts of his 'secret' mission. Registering at his hotel under an assumed name and growing his beard were not precaution enough.

'You're too easily recognisable,' William mused. 'You look like Napoleon.'

'Yes, in New York they call me a second McKinley.' President McKinley was often called the Napoleon of Protection because of his resemblance to the emperor and his changes to American tariff and import laws.

'You asked my advice about this meeting, Joseph. You should take the *Carabinieri* with you for protection.'

But Petrosino refused the police escort. It was one of their last conversations. Perhaps William should have insisted, because the resulting weeks have been the most trying of his life. Certainly he has not lost that life, yet, but if he keeps pressing the local authorities to find Joseph Petrosino's assassins there are strong indications he will.

Two letters, signed with a black hand, demanding that he do nothing.

In his heart he believes that the murderers will never be caught. No Sicilian will talk – *omerta*. Petrosino, although he had been born in Italy, was an outsider. It is little wonder the authorities can find nothing. But if William leaves on this steamship, who will press for answers? If he walks back down Thia's gangway, will he live? The detectives cannot remain by his and Sheba's side forever. Would staying in Palermo even make a difference?

And this city has given them a snarling adieu, a climax to all his unpleasant memories.

First, Thia is unable to take aboard any cargo due to a strike and so is to leave port quickly, transforming what should be a leisurely departure day into one that is harried. Then she changes her moorings from the dock to the offing, and the consular boat that is to take them out runs hopelessly for an hour in dangerous seas before giving up. Instead, they are forced to join the tender boat leaving from the emigrant pier. But the shipping agent resists lading their baggage. Eventually, William and the vice-consul and his aide of health are forced to go out and sit upon the bags and refuse to move unless they are loaded. William suspects the agent is in league with some evil gang, and that he means to detain their baggage and loot it in the belief it contains Petrosino's papers, the work he completed before his murder.

As the consul stands at Thia's railings and stares across the harbour, a violent sirocco stirs the air. The hot dusty wind abrades, like the city. Like the Mano. He will be glad never to feel it again, so long as he lives.

There is much to do in New York and he chooses to look forward, not back. He must deliver information about his investigations into Petrosino's death to the police commissioner – he has far more to say than the brief telegram of weeks ago that began *Petrosino shot* and ended *Dies a martyr.* He must deliver a plan to the State Department that will, he believes, reduce the instance of Italian criminals travelling aboard ships such as Thia, making their way to America's Atlantic ports. Passports should have photos, not just general descriptions. Immigration laws need to be enforced, new ones enacted.

And he'll get to visit his son at Annapolis.

The Italian detectives remain aboard only until Thia clears Palermo. As though once she's out of the waters around the city, the Bishops will be safe from the Mano. As though no Black Hander ever boarded a ship and crossed the Atlantic.

1912

When the Black Hand insignia appears on Thia, three years later, soon after Arthur becomes her captain, centuries of inculcated oppression from the east of the Atlantic join three decades of new terror from the west. The *Unione Siciliana* slaughterhouse, the bombings and kidnappings, the fall of the Mano's staunchest opponent Joseph Petrosino, the American consul's escape aboard Thia: all of these events, and the thousand other stories of the Mano – cross yourself – swirl in the minds of those in steerage when they see that symbol. And really, why should the Mano bother to conceal their presence? In the three years since Petrosino's assassination, Black Hand crime has doubled. Thia's sleek black hull may protect her passengers from the icy Atlantic, but there is little to be done about the scourge within her steel plates, about the symbol that she can't seem to be rid of, reminding them that no matter what ocean they cross, monsters follow.

HUNTING

2000

'SO, YOU BEEN HUNTIN'?'

Prominent maritime archaeologist James Delgado directs his question to the man sitting adjacent, Clive Cussler. They're in a small office teeming with bookshelves, in Vancouver's maritime museum: a glass and brick A-frame that sits on the south shore of the harbour between the city's tallest skyscraper, crowned with a revolving restaurant, and Stanley Park. On the far side of the park is Lions Gate Bridge, named after the twin mountain peaks visible to the north.

In front of James and Clive, the surface of a coffee table is covered by a hydrographic chart and a black-and-white still of a lifeboat.

Most people who wonder about Thia in the years after she sinks only ever wonder. They might possess the inclination, but neither the resources nor the expertise to find her. While there's more than one man with this trinity, the one who goes hunting is Clive. He's found dozens of lost shipwrecks over the years. *Mary Celeste* off Haiti. *Invincible* off Jutland. *Ivanhoe, Rattlesnake,* another *Invincible* – these three American vessels. Ship names are often reused, even Thia's one day.

As a bestselling author, when Clive first started looking for wrecks he funded the expeditions out of the proceeds from his novels, some of which feature a hero who belongs to a fictional marine exploration organisation. Eventually, Clive set up a non-profit foundation dedicated to preserving maritime heritage. In a humorous tip of the hat, the new board of trustees named the foundation after Clive's fictional one: the National Underwater and Marine Agency. NUMA.

A while later, when Clive wrote a book about his real-life wreck-hunting experiences, it sparked a documentary series. A team formed comprising him, James, father and son dive experts Mike and Warren Fletcher, and the documentary's producer, John Davis. The men collaborate in their searches for lost wrecks. All three – the book, the documentary series and the men – are called The Sea Hunters.

The first ship in their sights is Thia. Clive is curious about her fate, so in early 1999 he started researching. He located British and French hydrographic charts that show an unidentified wreck near Thia's last reported sighting. It was a promising lead, enough for him to bankroll an expedition; while he wished he could head it, his wife's poor health kept him close to home.

Clive hired Graham Jessop and his company Argosy International to investigate. In 1981, when in his early twenties, Graham helped his father recover roughly US$80 million in Russian gold from the sunken HMS *Edinburgh*. Graham chartered *Ocean Venture* and in September 1999 he, Captain Gary Goodyear and *Venture*'s crew sailed out of Penzance and headed south-west to the wreck site recorded on the charts. But it wasn't as simple as arriving at the right latitude and longitude. That only put them in the vicinity. They still needed to find the exact location below, in an area which, courtesy of German U-boats, is a mecca of underwater gravesites.

After hours of hunting with sonar, methodically, patiently – ask anyone who hunts wrecks and they'll say what's needed, above all, is patience – they found something. Something the size and shape of Thia, eleven kilometres east of her last reported position. The monotony of the search gave way to anticipation and growing belief. A belief so strong, Graham publicly announced that Thia had been found. It was too deep for their divers so the crew dispatched a rover. It sent back images of the wreck.

'Yeah, we went out in September,' Clive replies to James's question about hunting, hands linked on his left knee, thumbs steepled. He's an older man. Weathered, but still fit. He says *we* as though he was aboard *Venture*. As though he wishes he was. 'Thought we had it.'

When he talks there's so much life in his face, which, coupled with his silver hair and beard, would make him a dashing Saint Nick. Fitting, as Nick's the patron saint of sailors.

'But it turned out to be the *Isis*. Soon as we got a ROV down we found four blades instead of three on the propellers,' he continues.

The media, however, had reported the discovery of *Isis* as the discovery of Thia, based on Graham's misidentification. It was from then that Ric and the Northern Gas Team started thinking about diving Thia, unaware that she had not actually been found.

'Then we brought up a dish that said Hamburg American Line,' Clive says, 'so we started researching.' They found out that *Isis* went down in a storm and only the cabin boy survived. 'Then the weather turned bad and beat us out, so we're going back next month to try again.'

———

Mike Fletcher and the Sea Hunter documentary crew join the second expedition in May 2000. With the chart wreck eliminated, a search area is calculated based on different but nearby sets of coordinates uncovered from the logs of Thia and two other vessels in the vicinity when she sank, HMS *Snowdrop* and SM *U-55*, which each recorded what they believed was her last position.

The search area is almost five hundred square kilometres. Although *Snowdrop* and Thia both report she sank at its southern end, *Venture* begins the hunt using the numbers she'll encounter first: the northern position reported by *U-55*.

'Fish goin' over,' first mate John Mayo Evans, who'll eventually skipper *Dancer* for the lads, says into his radio as Mike guides the side-scan sonar across the gunwale and down the hull. Then *Venture* oscillates in a grid pattern, sailing parallel lines while scanning with both forward and side-scan sonar, as well as her magnetometer, mapping the ocean floor. They call it 'mowin' the lawn', because it resembles the way a lawnmower moves back and forth cutting grass.

A magnetometer detects metal, like a metal detector, and also the Earth's magnetic field, like a compass. Today's prevailing theory is that the combination of the Earth's rotation and its molten metallic core creates a self-sustaining dynamo, causing magnetic currents to flow between the north and south magnetic poles. The currents extend thousands of kilometres into the cosmos, creating a force field that deflects solar wind, a deadly combination of charged particles and plasma that flows at hypersonic speed from the sun. When the planet's outer magnetosphere is overwhelmed, as during a solar flare, plasma is funnelled along the field's magnetic lines to the poles. What results is the most extraordinary light show in the world. The auroras are solar winds knocking hard, and Earth's shield answering. Iron and steel carcasses on the seabed attract Earth's magnetic fields, creating anomalies. Magnetometers detect these, and use them to find the things the sea hides.

The side-scan sonar looks like a featherweight torpedo with fins. It is trawled behind *Venture*, emitting sound waves from either side that angle down to the seabed. The reflected waves produce an acoustic underwater map.

For three fruitless days this map shows only virgin seabed as *Venture*'s crew search the north side of the grid until they are well south of *U-55*'s numbers. Conscious that the mid-region is the least promising, they bypass it and head for the southern reaches, near the numbers reported by *Snowdrop* and Thia. Twelve hours later the sonars ping.

The men look to their other instruments. 'The mag is decreasing,' Mike says. 'We've passed the strongest part of the target.'

The crew hover as Mike and Gary inspect the black-and-white image the side-scan returns. But as with their first expedition, Thia resists being found. From the sonar they can tell it's part of a destroyer, name unknown. Before they can continue the search, reports of gale-force winds send them scurrying to Baltimore, Ireland, the nearest port. The village is almost as far south as one can go in Ireland. A lush emerald jewel that meets the wild Atlantic, littered with summer homes and a bay full of shipwrecks.

When *Venture* enters the channel between the mainland and Sherkin Island, heading into the harbour, she passes a stark white pillar high on the eastern cliffs. A beacon for sailors; locals call it Lot's Wife. Soon after arriving, Graham and John Mayo Evans head up Castle End, a road which fittingly does end in a small castle, to the local dive shop, Baltimore Diving and Watersports Centre.

It's a logical place to ask about shipwrecks. There, they meet John Kearney, the dark-haired Irishman who owns the centre, and tell him about their search for Thia. Kearney has a friend who runs a Spanish trawler in the area, and he gives them some old charts showing hook-ups off the coast. Nets are expensive: when they snag on the seabed, trawler captains are careful to mark the numbers so they can avoid the area in the future. Kearney examines the charts with the Sea Hunters and they find seventeen possible targets while waiting for the weather to clear.

When it does, they return to the search area. Then they mow the deep blue, day and night, sailing from one number to another, like a dot-to-dot puzzle. Over the next few days they eliminate sixteen targets, until only the last remains. There's a saying: it's always in the last place you look. And that's true. But it's never in the last possible place. Just the one that ends the search.

Time is not on the Sea Hunters' side. *Venture* must return to Penzance at day's end. So when the side-scan hits on the seventeenth and last hook-up, they claw hope down, afraid to trust. It's unlikely that this is that last place. But hope is relentless, not least because the sonar paper shows a clear profile and the mag readings indicate a strong anomaly. Even with inclement weather approaching, there is no debate. They have to send down the rover.

Mike hauls out the bite-sized explorer from a small cargo container on deck, conscious of the grey swells and clouds that extend to the horizon. They load the rover into the white metal casing that will house it until it reaches the seabed, and act as a relay point with the ship. The casing rocks as they lower it over the side, thudding against *Venture*'s hull. But it never makes the ocean floor.

Somewhere in the many metres of umbilical that runs from *Venture* to the housing, and the hundreds more on to the rover, there is a tear. Salt water shorts the system and the monitors stay stubbornly blank. They haul the rover back in and take it apart, but the damage can only be fixed on land.

Maybe the wreck is Thia.

Maybe it's not.

But time is up, and the question remains unanswered.

VIRGIN WRECKS

2000

BEFORE THEY TRY FOR THIA, RIC WARING AND OTHER members of the Northern Gas Team first dive *Dasher*. A commercial fisherman tells Richard 'Richie' Stevenson about the virgin wreck four, five years before they attempt her. *Dasher* is an Avenger-class escort carrier. Her keel was laid down in Pennsylvania, 1939, and when she launched it was as the merchant ship *Rio de Janeiro*. Then the war happened, the second one, and she became just one more thing that didn't turn out as planned.

In New Jersey they made her over as a carrier, then she was commissioned into the Royal Navy through the lend-lease scheme where US resources, including ships, were supplied to the Allies. In 1943 she went down from a cata-strophic internal explosion, cause unknown – but, you can be sure, widely speculated upon. The United States blamed the British for poor fuel-handling procedures and the British blamed the United States for poor design. Whatever the sin, it hardly matters now. She is where she is, at the bottom of the Firth of Clyde, the deepest coastal waters in the British archipelago, between the Isle of Arran and Scotland's wild west coast.

No one knows exactly how deep, but she's rumoured to be close to five hundred feet. Richie tells the lads about her. Only a few years ago, amateur diving of anything deeper than 165 feet was prohibitive. While *Dasher*'s depth is now possible, if they dive her using open-circuit scuba tanks then the hours needed for decompression – the penalty – will leave them with virtually no bottom time. So they let her be.

But they don't forget her.

In 1999, the lads reconsider *Dasher*. Richie, who operates his own dive business, has got them certified to use Trimix gas. To complete his qualifications to be able to teach other divers to use the mixture of helium, oxygen and nitrogen, he had to conduct his first training course while monitored by an instructor. He persuaded the lads to be guinea pigs and gave them a deep discount. Ric Waring probably wouldn't have bothered otherwise. But he's damned glad he did.

Breathing regular air at depths below 165 feet is like diving with cotton wool in your head. Your vision narrows. You feel drunk. Look at your contents gauge and instantly forget what it says. Forget what you've seen post-dive. That's all happened to Ric. You can even lose consciousness: it's called nitrogen narcosis and comes from breathing air, which is 78 per cent nitrogen, while it's under elevated pressure. Trimix uses helium as a substitute to lower the nitrogen level, which alleviates the narcotic effect.

Also, by this time, the lads are using rebreathers instead of scuba tanks. Rebreathers look like rectangular, hard-shell packs. One of the most popular brands is Inspiration, nick-named the yellow turtle because of its canary shade. Where an open-circuit scuba-tank system discharges exhaled gas directly into the water, in an effervescent trail of bubbles, a closed-circuit rebreather has a scrubber that absorbs the carbon dioxide and recycles the unused oxygen so it can be 'rebreathed'. Trimix and rebreathers mean divers can go deeper and stay longer, pay higher decompression penalties.

The Northern Gas Team belong to a small number of elite divers who have pioneered technical diving in the United Kingdom, eroding depth limits in pursuit of virgin wrecks like *Dasher*. Like Thia.

In bounce dives, divers are hardly at depth for more than a moment. It's about how deep they can go. Saturation diving, on the other hand, requires divers to live for extended periods in pressurised underwater habitats. This allows them to undergo fewer decompressions, and these are gradual, measured in days. Technical divers can under-take the same number of decompressions in a week as a saturation diver does in six months. The longer a diver is down and the more frequently they decompress, the greater the risk of decompression sickness.

Most technical divers know someone who has died from this condition, or from hypoxia or hyperoxia or hypercapnia . . . or any of the things that can kill a diver besides simply drowning. Divers who use an Inspiration rebreather have another name for it: yellow box of death. Other brands have their own macabre nicknames. Divers and their black humour. Sometimes it's all they've got.

The month before they dive *Dasher* in September 2000, the lads lose one of their own on a practice dive. His name was Andy Wilde. They had been diving a deep wreck off the coast of Plymouth. During decompression, Ric sees Andy spit out his mouthpiece then hit for the surface. He never sees him again.

2007

Diving Thia, more than 250 miles out to sea, puts them far from help. Much further than they're used to when diving coastal wrecks. The Sea King helicopters at Culdrose navy base have a range of 200 miles. It would take *Dancer* seven hours to reach a rendezvous point. With land almost 20 hours away, they chose her because she can withstand a gale at sea – touch wood – but she also has a recompression chamber aboard.

The hyperbaric chamber can be used to treat decompression sickness, which occurs when gases that dissolve under pressure solidify into bubbles inside the body after depressurisation. It's most common in the joints, and the lads have all had the bends, as it's called, but this normally wears off after a couple of days – though they might suffer when they get older, who knows? More seriously, decompression sickness can cause seizures and paralysis, and can affect the brain, spinal cord, heart and lungs. Severe cases can kill and, given the depths they will be diving on this expedition, it's a significant concern.

During the voyage out to Thia the lads test the hyperbaric chamber, but when they blow it down to pressure one of the pipes bursts. Fortunately, the chamber is empty. Being inside during instant depressurisation would be very bad.

2000

In early 1999, while Clive Cussler's thinking about Thia, Ric and a few of the lads drive up to the Clyde and take a boat out to survey *Dasher*. See whether she really is feasible. They find her lying deeper than expected, at around 550 feet, but her shallowest point is only 425 feet. They decide to try her, and begin to organise an expedition and look for sponsorship. But the most important thing they do is seek permission from the Ministry of Defence.

When *Dasher* sank, she took men with her. More than half her complement. One moment she was home to over five hundred sailors, the next their fiery prison. They screamed in pain. Called out to one another. Called out for help that did not come. The air smelled of petrol scorching alongside metal and flesh. Men were plunged into icy, hypothermic water, and searing flames as the ocean burned.

The British authorities tried to conceal the accident. Perhaps to stop the casualty of morale that accompanies such a meaningless loss, but more likely they were anxious not to alienate their wartime benefactors. They may have believed the Americans were at fault due to poor design and construction, but they weren't about to say that. Instead, they told the fourth estate not to report on the disaster; they told the survivors not to speak of it; and, in the final abuse, they told the families they were burying the dead in unmarked graves. And that is what they did.

The team spends months working with the Ministry of Defence to alleviate the concerns that arise from diving such a sensitive wreck, a war grave, but they are finally granted permission and issued with a comprehensive code of conduct. But waiting for this permission costs them.

If the Northern Gas Team had a rival it would be the European Technical Dive Centre. The lads aren't happy that in June 2000, three months before they plan to dive *Dasher*, their rivals beat them to her. It's a small community and their plans were no secret. The lads see it as deliberate poaching and it breeds ill feeling between the two dive groups.

The European Technical Dive Centre conduct a bounce dive and lay a memorial plaque on the wreck. They're only there for a few moments, but there are no prizes for second place and now that they will no longer be the first, the Northern Gas Team lose their sponsorship. They wear the expense and continue anyway – Ric, Richie, Mark Elliott and a few others, since these expeditions rarely comprise people from only a single team. There are always divers who have to pull out at the last moment, substitutions, and those keen on a particular wreck who know someone who knows someone who gets them an invitation to join the group.

Zaid Al-obaidi and Richie like fast descents and they have a bet about who will reach *Dasher* first. Zaid wins. The lads call him the Bald Iraqi, after his hair fell out when his home was bombed during the Iran–Iraq War. Mark – who is English and lives in Cheshire – they call Eric the Viking on account of his thick blond hair.

When Graham Jessop announced that Thia had been found in September 1999, she became the talk of the dive world. *Dasher* lies at almost the same depth as Thia, but much closer to shore. And so, *Dasher* becomes a trial run for Thia, who is now the prize mule, the most coveted wreck in the United Kingdom.

And the lads are determined.

No one will beat them to *her*.

MULE SHIP

1912

ON SUNDAY MORNING AT 7.30, AS IT HAS EVERY MORNING
since embarkation, a gong sounds in second class. Katherine
Hurd snuggles deeper under the blankets, reluctant to stir.
There's a polite knock at the door and a maid calls good
morning, before moving on to the next cabin. Finally,
Katherine and Carlos rise and begin dressing. They leave
their room and head to the dining saloon. Breakfast is
the usual buffet offerings: fruit, oatmeal porridge and
milk, fish cakes, hot rolls, soda scones, corn bread, toast
and preserves, scotch pancakes with golden syrup, and a
selection of hot cooked meats and fried foods.

After breakfast they retire to the promenade deck.
Inevitably, someone from first class comes to the little division fence between their two promenades and peers over

curiously at the second cabin passengers who in turn peer over the end of their deck down at steerage, though no one dares to cross those divisions, and the social milieu of Edwardian society remains properly observed. Carlos tugs two deckchairs together in the sunshine, and Katherine huddles next to him under a blanket they share. It's bright and fine but these St Louisans are still chilled.

Overlooking them, two decks up, is the Marconi shack. Inside the small square deckhouse, young Harold Cottam sits at the instrument table and listens through his headphones as he waits for the day's passenger traffic to commence. Thia's antiquated wireless equipment consists of two coils, one of them punctured, a tuning device, a detector and receiver, a sending key, and condensers that are older than he'd like. The set transmits Morse code by radio wave. Often, if he's free, Harold will pick up news or chat with other operators. Anyone within receiving range can tune in and listen. He's already heard from *Antillian* and *Hellig Olav* this morning.

He rather thinks he might see Dr Blackmarr again today. Curious passengers often venture to the Marconi shack, but the nature of his work means the Chicago radiologist has a more considered knowledge of electricity than most, and possesses a keen interest in the wireless apparatus and learning how it works. Harold likes how the doctor makes him feel. Respected. Knowledgeable.

When Harold hears a spark through the headset he adjusts the receiver and listens as the letters come through.

dah-dah. M.

dah-dah-dit. G.

dah-di-dah-dah. Y.

MGY MGY MGY DE MSF MSF MSF. *Titanic Titanic Titanic this is Caronia Caronia Caronia.*

One of *Titanic*'s wireless officers answers and *Caronia* sends her message: *Captain, Titanic – Westbound steamers report bergs, growlers and field ice in 42 deg. N, from 49 to 51 deg. W, 12th April. Compliments – Barr.*

Harold knows both wireless operators aboard the new White Star liner. The senior telegraphist is Jack Phillips. He met Harry Bride – really another Harold, but to avoid confusion we'll call him Harry – the junior operator, when the latter came into the London post office to inquire about the cost of telegraphy school. The set they're using on *Titanic* is the newest thing. Thia's only has about a 150-mile range: a little over 200, perhaps, at night when the atmospheric conditions are more favourable. *Titanic*'s is at least three times as strong.

Caronia's Captain Barr sends the ice warning to other ships in the region, and Harold takes it to the bridge where Second Officer James Bisset is on watch, then returns to his post.

James glances at the slip of paper, not overly concerned. The ice is miles north. Still, when the captain returns to the bridge James hands him the ice warning.

'It seems to be a big field,' Arthur observes. Thia is south of *Titanic*, on the eastbound Atlantic track. She's unlikely to be affected, but the location of the ice is two days old and the field may have drifted. 'Keep a sharp lookout,' he orders James. 'Carry on.'

In a little while Arthur is joined by Thia's department heads: Chief Officer Hankinson, Chief Engineer Johnston, Chief Steward Hughes and Purser Brown. They accompany the captain as he begins his Sunday inspection. It's part necessary chore, part tradition, part authorial display. Played out in a time when social discourse is theatre, before an audience of passengers who know their roles well.

Saloon-class passengers politely greet the captain and his entourage, who are attired in their best uniforms. Starched collars. Brass buttons. White caps. The men inspect Thia from top to bottom, ensuring she's as shipshape and as tidily turned out as they are.

Thia is a pretty ship, but it's hard to define what makes her so. Whether it's her finely executed proportions, the stark contrast of her black and red hull, the cut of her bow, the curve of her stern. Maybe it's the sum of all things.

The boat deck is at the top of her superstructure. Harold's little shack is located aft, on her highest point, to aid signal transmission. Amidships, the lifeboats for which this deck is named surround her red-black funnel. Then come the officers' quarters, Arthur's quarters, and the chartroom, with the bridge and wheelhouse above.

On the doorstep of the Marconi shack is a glass skylight that peers down onto the bridge deck, into the second-class gentlemen's smokeroom. The room is panelled in walnut and fitted with a bar that houses cut-crystal decanters. The furnishings are upholstered in moquette and smell faintly of cigars. The men inside are occupied at games of whist, or chess. To the port side of the smokeroom is the second-class ladies retiring room, then a well deck that serves as the promenade area, where Katherine and Carlos huddle under their blanket.

Small gates mark the transition to the first-class promenade, two long thoroughfares that run starboard and port alongside the staterooms and the library. Fitted out with an Axminster carpet, gold silk tapestry window hangings and plump easy chairs, the library serves as retiring room for the ladies of first class, with lounges and occasional tables, writing desks and an oak bookcase. Another well deck surrounds the foremast, providing an ideal location for socialising, before the deck terminates at the first-class gentlemen's smokeroom.

The shelter deck is the first deck to stretch from Thia's stem to her stern. The aft is open and exposed to the weather, with derricks, winches and hatches that lead down to cargo holds. The second-class dining saloon is in the superstructure, along with the second cabins, the barber shop, galley, baker's shop and stillroom. There's also accommodation for the chief steward, purser and doctor nearby. Forward in the superstructure is the first-class dining saloon. A decade ago, when Thia was built, she wasn't intended to serve first-class passengers and this area was a covered promenade for steerage passengers – a practically unheard-of luxury. When she was refit for first class the area was converted into the dining saloon. Only the foredeck has been retained as steerage promenade.

Because of this reconfiguration her divisions are not as tidily segregated as they might otherwise have been, though this is the only deck that sees all of her passengers allocated space, irrespective of class. Otherwise, the social hierarchy between saloon and steerage is strictly observed. The former above, the latter below.

The upper deck, the first contained within her hull, houses the stewards' quarters nestled in the stern, the male and female infectious hospitals, for quarantining the outbreaks of measles or smallpox that are common on immigrant liners, and several large compartments full of hundreds of berths for steerage passengers. Portside amidships are the engineers' quarters, the electricians' shop, and the carpenter and joiners' shop. Centrally positioned alongside them is the dynamo room and switchboard, and the casings that house her quadruple expansion reciprocating engines and the massive boilers that feed them.

Nearby is Thia's donkey boiler. Unlike her six other boilers, which are banked when she is berthed, the small donkey always needs to be ready. It's used for everything from powering the steam winches for loading and unloading cargo, to heating Thia while she's in dock, to providing auxiliary power to the engines during an emergency. Even the furnaces of the main boilers are lit by throwing burning fuel into them from the metal donkey.

In fact, Thia owes her existence to donkeys, or, at the very least, to mules.

1900

Mules are man's creation. The product of breeding a jack, a male donkey, with a female horse. The resulting hybrids are plebeian. More sure-footed, strong and hardy than their dams, and more tractable, intelligent and domesticated than their sires. As they are superior to their progenitors, Darwin says that mules are art that outdoes nature.

The majority of mules in the United States descend from George Washington's stock. The most prized are those sired by Andalusian donkeys, from the same Spanish region as the Andalusian horse. Washington wanted to breed them on his Mount Vernon plantation, only their export was prohibited. But he was in luck. King Charles sent him two jacks and two jennies as a diplomatic gift. Only one of the jacks, Royal Gift, survived the crossing. He was joined a year later by Knight of Malta, a Maltese donkey gifted by the Marquis de Lafayette, who'd been Washington's protégé during the Civil War. Gift and Knight were put to stud and founded a dynasty of millions of descendant mules.

In 1900, Thia's story begins with these mules.

Mules that Britain needs desperately for the Boer War.

Fourteen hundred and fifty of which are loaded aboard the steamer *Carinthia* at the New Orleans dock. She's one of Cunard's first cattle ships and is ably suited for use as a mule transport.

Mules are critical to waging war. The cavalry may ride horses, but mules carry supplies and munitions, pull artillery, wagons and ambulances over deserts in Africa and, one day, endless bloody mud on the Western Front. For this honour they endure monstrous suffering: service, fear, pain, death. On *Carinthia* they are cattle, crowded aboard, with only humans to depend upon. Ironic, since it's mules who've proved to be the far more dependable species.

When *Carinthia* leaves New Orleans she sails for Cape Town via the Caribbean. Following the most direct route, her master, George Campbell, sails her between the islands of Jamaica and Hispaniola. As they approach *le Tiburon* on Haiti, a squall gathers and obscures the coast. As night falls and lightning flashes, Campbell is sure he can see *Pointe de Gravois* four miles to port. He alters course inshore. Hours later, as the rain lashes hard and thick in a torrential wrath so heavy that the crew can scarce see her bow, *Carinthia* runs aground.

Poor judgement on Campbell's part and inclement weather is only one story. The captain's story. Here is another that the muleteers tell; 64 men recruited from St Louis – those in New Orleans already wise to the hardships – and promised a voyage to Cape Town in return for the simple task of caring for a few mules being transported aboard. It sounds like easy work and though the pay is only $15, the voyage will be an adventure. According to the muleteers, the night *Carinthia* slams into the rocks at *Pointe de Gravois*, the weather is clear but the officers are drunk. Later, when German steamer *Valentia* attempts to tow them free, she leaves *Carinthia* noticeably listing. When Man of War *Proserpine* arrives and fails at the same feat, *Carinthia* is so much inclined that walking about deck requires lifelines. For days the muleteers, who have to sleep on the slanting deck, lash themselves down so they don't slip through the scuppers and into the blue.

In the pens, mules trample atop one another, dying by the dozens. The stench of excrement, acute distress and necrosis is overwhelming.

On *Carinthia*'s first voyage as a mule ship, in optimal conditions, she lost thirteen mules en route. Now, the muleteers, forced to work amidst the terrified beasts, dispose of 260 carcasses overboard. When *Proserpine* returns she refuses to take the mules off for fear the wretched conditions have bred Yellow Fever. It's the native Haitians who finally assist in landing the animals. The muleteers throw the remaining livestock off *Carinthia*'s port bow and the Haitians' boats guide them to shore. Despite their best efforts, another 500 mules drown.

Stories are complicated truths, the way they change depending on the teller. If the muleteers' tale is true, then the better part of a thousand skeletons lie on the Haitian seabed. Regardless of who you believe, the captain, the muleteers, or this account, the story ends with *Carinthia* stuck fast upon the rocks and her belly stove in.

This is how *Carinthia* becomes *Carpathia*'s progenitor. How Cunard's loss of her precipitates Thia's life, though the similarity in their names is happenstance. *Carinthia* was a four-masted, single-stack cargo ship with no real superstructure, only a few deckhouses. Thia is much more. More than the sum of her decks, funnel and engines, of the men who sail her and the people who sail upon her. Each part and each person is a fragment of the whole, but she's extraordinary in a way that their simple addition cannot account for. They meld to create a life that is all her own. One that's humble and complicated and inexplicably real.

1912

Arthur passes Thia's donkey boiler as he continues his inspection. On the starboard side of the deck is a large linen room, the flour store and the potato store, all close to the third-class pantry. The steerage dining saloon runs the breadth of Thia. Then there is an operating room and two general hospitals, one for women, the other for men, which, before she was refitted for first class, were the third-class ladies' room and the men's smokeroom. The male and female berths in steerage are also segregated. Men are at the stern and women are at the bow. Passenger lavatories and washrooms are followed by the refrigerator room, amenities for the boatswains, master-at-arms and quartermasters, and then the paint room, at the tip of Thia's bow.

Below the upper deck is the main deck, the principal deck of a vessel. From stern to amidships are more third-class compartments. The casing containing the boilers and engines extends from the upper deck down here. There are quarters for trimmers, firemen and greasers nearby. Forward are third-class cabins, simple but private, and stewards' quarters.

As Arthur passes through these steerage spaces, the passengers are far more reticent about greeting him. Socially, he's superior, not that he would ever be discourteous. Then he inspects the lower half of Thia's hull, which is given over to cargo holds, ballast tanks, additional engine and boiler space, coal bunkers, insulated compartments, storerooms, and the chain locker, with tunnels and companionways amidst the mix. An ocean liner is a city in miniature while at sea, with all the needs of a city. Arthur finds a few small quibbles – it is an unwritten law that there is no such thing as a perfect captain's inspection – but nothing of note.

Later that morning he stands in the first-class saloon and prepares to deliver the Sunday service. Some captains don't favour the role of cleric, but Arthur could never find serving the Almighty a chore. As the passengers settle the air becomes reverent.

There's a quality, when giving thanks to God at sea, that Arthur has never observed in any earthly counter-part. As though these people who have spent their lives on land come closer to God than they have ever been before. There's a psalm that all sailors know: *They that go down to the sea in ships, that do business in great waters; these see the works of the Lord and his wonders in the deep.*

Amongst the parishioners are Katherine and Carlos, for once permitted to trespass across the class divide – a tacit recognition that it is only humans who judge each other's worth by social standing. They listen as Arthur gives thanks, as he asks for God's blessing on King George, and, diplomatically, President Taft.

After the service Arthur spends a few moments exchanging pleasantries before excusing himself. Then he meets his three ranking officers on the starboard bridge wing to take the noon sighting. He looks through the sight on the sextant and adjusts the brass arm, until the sun, reflecting off the instrument's mirrors, aligns with the horizon. He reads the degrees indicated where the arm rests on the curved scale.

Beside him, Chief Officer Thomas Hankinson takes his own sighting, as does First Officer Horace Dean and Second Officer James Bisset. Once they've determined the sun's noon altitude they use it, along with an estimate of their speed over the past 24 hours, accounting for the influence of wind and currents, to calculate the distance travelled since noon yesterday.

While one crewman displays the result on the passengers' bulletin board, another sounds the siren. As the deep horn washes over Thia's decks and through her hull, her saloon passengers gather. With little else to do at noon, the outcome of the daily run is eagerly anticipated. Good-natured joviality permeates the small crowd of ladies and gentlemen. The purse for the winner is modest. There is far more satisfaction in being the person who guessed closest.

With a top speed of just over fourteen knots, the furthest distance Thia can conceivably cover in 24 hours is 345 nautical miles. The fastest liners all easily exceed twenty knots, and *Mauretania*, Cunard's crown jewel, holds the eastbound Blue Riband, the record for the fastest North Atlantic crossing, with an average speed of 25.88 knots. There's some speculation, as there always is, that White Star's new liner, *Titanic*, will relieve *Mauretania* of this record. Perhaps even on her maiden voyage. But it's unlikely. The new ship is built for luxury over speed.

In the Marconi shack, Harold listens to the afternoon traffic. He overhears two ships talking about ice. One is the *Parisian* but he is unsure of the other. Possibly she's the *Californian*, since he's heard traffic from her all afternoon. She's close and her signal comes in strong. He also hears *La Bretagne* and two hours later *Masaba*, and notes them in his log. Just before five he exchanges ship's time with *Parisian* and a little later takes a commercial message from *Titanic*.

That evening at dinner, Thia's purser discreetly approaches one of the tables in the first-class saloon to deliver that message. 'A marconigram for you, sir.'

Sixty-seven-year-old Charles H. Marshall takes the slip of paper, looks at it briefly and hands it to his wife. It's a reply to a ship-to-ship message she sent earlier that day to their nieces, Charlotte, Caroline and Malvina. He picks up his silverware and looks down at his plate, at the blue-and-white pattern bearing Cunard's rampant lion. Over a decade ago, he sat in his office in The Liverpool and London and Globe Insurance Company and wrote a letter to Cunard's commodore about the ship he now dines aboard, named after a magnificent mountain range.

Josephine skims over the official particulars in the message but her eyes catch on the office of origin: *Titanic*.

To: *Marshall Carpathia*.

Message Received Love Lottie.

There are so few words. Not enough to judge how the girls are faring with the loss of their sister Elizabeth. They are returning home from her funeral, after having travelled to Paris when it became clear the end was near. Though Elizabeth lived abroad with her husband for the past three decades and her illness was one of gradual decline, the reality of such a permanent loss is keen, and there is altogether too much time to think aboard an ocean liner, in the middle of nowhere. No place for the sisters to escape their grief. Josephine passes the telegram to her daughter, Evelyn. At least *Titanic* will offer them more in the way of diversions and company, for she's designed with the comfort and entertainment of her passengers in mind, far more so than their little ship.

———

After supper that evening Dr Frank Blackmarr strolls about the second-class promenade, almost ready to retire. The warm afternoon sunshine that turned the North Atlantic into a glittering seascape has ceded to a night so dark he can't help but notice how brightly the stars shine. Like some careless hand has strewn diamonds across the sky. His heavy overcoat protects him from the cold air that's turning his cheeks ruddy. Thia's lights here seem dimmer than elsewhere. Without them, he would be unable to see even his hand before his face. He walks to the side of the ship, rests against the gunwale, and looks down into the abysmal depths. It's an uncanny night.

In the Marconi shack, Harold tunes in to the news from Cape Cod, which transmits every evening at ten-thirty, New York time. He listens for any word about the coal strike in England. After the relay finishes, the station begins to transmit a batch of messages for *Titanic*. He's heard Harry and Jack signalling all afternoon, trying to keep pace with the commercial traffic, so Harold takes down the messages to retransmit in the morning.

After Cape Cod finishes he keys in the call sign for *Parisian*. He wants to confirm their earlier time rush before retiring. Hopefully that will be soon, since the previous two nights he did not get to bed until the early hours. He hears a return of *dits* and *dahs* almost immediately. But it's not *Parisian*.

MPA DE MLQ. *Carpathia this is Mount Temple.* GN OM. *Good night, old man.*

Harold responds, signalling his own goodnight. While he waits for confirmation from *Parisian* he writes up his daily list of communications. By the time he's finished she's still not replied, so he puts on his coat, for the night has become cold, picks up the list and goes to the bridge. 'Communications of the day, sir.' He hands the paper to James Bisset, the officer of the watch, then returns to his shack. He slips the telephones over his ears, hoping he hasn't missed *Parisian*'s reply while he removes his coat and makes what other preparations he can to retire, while still tethered to the receiver.

Nothing.

Bed is only a few metres away, in a curtained-off area of the shack. He's already run half an hour past the end of his shift and he's not going to wait on *Parisian* all night. He notices the batch of messages for *Titanic* and on impulse signals: *MGY MGY MGY DE MPA MPA MPA. Do you know that Cape Cod is sending a batch of messages for you?*

Harold bends down and begins to unlace his boots, listening for a reply through the 'phones. *Titanic* responds immediately: *Come at once. We have struck a berg. It's a CQD OM. Position 41° 46' N., 50° 14' W.*

CQD. All stations, distress.

WHAT'S THAT LYING IN THE SAND?

2000

'WHAT'S THAT LYING IN THE SAND?' JOHN DAVIS, THE producer of the *Sea Hunters* documentary series, asks.

It's almost four months later, in September 2000, when the Sea Hunters go back to the mystery wreck, and Davis could be asking that question about any number of the things lying in the sand. When they arrived, they sent down *Venture*'s upgraded rover, controlled by skipper Gary Goodyear. On the monitor they finally see the images they've been waiting for. Counting on.

The backscatter is like distant stars slipping past, particles streaming thorough the currents, catching on the rover's strobe lights. Then the water swirls and the world becomes a grey blizzard, a cloudy mess of silt that unfolds like silk in the wind.

The images are silent, distant. Visibility is poor, six or seven feet.

In the lights of the rover a fish darts along the seabed, zigzagging. Hermit crabs creep away as the rover circles, searching the ocean floor for signs of debris. It sets off, gliding through the water, and soon the sand gives way to a rough, textured seabed, flecks of wreck life beginning to appear. There's a mound, covered in silt, long and cylindrical. Like a dune on the ocean floor. The rover sets down, pausing at one end, before gliding along the surface. Somewhere near the middle the silty deposit thins. The rover pauses. A hue is visible beneath the granules resting like a fine dust over this one small area. The tincture is just strong enough for them to know what colour would be exposed if a hand could reach out and clear away the muck.

Red.

Cunard red?

Another object lies in the sand nearby.

Brass whistles, perhaps?

The rover moves on and more debris on the seabed comes into view, this time not buried in the sand, but tangled and encased in brittle stars. The debris grows, and as the rover turns to port, almost from nowhere the field of vision transforms into a vertical wall of marine growth. The rover pans up, then begins to rise, too close for anything other than a single square of hull to be visible. If they pull back, the wreck will fade into the deep dark.

The rover rises and rises. Then, almost unexpectedly, it breaches the limits of the hull, and the shadowy deck appears. The port side is just visible across the way, stark against the black ocean beyond.

The rover turns and glides along the deck. Every surface is shrouded in encrusted growth: the remains of the collapsed superstructure, the fallen derricks and twisted metal, repurposed into an eerie haven of underwater life.

The rover makes forays along the starboard edge of the deck, occasionally crossing to the port periphery. It descends the ship's side and returns to the stern. Glides along the massive, encrusted hull, past a jagged puncture in the metal plating.

Torpedo strikes? Her ribcage torn open from boilers erupting?

Past cavernous gangway doors – left open from an evacuation?

Until finally the starboard propeller shaft comes into view. The rover's lights slide down the shaft and a silhouette appears.

Two blades.

But their position, at ten and two, indicate a third, entombed in the sand.

Three blades.

There's a second screw on the port side, bracketing the rudder. Steamship rudders are like monoliths. They have to be, to turn thousands of tonnes of metal. Thia's rudder is so large it spans the height of her hull from the ballast tanks that line her keel, up her cargo holds, to her lower and main decks. The wreck's rudder is connected to the sternpost by six gudgeons that once allowed swing but are now seized like a locked hinge.

The monolith, the set of triple-bladed screws, the pattern of portholes, the curve of her stern in the grey light – all sleek lines – are like a calling card.

Nearby shell casings, the bow keel, crumpled from the violence of its impact with the seabed, the scars of the torpedo strikes, tell *this* story.

The story of Thia.

In a few days, when the Sea Hunters are in Halifax comparing rover footage with photos of Thia, measuring the wreck up against plans of Thia's general arrangement, James Delgado will confirm her identity.

But the men watching the monitor already know it's her. It's just that they've learned from misidentifying *Isis* and won't publicise it yet. They will wait for official confirmation then hold a press conference and announce her return to the world.

'What's that lying in the sand?' Davis asks.

It comes into view when the rover turns away from the stern, just beyond the shell casings.

'By God, a ship's bell,' mutters Gary. 'It's *Carpathia*'s bell.'

THE BEGINNING OF THE END

1914

THIS SAD STORY SHOULD START HERE, *NOW*. AT THE END of Franz and Sophie's fairytale. The part where they die, because that's where this chapter of Thia's life begins. But she has no love story of her own, too little of any kind of love, so instead it will start here: once upon a time – a few years before the turn of the century – a prince falls in love with a commoner, as they tend to do. His name is Franz and hers is Sophie. They meet when she is lady-in-waiting to an archduchess, and when the prince, heir to the throne, pays marked attention to that household, the kingdoms of Austria and Hungary take note. They, like the archduchess, believe his interest is in one of her eight eligible daughters. When she discovers the truth, the archduchess's rage is vindictive. She dismisses Sophie, knowing the terrible damage it will cause her reputation, that the court will infer her conduct unchaste, when her real crime is not that she fell in love, but that *he* fell in love back.

If this had been a mere dalliance on Franz's part, or he a lesser man, he would have abandoned Sophie. But that is not what happens. As required by Habsburg imperial law, he requests permission from the Emperor to marry her.

The Emperor refuses: a Habsburg may only marry from within the House or reigning dynasties of Europe.

Yet, despite the forces that conspire against their union, the objections of the Emperor, the laws that require Franz's wife be royal, and the disdain with which his kingdom views the match – unfairly, as Sophie is anyone's equal in intelligence, sensibility and good character – Franz truly loves her. So he scandalises Vienna by publicly declaring himself. He will marry Sophie, and only Sophie.

To say that the entire empire is against them is untrue. Entirely dramatic, but not entirely fair, though it is near enough the case. Not until Pope Leo XIII, Russia's Tsar Nicholas II, and Germany's Kaiser Wilhelm II, all concerned with the stability of Austria-Hungary's monarchy, pressure the Emperor to accept the match does he finally consent.

But there is a price.

Franz is made to agree that Sophie may never be styled Empress Consort, or any title that places her above the very many archduchesses and archdukes of the imperial court.

The insult is deliberate.

Franz will be Emperor, of the highest rank in the kingdom, while Sophie will remain of the lowest, and he must vow never to correct this once he ascends. As such, she can never be at his side in matters of state; will always enter last, least. And their children may *never* inherit their father's birthright.

Franz and Sophie agree. Anything, so they might marry.

And they should, despite all, live happily ever after.

But they don't. Live, that is. They are very happy for fourteen years and have three children, but as Thia sails beyond the Strait of Gibraltar having not long left Fiume, a port in their kingdom, a Serbian secret society called the Black Hand assassinates Archduke Franz Ferdinand and his wife, Sophie.

The day that Franz and Sophie die changes the world. It's a snowflake, tumbling down a mountain, until it can't be stopped. All in the time it takes Thia to sail to New York and back again. The voyage east begins poorly, fog leaving the way unclear. Her captain at this time is William Prothero and he remains on the bridge for three days, trying to see them through. They cross the Herring Pond, pass back through the Strait of Gibraltar, and, as they depart Naples into the Mediterranean, somewhere near Capri, in steerage, a baby boy dies. Night falls and they commit him to the deep with the usual religious rites. But with dawn comes another death. A grown man this time.

Boy and man join Franz and Sophie in the afterlife. By now, hardly anyone aboard can be unaware of the assassination and the resulting crisis. The Black Hand's motivation is a morass of politics, ethnicity, geography and patriotism, and yet a lesson in history, in the dates and the times of every incident that brought the world to this point, won't do any good. It's like Charlemagne learning about Attila, Caesar about Alexander. None of them ever learned what they should have learned about war. Still, some explanation of how the world almost annihilates itself is needed, so here is how the madness begins.

During a period of civil unrest in the Ottoman Empire, the Austro-Hungarian Empire takes advantage and annexes Bosnia and Herzegovina, the country on its southern border. This is poorly received by Serbia, which has that country's western border, particularly given the population of ethnic Serbs therein. In the years directly preceding and following the annexation, a network of alliances emerges alongside a focus, by all the European powers, on armament and naval expansion, a less than enchanting by-product of industrialisation. The United Kingdom, France and Russia ally in the Triple Entente, an understanding that they think seems wise in order to counter the threat posed by the Triple Alliance between Italy, Germany and Austria-Hungary. These central powers, lying between France and the United Kingdom on their west and Russia on their east, bisect the continent in a contiguous landscape stretching from the North Sea to the Mediterranean.

And so this foundation is in place when nineteen-year-old Gavrilo Princip – Bosnian, Serb, child – shoots Franz and Sophie and then, along with his conspirators, implicates neighbouring Serbia's Black Hand. The society formally style themselves Unification or Death, but no one calls them that. Their nom de guerre comes from the order they model themselves after, the Italian *Carbonari*, a semi-secret society who successfully, if bloodily, unified the states of the Italian peninsula, a hop, skip and a jump across the Adriatic Sea, into a single kingdom decades earlier. They would leave a charcoal imprint, a black hand, upon the doors of those opposed to their cause. A tactic that also inspired *La Mano Nera*, the Black Hand sect within the Italian Mafia.

Just as with the *Carbonari*, the Serbian Black Hand's guiding precept is unification, but of all ethnic Serbs into a greater Serbian nation. Though this sentiment has existed as long as the Serbian diaspora across the Balkan Peninsula, the Black Hand's formation is a response, a direct legacy, of Austria-Hungary's annexation of Bosnia and Herzegovina.

Although Franz and Sophie's murders were performed by a Bosnian in his own country, in the days that follow Austria-Hungary claims that the Serbian government is in league with the Black Hand, who count in their ranks several of the country's senior military officers, and issue the country a set of ten humiliating ultimatums, designed to be impossible to accept.

The Austro-Hungarians want war.

They want Serbia to stay out of their affairs with Bosnia and Herzegovina, and now they have a pretext to force the matter. A pseudo-legitimate reason to declare war. They use Franz's assassination as justification for issuing the ultimatums, knowing that no nation can voluntarily accede to so much foreign oversight and retain its sovereign dignity.

Serbia refuses.

Austria-Hungary, which has been assured of German support, declares war on Serbia and attacks Belgrade.

Russia, an ally and patron to small Serbia, mobilises troops along its shared border with Germany and Austria-Hungary.

Germany, which, most believe, is in favour of all-out war, demands Russia stop immediately.

Russia refuses.

Germany declares war on the Russians, then demands that France give assurances it will not support its ally Russia, but doesn't like its noncommittal response.

Germany declares war on France.

Germany then demands passage to France through neutral Belgium, which refuses.

Germany declares war on Belgium.

England, which Germany requests not interfere with events on the continent, warns that this will be impossible if Belgium's neutrality is not respected.

Germany stays its course.

———

These events unfold in a matter of days as Thia steams along the coast of the Balkan Peninsula from Patras to Trieste and then Fiume. The latter is the largest port in the Hungarian portion of the empire, and it's eight in the morning when she docks, her passengers at the rails breathing in the bright, beautiful atmosphere of the Adriatic. The old city rises in an amphitheatre of narrow, charming streetlets, a hilly backdrop crowded with houses, at whose foot new Fiume sprawls along the shore. Here, elegant, stately buildings grace the streets. Hidden a little way back from the water is the rotunda of St Vitus Cathedral, inspired by Venice's *Salute.* The market halls hum and somewhere along the shore is a factory where torpedoes are manufactured. Fiume is where they were invented, conceived of by an Austrian but built by an Englishman, several decades prior. The first of these that was effective, the Whitehead torpedo, has a striker in the head that rams back into a percussion cap of mercury fulminate, an explosive that's highly sensitive to impact, friction and heat, when the torpedo slams into a hull. The cap breaks and the fulminate expands exponentially, setting off a chain reaction that ignites a core of incendiary guncotton.

The original Whitehead, more effective than any previous sea weapon, had a range of only 600 yards. Now, it's 16 000 yards. Eight-and-a-half knots, slower than any decent steamer, has become 48 knots, faster than anything yet to sail.

It's soon after Thia docks at Rudolf's Quay when she learns that war – one, any or all – has been declared. Her passengers' sense of adventure and anticipation is instantly muted. She's due to stay in Fiume six days, but now, every hour they are in port, in the heart of enemy territory, is uneasy. It's on the third day that things come to a head. There's activity on shore and along the quays, and a certain tension on board. An alertness to the crew. Rumours begin to circulate amongst the passengers that Thia's been boarded and that the Austrian and Hungarian stokers have been removed to serve in the military. That her wireless office has been sealed by the Germans and that come morning the English officers will be taken as prisoners of war – though no official hostility has yet been declared on His Majesty's part.

Whatever the truth, Captain William Prothero knows that they are not welcome in Fiume. It's too dangerous, and all too clear that no port in the Austro-Hungarian Empire is safe. So he orders the crew to make ready, and quietly, quietly, Thia escapes in the middle of the night. While he knows they dare not stay longer, he still worries. The Adriatic into which they sail is hardly safer, home as it is to the enemy's fleet. It is not a large sea by any measure, hemmed in by the Balkan and Italian peninsulas, but it has never felt smaller. Though the next port on their itinerary is Messina, he cannot be sure of safety in Italy, allied as she is. So, conscious of the lives in his care, William lays a course to the closest sovereign soil: Malta, in the Mediterranean. Birthplace of Knight of Malta, Lafayette's gift to Washington.

The next day Britain declares war on Germany.

Had Thia stayed in Fiume, even until morning, she may never have left.

———

Three days later, as dawn breaks and the tiny archipelago of Malta appears across the bow, relief sweeps Thia's decks. The Baroque city of Valletta is even more beautiful than Fiume, with densely crowded stone buildings that rival any in the world in age and magnificence, and fortified cities that, more than anything, feel safe.

It's also the base of the Royal Navy's Mediterranean Fleet, whose number includes *Invincible*, *Inflexible*, *Indefatigable* and *Indomitable*. They are only a little larger than Thia, leisure cruiser to their battle cruiser, but they are the first of their kind. Every bit as well-armed as a battleship, but sleeker, faster hunters.

That evening, passengers, merchant marine and naval officers alike are tempted ashore by the cheering crowds, the snare of drums and the sound of horns as marching bands parade through Valletta. As the city demonstrates its support of the Entente, the patriotic strains of 'Rule, Britannia!' sound across the harbour in the gathering dark. But whatever comfort the revelries bring is short-lived. The next morning, Fleet Admiral Milne of flagship *Invincible* tries to take three of William's officers who are Royal Naval reservists. Their loss would put Thia at an extraordinary disadvantage during a time of war, William argues, until the admiral says he will be content with one. But the officers can't decide who it should be. They toss a coin and it lands on their second, Charles Bray.

But that is not where the losses end.

All told, Thia shelters at Malta, re-coaling and resupplying, some nine days. British warships come and go, themselves re-coaling and resupplying amidst the frantic activity on the docks, before returning to their Mediterranean patrol. They capture dozens of merchant ships that are escorted back to Malta, to the prisoner-of-war camp being established. The rumour that Thia's stokers were conscripted at Fiume is proved false when English officers board her and remove all of her Austrian and Hungarian crew members. They intern her stokers, bakers, stewards and cooks, as well as the chef, leaving her woefully shorthanded. Somewhere in the midst of all this the French fleet arrives, fresh from transporting troops stationed in Algiers home to France, and Thia's red-and-black livery is eclipsed by the 120-strong Anglo-French fleet in harbour, and by the war shadows that grow daily.

William weighs their options. They cannot replace the stokers at Malta and his only recourse is unorthodox. He's forced to importune the ship's stewards to undertake the dirty, backbreaking work until they make a port where they can enlist new crew members. He listens for whatever news the admiralty can give him. The French are preparing for a chase of the Austrian fleet in the Adriatic. Italy is safe: declaring the Triple Alliance a defensive measure, invalidated since Austria-Hungary took the offensive, they refuse to cast themselves alongside the empire and Germany. Thousands of American refugees are gathering there, trying to escape before the battle begins in earnest. The fleet has kept the Mediterranean open and the best course seems to be resuming their itinerary. Those refugees are depending on steamers for passage home, for whether America is part of the conflict or not, how safe can anyone be on a continent at war with itself?

———

In Genoa, Italy, American Consul General John Edward Jones brushes through the dense press of bodies that part to allow his passage to the table that occupies the centre of the largest room he has. Dr Jones – first a caregiver then a consul – leaps on top of the wood surface so he's visible to the crowd that spills out the doorway.

'I've just received word that the Cunard liner *Carpathia* will sail from Naples on August eighteenth for New York,' he announces without preamble. The atmosphere of tension in the room gives way to a faint hum of excitement. Ignoring the murmurs, he continues, 'Accommodations will be a little rough, but there will be no class distinction and those travelling in steerage will have first-class food and full privileges of the decks. Further,' he pauses, 'Cunard will not be raising the price of steamer passage.'

At these words, hope swells in the breast of every person present. Such as has not been felt since each arrived at the consulate's offices, saw the American flag snapping in the wind and felt some safety, some relief, that help was at hand. Only to have it snatched away by the frustrations and disappointments littered between then and now. And the fear. The ruthless emotion that makes each one desperate to return home from a place where even young gentlewomen have been forced to wander the city with nowhere to sleep because the banks have stopped cashing traveller's cheques and many people are without funds. Though they wire home for relief, cablegrams are taking eight or nine days to cross the Atlantic while funds dwindle further, eaten away by the cost of surviving in a foreign land.

The privileged amongst the stranded have already secured passage on *Principessa Mafalda*, pledging the astonishing sum of $184 000 for her charter. With no way for others to pay the cost, even if they could afford it, *Principessa* sailed with space for 200 more. When Dr Jones secured another charter, *Principe di Udine*, cabins went to the highest bidders. It is by no means democratic but there is nothing he can do. The American government has to realise as much as possible from the vessels, but even so will face a heavy deficit. The price of coal has increased 400 per cent, food prices have soared and labour is at a premium. He had to accept the highest bids, with scores paying over $1000, even as high as $15 000. Now, he can finally offer hope to the masses.

'Passage aboard *Carpathia* is set at the standard price of $82.50.' The room near erupts, but silently, as they continue to listen. 'The vessel is in need of a few stewards, if anyone is willing to work their way back to the states.' Dr Jones looks down at the sheaf of papers in his hand and delivers all other public announcements and instructions from Rome and Washington, as he has every day at ten and three, from the time the consulate first became overrun with refugees. He concludes as he always does. 'Though I have only limited funds at my disposal, I shall assist, as far as I can, any present who are penniless.' Then he climbs down from the table and exits the room, already preoccupied by the dozens of concerns requiring his attention. He's at the far end of the corridor when a hand catches his arm.

'Dr Jones,' a young man addresses him, 'how about this steward stunt?'

'Hustle down to the Cunard office as fast as you can make it,' he replies as he enters his office.

The young man does just that but is back not two hours later, a little after five o'clock, seeking an urgent audience with Jones.

'The Cunard agent phoned the ship at Naples,' he explains. 'They need three stewards but will only take me if I can prove I'm American. Can you issue me with an emergency passport?'

Like most Americans he doesn't have one. It's not required for foreign travel and obtaining one, especially overseas, involves a great deal of red tape. But war changes everything and if it gets one more American to safety . . . Still, Jones needs to establish that the man, who calls himself Ralph Benton, is an American citizen, for all he acts and talks like one. 'What evidence have you of your citizenship?' Usually this is provided in a letter or witness affidavit, or a certificate from a clerk or notary.

'Absolutely none,' Benton replies.

Since the ordinary measures won't work in this situation – Benton needs to be on a train to Naples today – Dr Jones casts around for some other way to verify his citizenship. 'Where do you come from?'

'Washington.'

'Your business there?'

'Newspaper reporter.'

'What paper were you last connected with?'

'The *Washington Herald*.'

There. That clinches it. He takes out a passport form. 'I was once in the newspaper game in Washington myself.' He completes the document, noting down the shape of Benton's head, his complexion. That his hair is dark brown whereas his eyes are light brown. That he's of medium height and build, et cetera, et cetera. Unmarried. Then he sends him on to the station to catch the 9.25 train to Naples, which won't reach its destination until the following evening. There, in a station swarming with Italian soldiers, Ralph finds 50 other Americans who are all intent on trying to get home on Thia.

THE BEGINNING OF THE STORY

2014

'WHEN I WAS BORN, MY FATHER SAW BLUE JAYS PLAYING outside the hospital window and said I was as sweet as a baby bird, and so they called me Jay,' I say, telling the version of the story I settled on long ago. Stories are complicated truths, the way they change depending on the teller. I've told this one so often that it trips off my tongue.

Like most people who encounter my name before they encounter me, Ric believed it was a man writing and asking him about Thia. He pictured, in his words, a bearded, nerdy, diver-type. For a while I suspected this misperception might be the case, but it was only confirmed when the reply to one of my emails included the phrase 'dick-swinging'. By this time, correcting the misunderstanding was awkward, but necessary, since Ric has invited me to stay with him in Manchester.

I'm not sure how I feel about this idea, so I weigh the wisdom of the action. But if I stay somewhere else, the best I'll get is a few hours of exchange between strangers, as shallow as a puddle. That won't do. Not for Thia's story. I want the intimacy of home.

When I arrive in Manchester Ric is working late so he sends a police officer to collect me from Victoria Station. That sounds more dramatic than it is – he's dating the slender, auburn-haired officer.

I like the two of them together. The fireman and the police officer. The idea and the reality. Later, Lynne tells me that Manchester cops call Manchester firemen 'water fairies', because firemen are higher up the hero totem pole than policemen. On quiet weekends when the red trucks roll up Deansgate for a spot of birdwatching, women migrate from the police to the firefighters like moths to flame. It amuses Lynne, who usually has a front-row seat when on patrol with male colleagues. She tells the best stories about Ric. Like the one about rescuing the cow in the canal.

That first night Ric cooks chicken stir-fry while we chat in the kitchen, but I don't ask any questions about Thia. I watch him chop vegetables and think about bachelors and economy of movement. The kitchen is small and too cluttered for more than one person, so I don't offer to help. Instead, my gaze is drawn to a half-dozen bronze ship's bells clustered at my feet. Ric's just bought this townhouse in Little Hulton. Moved in only a few days ago and things are still out of sorts. We eat dinner sitting on his mustard-coloured chesterfields and drink blackcurrant cordial. Dessert is chocolate Hobnobs.

The next night, after Ric and Lynne return from a running meet, he makes dinner again. Salmon, potato, broccolini and Hobnobs. There's more chatting that goes on until late, until we talk ourselves comfortable with one another and laugh at the misunderstanding about my name.

All told, I don't stay very long. But it's long enough to take measure. One night, Ric invites me to the pub to meet some of his friends. The men are polite and I'm sure they've been told to mind their manners. I love the place – the gleaming wood; the ladies room with its formal sitting area, a relic of a bygone age – but it's clear they chose it with me in mind. They're uncomfortable here. Don't know where to sit when they first walk in the doors.

Another night Lynne takes me to the Christmas Markets in the heart of Manchester, where I taste mulled wine for the first time and help pick out a new Oxford shirt for Ric, in a pale thistle colour. It will look good on his lean frame, against the warm brown of his hair and the creases in his face.

The couple make me feel welcome and I'm grateful. There are other things I like. The ancient Land Rover that Ric drives, with holes in the floor and exposed wires under the dash, and the way he makes sure the heat is turned up high and directed my way. But my favourite thing is the three rubber ducks on the dashboard. I can't resist asking about them.

He tells me it was a quiet shift on a rainy day, and the lads are wont to amuse themselves at such times. They used to have recliners where they could stretch out and sleep if they weren't on a call, but those times have since gone. When Ric came out from the station he found a little yellow duck bobbing in water that had pooled in the spare wheel cover on the Land Rover's hood.

Water fairies and their rubber ducks.

The third time it happened he took the cover off the tyre. But the rubber ducks line his dashboard, bright splashes of yellow in the dark interior.

On the third day, he tells me the story I came to hear.

THE FIRST EXPEDITION

2007

WHEN RIC STEPS OFF *DANCER*'S DECK HE HITS THE WATER with a slap. For a moment he's engulfed by the effervescence of the plunge. The ocean takes the weight of his rebreather and emergency cylinders, and in an instant he transforms, like an ungainly yellow turtle returned to its natural element.

The men diving with him today are Tim Cashman, Helmuth Biechl, Mark Elliott and Duncan Keates. When Tim enters the water, he drifts over to the shot line and follows his usual routine. He checks his gear, making sure it's hanging correctly, that nothing is tangled, and that his rebreather is working properly. Then he drops to 13 feet and checks everything again. He did the exact same thing a few months before, when he dived RMS *Niagara* off the coast of New Zealand. Launched early in 1912, she was given the appellation 'Titanic of the Pacific' though this was soon changed to 'Queen of the Pacific'. On that dive, a teammate recovered *Niagara*'s main mast bell. Tim can only hope they will have the same luck with Thia.

Several divers who were supposed to be a part of this expedition, Leigh Bishop, Teresa Telus and Pim van der Horst, had to pull out late in the game. Pim brought Helmuth on as a replacement, but he's from Germany and has never dived with any of the lads before, so hardly knows them. But he fits in well, and he's experienced. Helmuth's been diving and instructing since the seventies, and he runs the Deep Wreck Diving centre. He prepared for this expedition by diving deep lakes in Germany and Italy.

As Ric begins to descend the shot line, he thinks about the last time he was here. His first pilgrimage to Thia – which, depending on who you ask, did or did not take place.

2001

After the team dived *Dasher* it gave them the confidence to dive Thia; the knowledge that they *could* dive to those depths, even far offshore. They organised an expedition in July 2001, led by Richie Stevenson, who'd long been fascinated by Thia. They chartered *Ocean Venture* from Gary Goodyear, who had Thia's numbers from his work with NUMA. But *Venture* was for sale, and when a buyer turned up just before departure she became unavailable.

Then there was another death in the group.

It seemed like things could hardly get worse.

That is, until Richie's own charter boat became available. *Loyal Watcher* had been hired by a friend who offered to delay his own expedition by a week to give the lads enough time to find Thia – since they'd no longer have a skipper with her exact numbers – and dive her.

A week is not ideal but it is all they have. Then, for days the wind howls in from the Atlantic so wretchedly that the expedition once again seems uncertain. A few months earlier the weather had also forced the European Technical Dive Centre to cancel an expedition to Thia, when their boat couldn't cope with the rough ocean conditions. The lads, you can be sure, were unsympathetic, but now it seems the same thing is happening to them. It's like she doesn't want to be dived.

But they're determined not to lose out on being first. Not again. Then Ric receives a text that makes him drop everything, throw his kit in the car and start down from Manchester that night: *It's on.*

What with the uncertain weather, some of the lads have made other plans and others don't have enough time to drive down to Plymouth before *Watcher* has to leave port if she's to make it back on time. In the end, the beleaguered expedition comprises just Ric and Richie, Zaid Al-obaidi and Bruce Dunton.

Two days out of Plymouth they arrive in the area where they know Thia lies and begin to run search patterns with the magnetometer and dual scan sounder. They're walking around in shorts and T-shirts at nine that morning, just as the sun breaks through the cloud cover onto the mirror-flat sea, when the sounder shows wreck. Lying between 475 and 518 feet down.

It's the right depth, but is it the right ship?

———

Richie and Zaid close the distance between the surface and the seabed. Richie looks at his dive watch: 360 feet. So deep, but such a pure blue. So bright, he can easily see the wreck below.

They reach the bridge at 482 feet in four minutes with a slight current running, then tie in the shot and release the pellet to give Bruce and Ric the nod to start their dive. It rises quickly.

The leviathan bodies of two lings slide past.

Visibility is extensive, enough so that they don't need torches or instruments. They can use pilotage: navigation by sight.

There are telegraphs on the bridge, and when the men swim past the cargo holds they note a surprising amount of chinaware.

The lings follow.

Beyond the holds the bow is very flat and there are winches all over the deck, which rests lower at 502 feet. It doesn't feel that deep. The current is too slight and the temperature too sweet. With the bow direction confirmed they head back to the more intact midships, pausing when they reach the china.

Zaid holds open Richie's goodie bag. Putting a china plate in a bag is a simple thing, but at depth, in current, kitted up in drysuit and gloves, simple takes a detour. They sort it between them then continue to explore, sifting through the wreckage, hoping for the bell. They don't find it but Richie is happy enough with the china as they'll be able to use it to help identify the wreck. He looks at his watch and wishes he had the bottle to take longer schedules. He's limited to eighteen minutes at 500 feet.

Richie signals he's leaving to Zaid, who has an extra four minutes of bottom time. He checks his position and estimates the strobes are no more than 130 feet away. Then time seems to slow.

His gaze follows the shot line as it disappears up into celestial blue, to meet the silhouette of two divers, fins curving gracefully, as they descend. A froth of bubbles languidly rises in their wake.

It's a perfect moment.

———

Before coming on this expedition, Bruce's wife made him write his will. When he reaches the wreck after a six-minute descent, he sees a porcelain sink on the deck bearing a familiar shipping line crest. He gazes through a porthole, wondering about past occupants, but doesn't linger. Instead, he clips his reel off and promptly jumps down Thia's side.

Why, with such a wreck to explore, would a diver choose to go down her side, to the seabed, rather than explore her stem to stern? If this is Thia she's not just deep, she's quite possibly the deepest wreck to be dived in or near UK waters. If that's the case, Bruce could become the man with the deepest descent on a record-breaking wreck dive.

But when his reel jams he has to stop, which is disappointing as the seabed is only 12 feet below. Instead, he fins up to the deck, where, in the distance, he can see Richie rummaging through plates like he's at a car boot sale. Soon after, Richie swims to the shot line and begins his ascent. With a jammed reel Bruce doesn't want to venture far and before long he too is heading up to the surface. At eight minutes it's a shorter bottom time than the other three, with a smaller deco penalty to pay. He's using a different decompression system to the other divers, something Richie doesn't know. So when Bruce shoots past him at a deco stop, Richie starts shouting through his mouthpiece, sure Bruce is going to kill himself.

―――――

As Ric descends beside the shot line the viz is perfect and he looks around in wonder at the soothing, ambient light. It's the alpine blue of a glacier-fed lake. The line went down on the bridge. Sometime in the years she's lain here, the

Atlantic has claimed the wreck's superstructure. All that marks her bridge are the remains of three large telegraph heads, lying useless on the decking.

In steamships, speed ahead or astern was controlled from the engine room at her heart, mid and low and blind. The bridge, high and forward, served as her vision.

Thia's telegraphs, large dual-faced dials, stood on brass pedestals of waist height. Like a clock face, each dial had its own set of hands. The long hand extended out and acted as a lever, and the short hand acted as an indicator. The dials mirrored each other, but instead of roman numerals they were divided into wedges that each contained a different order. Upright, or twelve o'clock, was 'all stop'. Pushing the lever forward, towards the bow, indicated speed ahead: dead slow, slow, half speed or full speed. Pulling the lever back indicated the same commands astern.

When a change in speed was ordered, the bridge telegraph operator pushed one of the levers and overshot the command. Wires and pulleys snaked through the ship, down from the bridge telegraph to a receiving telegraph in the engine room, where the overshoot triggered a bell. The bridge operator then positioned his lever on the correct command, and at the other end of the wire a corresponding lever on the engine room telegraph changed position to match. The engineer followed the same process using the second lever and dial, positioning it to mirror the command just relayed. A bridge bell rang and the second lever on the bridge telegraph moved into place, acknowledging 'command received'.

Ric clips his strobe light to the shot line then surveys the wreck as she lies before him, tonnes of steel on the sandy bottom. She's crusted with shell and coral and brittle star, so that none of her metal is laid bare. The tight, fine weave of trawler nets tangle her. He starts slowly finning towards the bow.

Richie passes him and salutes, unclips his strobe and begins his ascent. Bruce and Zaid are nowhere to be seen, and even with all his experience, and the practice dive of *Dasher*, Ric's still nervous.

Wise men always are.

This is the deepest he has ever been.

Nearby, the pair of lings glide though the water. They are at home at this depth. Impervious to the pressure. Gilled.

———

Thia was built with a triple band of portholes ringing her upper decks. Brass surrounds that gleamed like warm brandy in firelight. But the brass on the seabed is decades dull, encrusted with deposits and marine growth.

The etymology of *porthole* derives from fifteenth-century ocean warfare when cannons were mounted internally, through holes in a ship's hull. To keep out inclement weather the holes had hatches, or *ports*, from the French word for doors. Swan & Hunter called them sidelights since their purpose was to admit light and air.

But there is little light and no air at the bottom of the ocean. Once, this ship's portholes offered glimpses of the outside world. Now they're a means to search through her depths and scratch at her secrets.

After a longer dive than anyone else, Zaid sends up one of the wreck's portholes.

Not that he'll get to keep it.

———

Ric is hardly past the shot line when he spies plates scattered around the bridge. Later, he wonders why, of all things, Zaid bagged a bloody porthole at that depth, with limited bottom time, when there are all these plates he could have taken.

In some ways their attitude to removing artefacts from wrecks is old fashioned. They all know that there are people who frown on them taking portholes and plates and whatever else they find. That it makes them a little bit the pariah – more treasure hunter than archaeologist. And they can understand that to some extent. But they think differently.

The sea rots things. Disposes of them sooner than you might think. Shipwrecks aren't eternal. The deep blue will not keep them down there forever. It's hostile and destroys things that do not belong. Sediments abrade, bacteria consume, and objects rot and languish, corroded by salt and acids – even brass, like Ric's bell off the *Armenian*, which is soft and leached of copper and won't polish up.

It's not just artefacts that rot. The wreck is slowly being consumed by parasites feasting on her iron skeleton.

Let the sea have her, or claim back what can be wrested from the deep?

What's right seems to lie somewhere in the Narrows: there are some things that should be preserved, some graves that shouldn't be robbed.

Ric descends to the bridge, towards the plates. It's not unusual to find artefacts in odd places. The debris field of a wreck is subject to how she sinks, the whims of the ocean, and time. As Ric rescues one of the plates he turns it over and gently wipes the muck from its surface. Silt clouds the blue water then dissipates. In the centre of what was once pristine white porcelain is a rampant lion, clutching the world between his forepaws. An arched crown hovers above, and below an unfurled banner: The Cunard Steamship Company Ltd.

Carpathia.

Divers never know for sure if the virgin wreck they're on is the one they think it is, not until they've found a bell or a plate or some other means of identifying her. The Cunard crest is confirmation enough for them. This hulking mass of twisted, netted metal really is Thia.

Ric's still nervy. *I'm not messin' around gettin' me goodie bag out. It's just gonna get snagged on somethin'.*

He carefully tucks the plate inside the webbing on his rebreather before moving on.

———

When Richie surfaces after five hours of decompression he swims over to *Watcher* and climbs her ladder, his fins flicking out like the flippers of a seal. Where regular ladders have rungs with closed sides, dive ladders have a central spine with open rungs so divers can move their fins up and down with ease.

He's relieved to find that Bruce is on board, safe and sound. When Richie starts kitting off he hands Skipper Steve Wright his goodie bag. There are two plates inside. Steve examines them. The Cunard crest is in the plate well and around the everted lip is a blue-and-white wreath. When he is done with his inspection Steve carefully sets the plates down into an empty plastic box to keep them safe. Only, when Richie takes off his lead dive belt and glances around for somewhere to put it, he tosses it into the plastic box. To the sound of breaking crockery.

———

Ric checks his dive watch. Twenty minutes at bottom and he's hardly gone ninety feet from the shot line, a distance not even a quarter of her length, but he shouldn't stay any longer. He swims to the two flashing strobes still marking the line, unclips his light, then swims up towards his first decompression stop.

Bloody hell, no!

Ric grabs for the blue-and-white porcelain as it slips free of the webbing on his rebreather, but it sinks too rapidly, spinning into the blue ether.

Back down to the waiting ling.

In the dive world, a wreck's not dived 'less you can prove it. Ric's plate just flittered back down to the seabed. Zaid's porthole has no provenance, no way to show where it comes from. And the porcelain casualty in the plastic box, when taped back together, is a sad testimony. Even so, the blue-and-white plate demonstrates only that they have dived a Cunard wreck, not which one. It comes down to the word of four men who say it was Thia, but for many, simply saying it is not proof enough.

The team have only come out with enough time for two days of diving, and tomorrow's forecast is for wind-force five to seven. Force five results in moderate waves and spray. Force seven means winds over fifty kilometres, breaking waves and airborne spray. Near gale conditions. It won't even matter if the weather breaks quickly. There is no time for a second dive. No time to recover more evidence.

But they are not entirely empty-handed.

Underneath the blue-and-white fragments in the plastic box, Richie's second plate is intact. It withstood World War I, about eighty years at the bottom of the Atlantic and the unforgiving weight of a lead dive belt. It seems that little piece of Thia has earned its return to the sun and the sky and the world above.

CQD OM

1912

ALL IS QUIET. MOST OF THOSE ABOARD THIA HAVE RETIRED to sleeping quarters made cosy by the steam circulating through her pipes. In his cabin under the bridge, the mahogany of Arthur's berth glows warmly in the low light as he prepares for bed. At midnight eight bells sound, signalling the end of the watch. He slips between the empty sheets. On cold nights at sea, a man misses his wife.

Marrying Minnie was, and always will be, his greatest good fortune in life. He wishes he saw her and his boys more often. Thia's assignment to the New York–Mediterranean route only allows him to return home to England at year's end, when she receives her annual maintenance at Liverpool.

A whole year without his wife. His sons.

He reads their letters. Re-reads them on the small velvet sofa in his quarters, perfect for that task. As though the small luxuries in his cabin can compensate a man who lives his life absent from the family he loves. Not that there is any other life he would choose. He's always been for the sea and has always known it. He settles into a comfortable position in his berth and gradually slides into the world between sleep and waking.

―――

At the other end of the deck, young Harold comes sharply alert.

CQD. All stations, distress.

Perhaps a little hesitant, perhaps a little disbelieving – this is the ship they say is practically unsinkable – he taps out a reply to *Titanic*'s distress call: *Shall I tell my captain?*

Yes.

The moment of hesitation passes and he rips off the 'phones, grabs the chit of paper marking her latitude and longitude, and runs to the bridge.

―――

First Officer Horace Dean is on duty, having replaced the second officer at eight bells. His sharp, attractive face fills with tension when Harold tells him the news. 'Come with me.' Horace bolts down the starboard ladder into the chartroom and barges through the door to the captain's quarters without knocking, emerging at the head of his berth.

Arthur leans up on an elbow and frowns. He's about to issue a reprimand to the cheeky beggar when Horace's words halt him. 'Captain, we've just received an urgent distress message from *Titanic*. She has struck ice and requires immediate assistance.'

Arthur reacts instantly. 'Turn the ship north-west.'

Horace leaves directly to carry out the order while Harold remains with the captain. Arthur rises, uncaring that he is in his nightclothes, and grabs the young wireless operator by the sleeve. 'Are you sure it is *Titanic* and that she requires immediate assistance?'

'Yes, sir.'

But Arthur finds it hard to believe. 'Are you absolutely certain?'

'*Yes.*'

'All right.' Arthur straightens, releasing the youth. 'Do you have her position?'

Harold indicates the chit in his hand then waits in the chartroom while the captain dresses. When Arthur enters he picks up Thia's position from the chart on the table. 41° 10' North, 49° 12' West. He gives it to Harold. 'Tell him we are coming as fast as we can.'

As Harold races off, Arthur's voice sings out orders up to the bridge: 'Send for the chief engineer and the chief officer. Call all officers.'

As he waits for the men to report he sets to work determining the heading that will take them to the distressed liner. Cunard company policy allows a captain to act as his own judgement directs when a vessel requires assistance. At a sound outside the chartroom Arthur looks up to see the bosun's mate passing with the watch, on their way to wash down the decks.

'Mr Ascheri.' The captain's call halts the crewman. 'Knock off all work and get the boats ready for lowering. It's all right,' he continues, seeing the instant alarm on the man's face, 'we're going to another vessel in distress. Keep quiet while you're about it. If any passengers awaken, instruct them to return to their cabins and stay there.'

'Aye, sir.' The bosun's mate scrambles to comply.

When Arthur finishes plotting the course he climbs to the bridge to finds his officers assembled. 'North 52 West True,' he orders the helmsman.

'Aye-aye, sir. North 52 West!' The man turns the wheel while Arthur telegraphs down to the engine room *full steam ahead*. Indicating that the officers should follow, he returns to the chartroom. Having been unceremoniously roused from their beds the men are drowsy, but the drastic course change brings them quickly alert. At sea, when things happen, they have no one to rely on but each other. And Thia.

It is the deep of the night. The hours that are so quiet and still, so dark and far from land, that Thia seems their only anchor to the world beyond the water. Those aboard rest easy in the knowledge that she holds them securely, travels them safely. Their welfare weighs heavily on her captain. Because the order he is about to give may see Thia meet the same fate as *Titanic*.

'*Titanic* has struck a berg and is in distress 58 miles from here on the bearing North 52 West. We're going to her aid.' Arthur speaks quickly, but steadily. 'Mr Johnston,' he says to his chief engineer, 'call out an extra watch in the engine room and raise every ounce of steam possible. Cut off all heating and hot water and put it back into her engines. Make all speed possible. Spare nothing.' The Scotsman's bushy white moustache twitches as he acknowledges the orders. While Johnston hurries away, Arthur sends for Dr McGee, Purser Brown and Chief Steward Hughes.

———

As Harold is returning to the Marconi shack, an impulse takes him. He makes a quick detour to the shelter deck and knocks on one of the cabin doors. There's movement within and a moment later the door opens to reveal Dr Blackmarr and Cecil Francis, the doctor's travelling companion, the son of one of his neighbours.

'Doctor, I thought you'd want to know,' Harold says, 'the *Titanic* has struck an iceberg and we are going to her aid.'

The doctor and Cecil are astonished and disbelieving, but Harold assures them it's true and leaves them dressing as he quickly returns to the Marconi shack. As he slips on his 'phones he can hear *Titanic* working *Frankfurt*, but the distressed liner is having trouble. Her extinguished furnaces are venting steam, making the signals from other ships almost indistinguishable to Jack Phillips and Harry Bride. Harold taps out a message to *Titanic* that conveys Thia's position. She's close enough to *Titanic* that her signals come in strong to the White Star liner. Then Harold stands by to aid them, passing on traffic from more distant ships. Otherwise he's silent so as not to jam her operators – that is, clutter up the airwaves with his transmissions and thus drown out theirs. But the news that *Titanic* has struck a berg is bouncing across the Atlantic, from ship to ship to shore, as each vessel tries to determine their distance from *Titanic*, tries to determine who is closest, and if anyone other than Thia is going to her aid.

———

After the other officers assemble in Arthur's cabin he explains the situation. 'I don't believe there is any serious danger; nonetheless we must be ready to help possibly thousands of passengers.' Then he begins to issue more instructions. 'Dr McGee, you and your assistants are to remain in the first-class dining saloon and prepare it to receive survivors. See that Dr Risicato does the same in second and Dr Lengyel in third. Prepare a supply of stimulants and restoratives and have everything to hand for the immediate needs of probable wounded or sick.

'Mr Brown,' he addresses the purser, 'you, the assistant purser and Mr Hughes are to prepare to receive people at the gangways. Organise our stewards to assist the *Titanic*'s people to the dining rooms to receive medical checks. Get the names of survivors as soon as possible to send by wireless.

'Mr Hughes,' his attention shifts to the chief steward, 'all hands will be called so have coffee ready to serve to them. Also have tea, soup, brandy and whiskey ready in each saloon. Put blankets near the gangways, in saloons and public rooms, and also some in our own boats in case they are needed. See that all of the rescued are cared for and their immediate wants attended.

'All officers' cabins will be given up for accommodations. Use the smokerooms, library and dining rooms if necessary. Group our steerage passengers together and use all spare berths for *Titanic*'s steerage. The inspector, steerage stewards, and master-at-arms are to control our steerage passengers and keep them out of the third-class dining hall and off the deck to prevent confusion.

'Place stewards in each alleyway to reassure our passengers, should they inquire about the noise in getting our boats out or the working of the engines. Instruct them to remain in their cabins.'

Arthur has issued this litany of orders in less than a minute, but here he pauses.

'As far as it is possible, there is a need for absolute silence on this matter.' He surveys the small group of Thia's officers.

'Order and strict discipline must be maintained to avoid confusion.' If word gets out, the passengers' curiosity, questions and presence on deck will hinder the crew's efforts.

Arthur dismisses the doctor, purser and chief steward, and they leave to carry out his orders. He goes up to the bridge with his remaining officers and is soon met by Harold with news. 'Captain, *Titanic* called *Olympic* and asked them to ready their boats.'

Arthur's concern grows. *Olympic* is much faster than Thia but *Titanic*'s sister is also hundreds of miles away.

Harold's voice cuts in on his thoughts. 'They want to know how long we will be?'

'Say about four hours.'

Harold returns to the shack and taps out a message. He tells them Thia is *58 miles, coming hard*.

On the bridge, Arthur turns to his chief and first officer. 'Call all hands.' He issues more orders, as though he never stopped. 'Swing out all boats. Open all gangway doors.' There are four, two each side of Thia's upper deck. 'At each gangway put electric lights over the side; hook a block with line rove,' a pulley system, 'and chair slings for getting up any sick or wounded. Have canvas ash bags on hand for children.' The children could be placed inside the bags and raised to the deck. 'Boatswains' chairs, pilot ladders and side ladders at gangways.' When they arrive, the ladders can be dropped down Thia's side.

'Cargo falls, with both ends clear and bight secured, along ship's sides on deck.' The rope falls can be attached to *Titanic*'s lifeboats in order to raise them, since their own boats occupy the boat davits. 'Have heaving lines,' light-weight ropes, 'distributed along the side for lashing people in chairs. Forward derricks topped and rigged, and get steam on the winches.' They may need to bring luggage and mail aboard. 'Ready oil bags in the lavatories.' To pour onto rough seas and quiet them. 'Start firing rockets every quarter hour from 3 a.m.' By then Thia should be close enough for *Titanic* to see them. Additionally, Arthur gives each of his officers orders for manning Thia's boats, should it be required.

The ordinary complement of Thia's night lookout, in addition to the regular duty officer, junior officer and quar-termaster on the bridge, is one man in her crow's nest and another at her eyes, right forward on the deck. The posi-tion puts him nearer to the water than the man in the nest.

Arthur can hear the thudding tempo of Thia's engines, increasing in speed. 'Another lookout to the eyes,' he orders. Beside him, there are three other officers on the bridge and the quartermaster at the helm. He directs one of the officers to the port bridge wing, then calls the second officer, James Bisset, who has exceptionally good eyesight, to the starboard wing. 'Station yourself here and keep a special lookout for lights and flares – *and for ice*.' Spotting an iceberg on a calm and moonless night is no easy task. If a novice sees some dim shape upon the water they can take it for nothing at all, merely a shadow. But those with experience of ice know what to look for and can at once distinguish that it is a separate object. And that it must be only one thing. 'In this smooth sea it's no use looking for waves breaking around the base of the bergs. Look for the reflection of starshine in the ice pinnacles.'

'Aye, sir,' says James.

Satisfied the second officer will keep sharp to his duties, Arthur looks out into the black veil where Thia sails. The silence is broken when her bell tolls, rousing the crew, but the echo soon fades. For the first time since he was disturbed in his cabin, Arthur stops. All the orders a captain can give in such a situation, he has given. He trusts his men to attend them diligently.

There is only one other thing that may make a difference, and this he does willingly. His hand moves to his cap and he raises it a fraction. His head bows, his eyes close, and his lips move silently in the night.

PART
TWO

THE MAIDEN VOYAGE

1912

THE DARK SEA IS CALM. IT HAS THE APPEARANCE OF A quiet lake. There are rises and falls but no waves. The world seems wrapped in tranquillity, save the low mutters of officers carrying out the captain's orders. The sky is clear. Moonless. The stars glitter gloriously.

It feels like he's only just fallen asleep when Steward Robert Vaughan is awakened by tugging on his bedclothes. 'What's wrong?' he asks, sitting up. It's pitch-black – someone's swiped the lightbulb again, to discourage late-night chats – and he can't tell who woke him. They've already moved on to the next bunk.

Words hiss at him through the dark. 'We've struck an iceberg.'

Alarmed, Robert and four other stewards, hazy from sleep, stumble to dress in the small cabin in the dark. They brush against walls covered in pictures of loved ones, stage beauties, boxers and other sports stars, framed by cut-out menu cards. Bang against berths and the sea chests stored under them, against boxes nailed to the bulkheads containing knick-knacks and mementos of home.

Somewhere amidst the confusion sleep falls away. They realise that if Thia had struck a berg they'd have felt it. Their cabin is well forward, near her bow. When Robert makes it up on deck the second steward orders him and the others to get the spare blankets out from the lockers. Then he helps lay the tables for soup and coffee, for a full complement. As he follows orders he keeps an ear out for the furtive comments exchanged between the stewards, none of whom seem to know exactly what's about. But their curiosity is soon assuaged.

An order is given to muster in the main saloon. There, Chief Steward Hughes tells them about *Titanic*. He tells them that Thia is going to her rescue. That they are to keep this information from the passengers. He asks them, when the time comes, to uphold the traditions of the sea. When he dismisses them he says, as if a commander to his troops, 'Every man to his post and let him do his full duty like a true Englishman. If the situation calls for it, let us add another glorious page to the history of the Empire.'

And every man there salutes.

Before they're dismissed they are assigned stations to attend during the rescue. Until then, the preparations having all been seen to, they're free to do as they wish. Robert goes to the afterdeck where many of the crew gather to watch and wait. They mess about to stave off the cold. It's a bit of horseplay to distract themselves, even as they're all silently aware that something comes.

───────

The blasting of Thia's whistle awakens Augusta Ogden. Lying abed, she hears unusual sounds outside their stateroom. 'Louis,' her voice is soft in the dark, 'did you hear that? Is there a fog, do you suppose?' When there is no response she says his name louder, until he wakes. 'What's that noise on deck?'

'Don't worry,' he mumbles groggily. 'Go to sleep.'

'I think something might be wrong with the ship. *Please*, look outside and see.'

Blearily, he climbs out of bed, grabs a wrapper against the cold and cracks the door. There are stewards in the alleyway. 'What's this noise all about?'

'Nothing, sir,' one of them replies. 'Doing work with the boats.'

'What for?'

'I can't tell you, sir.'

Louis looks at the blankets the stewards are carrying. Blankets and lifeboats are a worrying combination. He relays the news to Augusta, and, as they listen, sounds creep though the walls: chocks being removed from the boats, boats being swung out on the davits.

'Why would they be working with the boats at this time of night?' Augusta asks. The Ogdens are seasoned travellers, but neither of them can answer the question. At least, no answer that they like. The harsh reality of being alone at sea plays on their minds until Augusta can bear it no longer. 'Try again,' she urges.

Louis opens the door once more and sees Dr McGee. 'What is the trouble?' he asks.

'There's no trouble,' the doctor lies. 'Please stay in your cabin. Captain's orders.'

Well that doesn't make sense. Why would the captain have issued orders for them to stay in their cabin? Certain that something is wrong with Thia, worried there might even be a fire aboard, Louis closes the door and urges Augusta to dress. After hurriedly pulling on their warmest clothes they slip their valuables into their pockets.

'Try again to see if you can find out what is going on,' Augusta asks her husband. For a third time he opens their cabin door and is again met by Dr McGee, who speaks before he can say anything. 'Please return to your cabin, sir, and remain there until the captain gives instructions.'

Now seriously concerned, Louis at last refuses to be put off. 'No. There is something clearly wrong aboard this ship. Are we in danger? Is she sinking? *What is the matter?*'

At this obvious worry Dr McGee finally relents. 'An accident, but not to our ship. Stay inside.'

'But *this* ship isn't in distress?' Certainty is one of life's great reassurances.

'No, sir. It's *Titanic*. She's struck ice.'

'You'll have to give me something better than that! *Titanic* is on the northern route; we are on the southern.' His tone is sharp.

The doctor matches it. 'We're going north like hell. Stay in your room.'

Louis relays the news to Augusta.

'But that's ridiculous – *Titanic* is unsinkable,' she says. 'Do you believe it?'

'No.'

Certain now that Thia is in danger and that they have to escape, Louis and Augusta sneak out on deck. They find a quiet nook and remain there, worriedly watching the crew's hurried preparations.

———

As Thia heads north-west the cold night becomes bitter. The bridge crew watch the falling barometer, measure the falling sea temperature. Deep in Thia's underworld, the chief engineer rouses a second watch of firemen. They fall out of their berths as soon as they hear the news. Some report for duty still in their union suits, though most work stripped to the waist.

In the midst of the sweltering inferno are six massive boilers with a combined 20 000 square feet of heating surface, to turn water to steam. They stand three to a row, back to back, towering above the firemen. There are four furnaces in each boiler.

Trimmers cart barrow after barrow of coal and pile it at the base of the boilers. They bring it through the tunnel from the adjacent bunker, where the icy chill of the water penetrates Thia's metal hull, and pour it down the shafts from the bunker overhead, caught in the rising heat from the boilers. Even in a crisis they are careful to mine the coal uniformly and keep Thia in trim.

A gong sounds the start of a new stoking cycle. Like a metronome, the indicator keeps the firemen in time. They use their slicer bars to break up the large lumps of coal at their feet. Then, rolling with Thia's pitch, they each open a furnace door. Heat whooshes out across sweat-slicked, soot-blackened torsos. They rake their bars across the coals, stirring the embers and breaking ash and clinkers loose, sweeping the cinders out into the pit.

Metal scrapes across metal and scratches across carbon as they shovel coal deep inside the glowing furnace. Again and again. Until there's an even layer several inches deep. Then they close the door.

On any other day they'd repeat the cycle, as many times as necessary before the gong sounds again, so that all of Thia's 24 furnaces were stoked. The more speed wanted, the shorter the interval between gongs; eight minutes for full speed, 30 minutes for dead slow. But the captain has asked them for as much speed as possible and the extra watch means each man has fewer furnaces to feed, and so they are stoked as never before. Without cease, in unspoken consensus, by men determined to wring every drop from Thia that is humanly possible.

The vapour produced by the boilers flows through the overhead pipes into Thia's steam plant – her two quadruple expansion engines – in the neighbouring chamber. In each engine four daisy-chained cylinders enclose pistons that pump up and down when the steam expands as it cools. Piston rods extend from the bottom of the cylinders, furiously working the crankshaft, which in turn spins one of her propeller shafts and screws. After the steam passes through the final cylinder it's piped into the condenser, cooled to water and recycled back into the boilers.

Thia's steam plant is three decks tall. Water drips from copper pipes and the rhythmic piston-pounding sounds like a train hard on the tracks. As the stokers work overtime, the chief engineer follows the captain's orders. He directs his men to cut off steam to the heating and hot water, and divert it back into the engines. They do the same with steam to the pantries, galleys and kitchens, leaving only that which is necessary to the rescue preparations. Then they close the safety valves, the ones that automatically purge steam if the pressure gets too high.

Like the mules that resulted in her genesis, much depends on Thia. She carries a heavy load and these men ask much and give little. And the more they ask, the further the pressure-gauge needle creeps towards the red.

———

Decks above, the English, Italian and Hungarian doctors carry out their orders. They prepare alleviatives and excitants as well as dressings and instruments. They set up stretchers, prepare splints, gather cognac and whiskey. When the stewards bring the blankets from storage they set about heating them.

Passenger Howard Chapin is awakened by the sound of footsteps overhead, such as he has not heard on any of the three nights since Thia left New York. As he lies in the top berth, his wife asleep in the lower, he recalls that there is a lifeboat tied to a cleat directly above their stateroom. If not for the deck between he could reach out a hand to touch it. He hears someone kneel down and he's certain they are untying the boat. He climbs down from his bunk, throws on an overcoat and hurries out on deck. It's pitch dark, although the stars shine overhead. And it's so much colder than when he and Hope retired. When he finds the sailor – who is, as he suspected, untying the boat – Howard questions him. Perhaps the captain's entreaty to silence has not filtered down to the sailor because he replies with the truth of *Titanic*'s situation.

Howard returns to awaken Hope. They dress in their warmest clothes and go out on deck. It is even colder now. They cannot see any other passengers but the deck is covered with lifebelts, breeches buoys – rope chairs – and blankets, and Thia's side is lined with rope ladders. The crew are readying more lifeboats: rolling back the canvas covers, unlashing them from their deck cradles, ensuring the oars and oarlocks are secure and the drain plugs are in place. Howard and Hope settle quietly out of the way and wait, watching as the boats are carefully swung out over the gunwale, first the bow then the stern, suspended from their davits. The small white boats are chained to stop them from swinging about until they are ready to be lowered. The time it takes to prepare the boats is considerable, which is why the captain ordered the task done now. They must be ready by the time Thia arrives.

The temperature of the Atlantic is two degrees below zero. Only the salt in the water prevents it from turning to ice. The human reaction to immersion in water this cold is uncontrollable, a physiological response.

First is the gasp reflex. Pray it happens while your head is above water.

Within seconds hyperventilation and cold shock set in. The heart races, blood pressure spikes and there's a chance of cardiac arrest. In less than two minutes the heat is leached from your limbs at a rate 25 times faster than air of the same temperature.

You lose dexterity. Feel it first in your hands and fingers before your arms and legs stop responding. Within ten, perhaps twenty minutes you slip below the surface; know you are drowning but are helpless to stop it. With a life-belt you have a little longer. Maybe thirty minutes before your organs fail and you die of hypothermia.

———

Down in the engine room, the needle creeps up.

In the wireless room, Harold listens intently to *Titanic*'s signals but *Frankfurt* keeps calling and asking, *What is the matter?* She doesn't seem to understand the situation. He hears *Titanic* use the new international distress code, SOS, then he hears her call *Olympic*: *We are sinking fast.*

Sinking?

Titanic is sinking?

No one aboard Thia imagined the other ship to be in mortal danger. The wireless messages simply said that she had struck a berg and needed aid. Then Harold hears something that makes him rip off the 'phones and run to the bridge once more.

'Captain,' he says, and there is something in his voice.

Arthur looks at the young man.

'Message from *Titanic*. She says: *Engine room full up to boilers.*'

———

The news whips through Thia's crew like wildfire and, for the first time, the spectre of what it means if *Titanic* goes down. It's at the forefront of Dr McGee's mind when he's summoned to attend one of Thia's cabin passengers. After he examines Captain Crain and prescribes a treatment, Mrs Crain sees the doctor out. Perhaps because her husband is a sea captain, perhaps because she has noticed the unusual activity aboard, perhaps because the spectre looms large, Dr McGee tells her that Thia is going to *Titanic*'s aid. That the other ship is on the verge of sinking.

Despite Arthur's order for silence, knowledge of the icy danger towards which they hurtle creeps through Thia's passengers. By now she has attained maximum speed. The chief engineer reports this to the captain, just as each officer, after having carried out his orders, reports to the captain.

Thia's stem cuts through the ocean, throwing up massive spray. On the bridge the cold night air coils around the officers and slides down their spines. It is full of unspoken words, until – 'Captain, are we sure this is the best course of action, sir?' One of the officers asks the question that all are thinking. They are sailing full speed towards ice. On the darkest of nights. 'Is not the risk to our passengers too great?'

The most important duty entrusted to a captain is to safeguard the lives aboard his vessel. That those aboard Thia are in danger, that this danger increases by the second, is unquestionable. But to do nothing would be unconscionable. At least to Arthur, and the decision is his. A ship is not a democracy. The rules that govern society cannot withstand a trial by ocean, even as they compel him to act. He knows where the icefield lies and has increased the watch for bergs. He will take every precaution save one: that of doing nothing.

Yet, even as he obeys the dictates of his conscience, even as he places his trust in God, he is anxious. An emotion best hidden. Thia's crew looks to him and *she* depends upon him. So while he respects his officers and listens to their concerns – it is only right that they voice them – they press on.

Below, the chief engineer places his cap over the pressure gauge.

Two hours after they first received word of the disaster, Dr McGee climbs the ladder to the bridge and makes his report to the captain, who listens while maintaining his lookout. As they discuss what to expect, Arthur sees a flash of green a half point off the port bow. 'There's her light.' His words are infused with renewed hope. 'She must still be afloat.' Thia is yet a long way off and it's only a flicker of green, but it looks high enough to be *Titanic*'s starboard navigation light.

After the last wireless message that said the water was up to the engine room, and with Harold having received no signals from *Titanic* for at least twenty minutes, Arthur had nearly resigned himself to the worst. But now . . . 'Fire a rocket,' he orders. 'And the company signals. Every fifteen minutes. Let them know we are coming.'

The first rocket is fired and 800 feet up the sky explodes in a white shower of light. A roman candle is lit immediately after. In quick succession, it shoots six sparkling blue balls 150 feet skyward, identifying Thia as a Cunard liner. The fireworks linger in the sky against the soft green northern lights on the horizon.

'Captain,' James calls from the starboard bridge wing a minute later. His face is ruddy from the frosty air, his night vision still recovering from the rocket's bright flare. 'Two points off the port bow.'

Arthur's attention snaps to the night beyond the bearing, the impenetrable blackness that comes before the soft green. There: the glimmer of a starbeam three-quarters of a mile ahead. But not in the sky. Reflected off the cold, hard facet of an iceberg.

1903

There are stages in a ship's life, as with any life. The laying of her keel and her launch are markers on that timeline, but there are few things as significant as her first sailing. This is when she comes into her own. Most stories about Thia are really about *Titanic*. They tell about *her* maiden voyage. So here is the tale of Thia's.

Thick moorings anchor Thia to the Swan & Hunter shipyard at Wallsend, which has been the extent of her world until now. After years of planning and endeavour she is about to fulfil the promise that is built into the curves of her hull, signalled by the red-and-black livery of her funnel, and evident in the red ensign – the flag that marks her as a British merchantman – fluttering from her mast. They're marks of all those who have invested in her. Not only Cunard and the hundreds and thousands of pounds spent on her creation, but also the men in the yards. The ones who, even now, perform the finishing touches that will make her perfect.

Sometimes the cost of such perfection is high. Men die in the yards. Not as often now as it once was, but often enough. Even when the cost of an ocean liner or wind-jammer or clipper or sloop – any ship – is not a man's life, each one still gifts some part of himself. A transference that enlivens her until she's more than the sum of her materials. Until she's imbued with an essence at odds with something wrought by man, and not God.

This transference has accompanied the building of boats since the beginning. It has ancient foundations from when men could whisper to wood. Could wrest vessels from living materials because they understood the nature of nature. And though this art is slowly eroding in the Western world, and iron has replaced wood, the essential legacy remains.

When Thia is released from her moorings for the first time, the cheers of the yardsmen are joined by those of the spectators who line the riverbanks, their exuberance carrying upriver as Thia steams downstream to the Tynemouth and out past the stone breakwaters, which extend almost a mile and took over forty years to build. Six years ago, a storm breached the northern seawall and it was almost completely destroyed. Sir John Wolfe Barry, of Tower Bridge fame, is one of the engineers working on a new seawall. It will protect the Tynemouth from waves that break as high as 75 feet in wild weather. Some of Thia's passengers stand on her decks, watching the walls pass. Really, they are the ones passing, but it seems as though it is the world that moves. It's the same with the sun. With life. With time. When the wall is completed a lighthouse will be built on its seaward end. Before long it will be as though it was always there.

After luncheon, Thia begins her sea trials. All ships undergo these trials. She'll prove to the Cunard representatives aboard that she is capable of the speed Swan & Hunter guaranteed when they bid to build her. Her first run over the measured mile – two points on land covering a nautical mile – is recorded by one of Swan & Hunter's naval architects in a small black leather notebook. He turns to a new page and carefully pencils in her name and her yard number, 274. He records tidal and wind conditions, propeller diameter and number of blades.

Then, precisely at 4 p.m., Thia begins her first run. South. Towards Sunderland.

In the first run column, the naval architect pencils in an array of numbers that represent screw revolutions, steam and vacuum pressure, engine gauge readings, and indicated horsepower. Thia covers the mile in four minutes, fourteen and a half seconds. Then Captain James Barr, her first, turns her north and at half past the hour they steam back along the mile to the Tynemouth. Four minutes, nine seconds. Distance travelled divided by time taken, calculated for each run, and the architect pencils in a mean speed of 14.344 knots.

That's a very respectable speed for a mid-size liner. Not record breaking, but then she was only commissioned to make a guaranteed fourteen knots. The results are good enough that they don't bother with the usual third or fourth run. In any accord, it's late afternoon and the sea is up.

A small paddle-box tug manoeuvres alongside Thia. Barr gives the order for Liverpool and the trial trippers clamber down a Jacob's ladder. When they reach the level of the tug, helping hands guide most of them aboard, except for those who, to the delight of the observers on Thia's decks, leap dauntlessly between the two vessels. The remaining crowd cheer, wave hats and kerchiefs at the departing tug, and are met by a similar farewell against the looming backdrop of the cliffs of old Tynemouth.

Above the cliffs, on Pen Bal Crag, are the ruins of a castle and a Benedictine priory where the bones of the kings of Northumbria lie. Dusk is approaching and the ruins are silhouetted against the evening sun. Thia's passengers stare up in wonder at the ancient edifice. Like the Roman wall uncovered at the yard when Thia was built, it's a testament to the ravages and the benedictions of time. What is old was once new. What is new may one day be old. A thing that's infinite and instant, a grain of sand and a wildflower. And now that Thia's left the sheltered Tyne with its protective walls, the only home she's ever known, and sailed under the rippling shadow of Pen Bal Crag, she steams into the gathering darkness.

———

Kate Smith was born in Manorhamilton, County Leitrim. The town is a stone's throw from the court tombs of Tullyskeherny, and if one were to walk further, say up to the plateau of O'Donnell's Rock, on a clear day looking west they could see the rise and fall of Ireland as far as Lough Gill, Knocknarea and, beyond, the Atlantic. When Kate married it was to an American, Richard Kelley, and they made a life together in Boston. After she conceived and it seemed safe to travel, she returned home to see her family and let a little bit of Irish green seep through the soles of her boots, up to the child that she carries. When spring closes he is almost due, so she prepares to return to America. Her son will always belong in part to Ireland, but should be born on paternal soil. Kate travels south, to Queenstown, and books passage on a liner.

The sun shines gently on the morning of 6 May when Thia docks at the Cunard Wharf in Queenstown, her final port before the open Atlantic. The ocean breeze stirs Kate's skirts as she carefully walks up the gangway, clutching the railing tightly, remembering, maybe, what it was like when she was one of these Irish, another Barry or Brennan, Connor or Kelly, sailing to a new world.

The local Cunard and press agents enter with the promenade and saloon passengers. They examine Thia's decks and dining halls, her staterooms and library, where some of them pause by a glass box atop a bookcase, curious about its contents. This same inspection will replay at each port until she is no longer new. The men disembark before Thia departs in the early afternoon. By this time Katie has found her berth, forward, in the women's steerage quarters. The men are aft and segregation is strictly maintained after lights out. She inspects the room with the curious interest all passengers exhibit when they first encounter their at-sea accommodations. The compartment sleeps four. There are two berths, top and bottom, against the starboard wall and two against the port wall. Each coverlet bears a Cunard lion, rampant and blue against the crisp white of the bedsheets. There's also a washstand and mirror. From the woodwork to the linen to the electric lighting, there is no other ship in the Atlantic service with steerage accommodations to match.

Katie meets the other women who will share the cabin. They ask her when she's due – *soon*. They exchange pasts – *Manorhamilton, but my husband is American* – and pleasantries – *how nice it is to be sailing on the maiden voyage of such an agreeable ship, with our very own ladies' room and promenade.*

Katie has one of the lower berths and that night she slips between the covers and falls asleep to the distant hum of Thia's engines as they leave Ireland in their wake. It's still dark when she stirs. She places a hand over her stomach and braces against the contraction. Fingers grip the bedsheet and she calls for help from the other women. They hold her hand and reassure her. Summon help from the stewardesses, who take Katie to Thia's hospital and rouse the ship's surgeon.

As Katie labours in the dark, Thia passes through the Southwest Approaches, the offshore waters between the Atlantic and Great Britain. It's roughly eighteen hours since their departure and they've travelled a little over three hundred miles, putting them on the edge of the Celtic Shelf, the place where it drops away into the abyssal plain, the most remote region on Earth. This is where her child is born, as the sun rises behind Thia and lights the path ahead. It is Thia's first daybreak far from land and the child's first in this world.

The sea breeze carries the news from dining hall to dining hall, across class divides, and the whole ship celebrates. Captain Barr writes the details in Thia's log, but when he asks the child's name there is none to record. Katie, perhaps, does not want to name their son without her husband. But some of the officers think he should be named Carpathius. Thia means *divine*.

No better masculine derivative can be found so this is what the passengers call him, regardless of what his mother may say about it. Carpathius Kelley. But his name is not all that is of interest about this child. There is the question of nationality: Irish mother, American father, ship British registered, born in transit.

Not far north of their position, on the edge of the shelf, is the trough *Clais Sgeir Rocail.* In all the world the waves are not higher than they are here, near Rockall – the sea rock of roaring. And even closer, somewhere just off starboard, is an island. It cannot be found on any prevailing map, only those inked half a millennium ago during cartography's renaissance. The isle lies west of Ireland. It has many names but most call it Hy-Brasil. The Lore says it can only be found one day every seven years, though reportedly there have been several successful expeditions. Two by English seafarers from Bristol; one, later, by the Italian explorer Giovanni Caboto; and one by Saint Brendan. The Celts say it rests where the sun touches the horizon. That the High King of the World holds court there. That it rises and falls, a sunken island. One of its names is *Tir fo-Thuin,* the 'Land Below the Wave'.

Phantom islands are like sea monsters – they may or may not exist. But most people want to believe.

Just as they would want to believe that the child is born in the waters of this island. That the land observes *jus soli,* and citizenship is his birthright. That he is Carpathius of Hy-Brasil. That any man with such a name and such a birthright will have stories written about him. That he will be forever connected with Thia by virtue of life strands woven together in their first moments, and whispered about by the deep blue when its waves break upon the shore.

But, in the end, they call him John.

1912

Arthur issues a command to starboard the instant he sees the iceberg looming ahead of Thia. He strides out to the port wing and waits tensely for her to respond as he sights the berg more clearly. They are far enough away that she has plenty of time to turn. But the encounter places every man on notice.

Arthur scans the water as he looks for other telltale glimmers. With no further obstructions in sight, he orders Thia to resume her former course. And though they have avoided the same fate as *Titanic*, the tension of every man on that bridge is at a rare pitch. That was only the first test. More will come before this night is done.

SALVOR-IN-POSSESSION

2007

SIX YEARS AFTER THE FIRST DIVE EXPEDITION TO THIA, Richie Stevenson, Ric Waring, Bruce Dunton and Zaid Al-obaidi are still the only ones to have ever dived her. Partly because it's an expensive endeavour, especially with the cachet of being first gone, but also because she's logistically challenging.

Most dive expeditions are land based. They start and end the day on shore. Thia is 268 miles out into the Atlantic from Plymouth, a 30-hour boat journey. Southern Ireland, 160 miles to the north-east, is the closest land, making her one of the most exposed and challenging dives in the world. And she's deep, right on the edge of the continental shelf.

It is difficult to pull together a group out of the fifty or so divers in the world prepared to descend to 500 feet. A group who can share the costs of hiring one of the few appropriate dive boats coded to go that far off shore, carve out the same two weeks of their lives, and be prepared to forfeit the £2000 the attempt will cost them if the British weather, that hemmed and hawed the first time they tried, doesn't hold.

There have been other failed attempts. The European Technical Dive Centre tried just a few months prior to the lads' hard-wrought victory, but lost out to the elements and a boat that couldn't withstand the rough Atlantic.

But still, it is the men who were there first who are most compelled to return. That single Cunard plate was not enough. Doubt met them, when they said they'd dived Thia. Whispers. Even amongst friends. In a country of millions these men are from a community of hundreds. And the rivalry is intense. To have their ability – their word – questioned, burned.

The whole affair made for a strange dichotomy. There was enough validity that no one else could make an unchallenged claim to have dived Thia first, yet enough doubt that their own claim could not go unchallenged.

But silencing the doubting Thomases is not the only reason that compels Ric's return. There are other motives. Thia's history and her ties to *Titanic*. The challenge of where she is, right out there in the Atlantic, and how deep she lies. The desire to dive her properly, to see more of her, photograph and film her. To do other than scratch the surface.

So here he is, six years later.

Once more into the fray.

———

The expedition divides into two teams, so they can dive Thia's wreck on alternate days. Team Two, diving today, comprises Ric Waring, Tim Cashman, Helmuth Biechl, Mark Elliott and Duncan Keates. When Ric finishes his descent he heads straight to Thia's bow, intent on finding her bell. On that brief dive six years ago he didn't know if he was on the right ship. Now he does. The ambient light is slightly dark, like dusk, and the atmosphere is strange. Different. The water feels deep. Atlantic water, rather than coastal. It plays in the back of his mind.

The temperature is pleasant, about eighteen or nineteen degrees. The current is easy, viz good. Thia's collapsed quite a bit since he was first here. Her bow lies lower. The deep blue is hastening its claim.

Thia's consumed by marine growth that's alien to anything he's seen in decades of diving. It's because she's farther offshore and in deeper water than any ship he's dived before. He pulls at twisted trawler nets and wreckage lying over the front winch, stirring a small cloud of coral and sand. Her bow is a graveyard of debris: encrusted vents, derricks, hawsers, broken railing, plating, masts and rigging.

If her bell's here, it's well hidden.

The bell is not all the lads are after, just the thing they want most. There's also supposed to be a trophy cabinet that showcased the tokens of appreciation showered upon Thia and her crew. They think it's in the main saloon. The

Marconi installation should be in the shack above the aft smoking room. The large silver loving cup awarded to her captain may also still be aboard – they weren't able to find out for sure – perhaps in the library. Retrieving any of these artefacts will require penetration diving, which is even more dangerous than what they're doing. Whether it's possible, with Thia, depends on how well she's held up. How safe it is to go inside. Getting lost or trapped in a wreck will kill a diver.

Whether it's worth the risk is debatable. Normally, there are good odds the Receiver of Wreck will let them keep what they salvage. But there's no chance of that here. Anything they find, the team on *Janus* will confiscate on behalf of RMS Titanic Inc.

That's what happened in 2001, after the first dive. Because it came from Thia, Titanic Inc. took Zaid's port-hole. Things got heavy. There were solicitor's letters. Threats of litigation. Demands that the divers surrender artefacts and sign contracts abdicating salvage rights.

On one hand, Titanic Inc. paid significantly to own Thia's wreck. It's not hard to understand their desire to protect that investment. On the other hand, it was the lads who mounted the first expedition, at their own risk and expense. Under the laws of salvage, which are ancient and universal, that gives them rights – at the very least, to compensation.

But after that first expedition things became quite nasty, for a time, and the lads *do not* want a repeat. So when Ric began planning a return to Thia, he informed Titanic Inc.

and proposed they work together to photograph and film her and raise some of her artefacts.

At first, Titanic Inc. was receptive to the idea. The team had several conference calls with Arnie Geller, the chief executive officer.

————

When Robert Ballard and Jean-Louis Michel discovered RMS *Titanic*'s wreck in 1985 they refrained from plundering her artefacts. But this left the door wide open for others to claim salvage rights. All they had to do was be first. Titanic Ventures, later RMS Titanic Inc., won the race, but not without challenge from other salvors. So in 1994 the US Federal Court awarded the company exclusive rights to *Titanic* – but as salvor-in-possession. They could salvage, *but not own* the ship and her artefacts.

Under CEO George Tulloch, the company favoured the policy of guardianship instituted by the courts and exhibited the artefacts all over the world. But the company philosophy changed dramatically in 1999 after Tulloch was ousted during a hostile takeover, the improprieties of which caused the Securities and Exchange Commission to levy over $400 000 in fines on those involved.*

The real money in *Titanic* artefacts is not in exhibiting them but selling them. They command a premium at auction. But the company cannot sell what they do not

---

* Full sources for the events discussed in relation to RMS Titanic Inc. are listed in the endnotes to this chapter.

own. After unsuccessfully petitioning the court for owner-ship of the artefacts, or compensation to the tune of $225 million, in September 2002 Titanic Inc.'s board abruptly passed a resolution to voluntarily suspend its exclusive rights as salvor-in-possession. This meant that the first operation to subsequently retrieve artefacts from the ship could stake a new, exclusive salvage claim, unhindered by the guard-ianship restrictions preventing the sale of artefacts that burdened the existing salvors.

Coincidentally, an expedition codenamed Bluelight was at the *Titanic* site poised to recover artefacts on the very same day in November that the board tried to relin-quish its rights in federal court. One of the expedition leaders was Graham Jessop, who was involved in the early expeditions to find Thia's wreck, and who, after selling her to Titanic Inc. in May 2001, began working for the company as salvage master. The other leader was its former vice-president and director of operations Derrick Barton, while the financial planning was handled by consultant in investor relations, David Hill. Barton, Jessop and Hill left their positions at Titanic Inc. only a few months before the events that saw the board try to relin-quish its rights and the simultaneous Bluelight expedition began salvage work.

Arnie Geller denied that Titanic Inc. was involved in Bluelight, but the timing of the expedition, organised and led by men who had only just vacated senior positions with the company, and which could have resulted in the ability to finally sell *Titanic*'s artefacts – well, it speaks for itself. In the end, if Bluelight was an attempt by Titanic Inc. to exchange salvor-in-possession for unrestricted salvage rights, it failed. The US court ruled that since these rights were the company's main corporate asset it could not relinquish them without consulting its shareholders – who were becoming increasingly disillusioned.

A shareholder lawsuit had already been brought against Titanic Inc. in April 2002 by Lawrence D'Addario, one of the founding investors in Titanic Ventures, who alleged that the officers, directors and controlling shareholders in its successor, Titanic Inc., had engaged in fraud and self-dealing. He accused Geller of mismanaging company assets when he gave $900 000 worth of company shares to Argosy International – Graham Jessop's company – in return for what Titanic Inc. called 'intangible assets that included confidential research data to be utilised in locating the wreck sites of twelve sunken vessels containing valuable cargo'.

In layman's terms, treasure maps.

Ones that Geller did not have appraised and which proved to be worthless. Further, the lawsuit took issue with the company's acquisition of another asset: Thia.

The value Titanic Inc. assigned to her as an 'asset' was $1 374 000. To acquire her, the company returned to Argosy International the treasure maps with an unamortised value of $555 000 but retained the right of refusal to salvage the twelve wreck sites, and also provided Argosy with more than a million additional Titanic Inc. shares valued at $819 000.

Arnie Geller had greenlit Thia's acquisition based on an independent appraisal that put the value of her rights at $4.5 million. However, this appraisal relied almost completely on the value of her contents, given her *Titanic* connection. The lawsuit contended that the company did not own the rights to these contents. That the rights Argosy had sold them were only for the sunken ship and did not even include any cargo. Easy to believe, since Argosy had acquired Thia's rights from the British government one year earlier for the princely sum of £500.

The lawsuit suggested that the company had exchanged hundreds and thousands of dollars of stock for what appeared to be essentially worthless rights to Thia and that this constituted a breach of its fiduciary duty to shareholders. After several years of litigation and appeals, the lawsuit was settled out of court.

Regardless of whether she would prove to be a wise investment, by the time the lads dived Thia in 2001 the company had committed assets well in excess of $1 million to acquire her.

So of course it couldn't let Zaid keep his porthole.

Almost six years later, in February 2007, RMS Titanic Inc. sold all of its rights, title and ownership interest in Thia to Seaventures Ltd. for $3 million. But they were keeping her in the family. Joseph Marsh, the principal of Seaventures – which registered as a business in Ohio the day before the sale occurred – was a major shareholder of Titanic Inc. and among those the Securities and Exchange Commission fined for the hostile takeover of the company. At the time of the sale, Seaventures and Titanic Inc. also made an arrangement whereby Titanic Inc. would be responsible for the recovery and exhibition of Thia's artefacts.

And although initially Titanic Inc. seemed receptive when Ric proposed a joint expedition, the company later rescinded. It informed the lads it would be going out several weeks before them to raise artefacts, and entrusted Paul-Henry and Comex to do the job.

It's understandable that Titanic Inc. would want maritime archaeologists with professional conservation practices to salvage Thia. Her depth, and the limited time – twenty minutes – the lads could spend there, would seriously hinder their ability to recover artefacts. But it felt like they'd been strung along. That all Titanic Inc. had wanted was to beat them to Thia. They were also gutted that they wouldn't get to dive her intact.

Though they're hardly in a position to quibble about that. They take artefacts themselves, leaving wrecks a little less intact than when they found them.

For once, inclement weather works in the lads' favour. *Janus* doesn't beat them to Thia by a month, like they feared, only a week. Her rovers recover artefacts while they dive. When Team One – Richie Stevenson, Carl Spencer, Edoardo Pavia, Andrea Bolzoni and Jeff Cornish – dived yesterday, two of the telegraphs Ric saw six years ago were no longer on the wrecked bridge. Presumably, Comex had already removed them. Only one remains, trapped under hull plating.

THE RESCUE

1912

IN THE DARK HOURS BEFORE DAWN THIA PASSES ICEBERG after iceberg, picking her way through like a snake. Too often her life, and the lives of her passengers and crew, depends on a sudden turn of her wheel. But she never falters.

Arthur occasionally sees the green light as he keeps his eyes skinned for bergs. At half past three, Purser Brown and Chief Steward Hughes report to the bridge: everything that can be done has been done. None too soon. Thia is almost upon *Titanic*'s coordinates.

Arthur pulls the lever on the bridge telegraph, signalling the engine room to *standby*. Meanwhile, Thia continues to send up rockets and Roman candles, as though reminding whosoever is on the other side of those lights in the sky that help is coming.

At 4 a.m. Arthur pulls the telegraph lever to *stop*. Below decks, the bell on its engine-room counterpart rings shrilly. The chief engineer glances at the brass dial and orders a reduction in revolutions. With the engines no longer labouring beyond capacity the world is suddenly, startlingly loud. Thia glides until she's stationary in the dark water.

They are there . . . but there is no *Titanic*.

If he's honest, Arthur didn't really expect to find her. There were moments, genuine moments, when he hoped, but he knows too well the signs of another ship at night. Knows that he should long ago have seen her brightly lit decks, guiding them to her like the north star.

He sees naught but clear skies, stars gleaming with the brilliance that only a keen frosty air brings. The seeing is as good as it can be for want of a moon, and every officer on the bridge scans the water, searching for any sign of life.

Those passengers scattered around Thia's upper decks do the same. As does the lookout in the crow's nest. The two at Thia's eyes. All searching for some indication that her race across the Atlantic tundra has not been futile. Foolish, it may have been – dangerous, reckless, it has been – but don't let it have been futile.

And then they see it. *A green flare.*

Low to the water, directly off her port bow. It must be a small boat but it's impossible to discern a shape. Arthur reaches for the telegraph. Thia's been idle only a few minutes and gets up to full speed quickly. He issues an order and her whistle blasts through the dark. For the time being, he refuses to think what it means that there is a boat in the water. Just applies himself to the task at hand. He'll enfold them along Thia's port side, using her bulk as a shield against the stirring wind and waves, harbingers of the dawn.

As Thia draws near, trying to pick out the lifeboat in the dark, Arthur's eyes chart a little further. Strain to discern . . . *Dear God.*

Simultaneously, an urgent shout comes from the starboard bridge wing. 'Iceberg dead ahea—'

'*Hard-a-starboard*,' Arthur orders, before the warning dies.

The berg is too close.

A few hundred metres.

Rapidly closing.

He can't account for how they missed it. From the nest, Thia's bell rings out three strikes. For the second time that night, at almost the same spot on the ocean, a ship is on a collision course with a mountain of ice.

'Hard-a-starboard, aye-aye,' the helmsman acknowledges as he spins Thia's wheel hard. It turns as smoothly as it ever does; it turns like it's mired in time's current. Like eternity in an instant. Most of the people aboard her are still asleep. They cannot know even half of what those in the waking world feel. Some profound experience of mortality. A lesson hard learned already this night.

And Thia does exactly as she's bid. As she's been bid all night. *All her life.* She works her heart out with dumb animal affection, the desire to please stronger than physical constraint.

It's as though she knows that the men on her bridge depend on her to respond, and although it seems like forever, only a few seconds pass before her stem angles right, her stern swings counterpoint, and Thia starboards away. Sails them clear of the ice. Free from oblivion. Away from the lifeboat.

For a moment it looks to those aboard the little boat as if she's abandoning them. Imparting her own lessons about hope and doubt and the ferocious unfairness of life. As though they won't keenly feel that lesson every day for the rest of their lives.

'All stop,' comes the command and she obeys, the iceberg on her port side, the boat starboard and behind. 'Full astern.' Thia backs up until she's abreast of the lifeboat. Goes a little further than intended before Arthur can get the way off her.

From far below a shout wends up to him on the bridge wing. 'We have only one seaman and cannot work very well.'

'All right,' he shouts back and turns to Second Officer James Bisset. 'Go overside with two quartermasters and board her as she comes alongside. Fend her off so that she doesn't bump and be careful that she doesn't capsize.'

'Aye, sir.' James takes two of Thia's crewmen to the foredeck where a Jacob's ladder hangs ready over the side. Arthur manoeuvres Thia as close as he can.

'Stop your engines!' the voice calls from the lifeboat. A lady seated at its tiller cries out, something about *Titanic*, but the words aren't strong enough to lift up to Arthur.

———

James and the quartermasters climb down the ladder and as the boat drifts past they spring onto its thwarts.

As James boards, he hears the sound of quiet weeping.

There are seventeen people aboard. Women, mostly. With pale, strained faces. Some clad in evening clothes, others night clothes. White lifebelts over the top. They are all numb with cold, and grief.

In the glow of the electric lights clustered along Thia's hull he sees an officer in the boat, near his own age. They work in tandem to stop from knocking into Thia's side and come astern to her open gangway. A line is lowered and they tie off the boat's painter to halt her drift. Then he glances about the miserable castaways and gently urges the women nearest at hand towards the ladder. Chief Officer Hankinson at Thia's gangway calls down encouragement.

Most of them are too afraid, but after a brief hesitation a young lady steps forward. James and the officer on the lifeboat, Joseph Boxhall, help Elisabeth Allen into a lifeline, secured under her arms, and she begins to climb. Her numb fingers clutch at the rungs and when the ladder swings against Thia's hull she cries out. The officers call out reassurance. It's such a simple, immeasurably difficult task.

When the swaying lessens she forces herself to continue. To not look down at the dark water.

Relief overwhelms Elisabeth when she reaches the opening in Thia's hull. The same feeling as when she first saw the ship's lights on the horizon. Strong hands help her the last distance, raising her to the deck where she tumbles into the safety of Purser Brown's arms.

'Where is *Titanic*?' he asks.

———

On the bridge, Arthur learns that there's an officer in the boat and orders Joseph to report as soon as he's aboard. Then he sees Louis on deck. Both Louis and Augusta's earlier fears for Thia have long been allayed. Cupping his hands around his mouth, he calls down: 'What about that new camera?' Louis's gaze shoots up to Arthur, and he throws up his hands as if to say he never thought of it and hurries away.

Other women begin to slowly climb the ladder but most are in no condition to make the attempt. 'Lower the chair,' James calls up to the chief officer. Similar to a tree swing, it has a board and ropes up to eight feet, knotted together and attached to a main rope. One by one the women are raised to Thia's gangway, some up the ladder but most in the chair, hair wild in the wind, nightclothes flapping around slim ankles, Edwardian propriety be damned.

As the women reach Thia's deck, officers cut off their lifebelts and stewards shepherd them to the surgery next to the gangway, where they are wrapped in blankets warmed on the steam pipes and hot drinks are pressed into frozen fingers. Heat pierces the numbness. As they arrive, Dr Lengyel, the Hungarian doctor who serves Thia's steerage passengers, assesses them – for both injury and class – before they're shown to the appropriate saloon.

A lady claims the attention of a passing steward. There are fine lines beside her eyes and lips. A wisp of grey in the brown hair framing her face. 'What ship is this?' Another dark-haired woman stands beside her. Their soft hands are red from rowing.

'It is the Cunarder *Carpathia*, ma'am.'

'*The Carpathia?*'

'Yes, ma'am.'

Charlotte Appleton shares a surprised look with her sister, Malvina Cornell, then makes a request that has the steward scurrying away. Anxious words pass between the two women, there in the midst of the small group raised from the boat. A group that no other circumstance could bring together.

Steerage passenger Anton Kink evaded *Titanic*'s officers and jumped into the lowering boat when his wife and daughter called desperately for him. It did not seem reasonable that the edict for women and children first should separate him from his family when the lifeboat was mostly empty.

Before that, steerage passenger Winnie Coutts had fought earnestly for her eldest son to be allowed a place. Nine years old is not a man. She's still anxious from watching her youngest son raised to Thia's deck in a sack. When has a sack ever carried something so precious? And if it should fall?

Then there's Elisabeth Allen, returning home to St Louis to gather her trousseau. With her is an aunt, her teenage cousin, and their maid. Another maid stands beside Mahala Douglas. Her husband saw them to safety but when she'd entreated him to come he'd replied only, 'No. I must be a gentleman.' All night she worked the tiller in the little boat. Wondered if those are the last words he will ever say to her. What good is a dead gentleman?

Unloading complete, James and Joseph shin up the ladder then head to Thia's bridge. Arthur's gaze fixes on the White Star officer and he sees the truth etched on the young man's face, so that when he asks, he knows with a terrible certainty what the answer will be. 'The *Titanic* has gone down?'

Everyone aboard Thia seems inclined to ask this question, a question for which they already know the answer.

'Yes.' Joseph's voice breaks. *Yes.*

With all the survivors from the little boat raised, the darkness gives way to a silvery light. It spreads over the sea to show Thia surrounded by monsters of ice. Magnificent, great white bergs, coming out of the dawn.

Many of her passengers, alerted by the stopping of her engines, stir from their warm bunks to find their cabins arctic cold. Frigid water falls from the taps. Those already on deck have to make sense of a new reality. They cannot believe that *Titanic* has sunk and yet it must be so. They have just seen a boatload of survivors brought aboard.

When *Titanic*'s passengers entered that lifeboat and others in the dead of night, every star was reflected in the water. For a few hours the Atlantic was transformed into a celestial heaven, even if it felt far from celestial. Words cannot convey how deep the claws of fear and sorrow scrape.

———

In one of the lifeboats the babes are sniffling, cold and afraid. A lady in a brown sheath dress, fox skins, and velvet slippers, one missing its diamond buckle, unwraps a blanket-covered bundle to reveal a small toy pig with black-and-white fur. She grasps the rotund belly and gently winds the pig's curly tail. A tune tinkles out into the clear night air and for precious moments, the tinny sound soothes the little ones.

But it's not the stars on the sea or the music box pig that the people in the boats will remember. It's the quiet beauty of the rising sun. Daylight means hope. With it, they see Thia's red-black smokestack on the horizon. She looks like an angel. A huge angel from heaven, larger than any ship they have ever seen.

She looks like salvation.

In another boat, a small boy clutches a soft toy. A polar bear. In the morning light he gazes around in wonder and exclaims, 'Look at the beautiful North Pole with no Santa Claus on it.' The words bring a smile to the lips of those near him, but even the act of smiling seems like a betrayal of some kind.

The sun has risen over the curve of the ocean by the time the next lifeboat draws near to Thia. For those survivors already aboard, the empty pews in the approaching boat are gut-wrenching. Though it has a capacity of 40 there are only twelve people aboard.

———

On the bridge, Arthur continues to question Joseph. 'Were all her boats got away safely?'

'I believe so, sir. It was hard to see in the darkness. There were sixteen boats and four collapsibles.' The latter are boat-shaped rafts with collapsible canvas sides. 'Women and children were ordered into the boats. She struck the berg at 11.40. The boats were launched from 12.45 onwards.' His words spill over each other. 'My boat was cleared away at 1.45, one of the last to be lowered. Many of them were only half full. People wouldn't go into them. They didn't believe that . . .'

'Were many left on board when she sank?'

'Hundreds and hundreds. Perhaps a thousand. Perhaps *more*.' His voice carries the weight of a thousand bodies in icy water. 'We had room for a dozen more people in my boat, but it was dark after the ship took the plunge. We didn't pick up any swimmers. I fired flares . . .' For hours, he's had people depending on his leadership. Now someone else leads and he can allow himself the luxury of despair.

'Go below and get some coffee,' Arthur murmurs. 'Try to get warm.'

Coffee and warmth sound enticing but as soon as the second boat arrives Joseph is on deck, helping Thia's crew pass up survivors.

There is silence on the bridge.

Finally, Arthur issues a new command. 'Lower the flag to half-mast.'

The red-and-gold Cunard standard sinks slowly down Thia's mainmast.

Encircling Thia are dozens and dozens of bergs, some close, others on the horizon, towering like cathedral spires. It's the sailor in Arthur that fancies they resemble ships under full sail. He knew there was ice, but had he known there was so much about he would never have run Thia under a full head of steam. Three miles away there is a huge icefield trending north-west to south-west as far as he can see, like an impenetrable wall between them and the North American continent.

Then Arthur scans the water for the other boats. In the light of the new day he locates them, dotted here and there within an area of about four miles. Some are in groups of two or three, pulling towards a common centre. Thia.

Most of *Titanic*'s wooden lifeboats were designed with capacity for 65 people. Some are dangerously overcrowded, others are half empty, rowing laboriously through the sea where countless calves and growlers drift sluggishly. Arthur turns to one of his officers. 'Go to the top of the wheelhouse and count the bergs that are between a hundred and fifty to two hundred feet high – like that one,' he says, indicating.

It's evident that Thia's boats won't be needed so Arthur orders them swung in and secured. Then they focus on rescuing the remaining survivors, manoeuvring about to meet the boats, ice swishing and grating against Thia's hull. Those not yet aboard are even now at risk of exposure. Some are miles away and it will be hours, still, until everyone is aboard. Some boats look in danger of capsizing, and the North Atlantic kills in minutes.

In the boat that contains only twelve survivors there are seven crewmen, mostly stokers, and five first-class passengers: amongst them, Sir Cosmo Duff-Gordon and his wife, Lady Lucy. The people in this boat are in the fortunate position of having experienced only material losses. Sir Cosmo even promises five pounds to each of the crewmen, to replace their lost kits.

The next two lifeboats arrive together. They drifted close during the night and tied up. From the first boat the crew use the chair to raise a middle-aged lady. She whimpers in pain as she's cut free from her lifebelt.

'Annie!' A male voice rings loudly across the way. After a night spent partly unconscious and otherwise in excruciating pain, on Thia's deck she experiences the nearest thing to heaven on earth she's ever known.

When her husband, Charles Stengel, saw her into the lifeboat then stepped back with the other men, obeying the edict of the officer loading the boat that only women and children were allowed aboard, they'd thought that launching the boats was merely a precaution. That *Titanic* could not really sink. Then, to spend the night hurting, with a score of empty seats nearby, not knowing if he'd been allowed a place in another boat . . .

'*Charles*.' His arms feel like home to her but as he tightens them she gasps in pain.

'What is it? *What's wrong?*'

'A man jumped into our boat as it was being lowered. He fell atop me. I was knocked unconscious and my side hurts terribly.'

Annie's husband escorts her to Dr Lengyel in the third-class saloon. The Stengels are first-class passengers so the Hungarian doctor would ordinarily send them to Dr McGee, but he can tell Annie's ribs are broken and has her placed on a stretcher and taken to the ward with the other injured survivors, accompanied by her husband.

Around him, in stark contrast to Annie and Charles, there are women crying. 'Bambino!' one of them frantically screams, drawing the attention of everyone in the saloon. She tries to explain, but she's Italian and cannot make herself understood except to say 'bambino' again and again. Only when an Italian steward is summoned do they learn she has been separated from her daughter and seven-week-old baby who were with her in the lifeboat. The stewards begin a search of the ship. The young girl is quickly found and, eventually, the baby. Someone had put the little one on the steampipes in the kitchen pantry to bring it to life.

This Italian mother is one of the few fortunate ones. There are other women desperately looking for their sons, or for their fathers. Most, for their husbands. It's terrible to watch.

———

When the steward dispatched by the dark-haired sisters finally returns, having discovered the information they sought, he escorts them along the promenade outside Thia's first-class staterooms. A knock at the door rouses one of her elderly passengers, Charles H. Marshall. It's still hours before breakfast. Far too early to rise.

'What is it?' he calls through the wooden door.

'Your nieces wish to see you, sir.'

His nieces? His nieces are on *Titanic*. But when he opens the door he finds that they are not. 'Lottie?' he asks, dumbfounded.

'The *Titanic* has sunk,' she cries. The sisters fling themselves into their uncle's arms. He soothes them, even though he cannot countenance what they are saying. Soon enough they are telling the sorry tale to him, their aunt Josephine and cousin Evelyn.

'But where is Caroline?' Their other sister, Caroline Brown.

'We do not know. She and Edith – our friend, Miss Evans – were not in our boat. Colonel Gracie,' a family acquaintance, 'was a passenger on *Titanic* and he escorted all of us to where the boats were loading, but the officer would not let the men any closer. In the crowd we were separated from Caroline and Edith. We do not know if . . .' Fear chokes her voice.

'I'm sure they made it to another boat,' Josephine consoles. Young Evelyn slips on a warm coat and goes out on deck to keep vigil.

In the next boat, four-year-old Washington Dodge Jr, clad only in his pyjamas and a life preserver, is hoisted aboard Thia in a mailbag. His mother is hoisted aboard wearing a fur coat over her nightrobe, and her shoes coupled with a pair of men's stockings, given to her by a kindly quartermaster with the earnest promise that they are clean.

From the same boat the crew raise Dorothy Gibson, famous silent film actress, in a white silk evening dress and a polo coat; Miss Margaret Hays, New York heiress, with her Pomeranian, Lady, on her lap; and two little boys with brown curls and no parents to be found.

In one of the lifeboats a refrain drifts across the waves. The occupants sing as if the words can hold numbness at bay:

> *Light in the darkness, sailor, day is at hand!*
> *See o'er the foaming billows fair haven's land,*
> *Drear was the voyage, sailor, now almost o'er,*
> *Safe within the life boat, sailor, pull for the shore.*

Only the shore is Thia.

This lifeboat is heavily crowded. Fifty-five women and children are brought aboard, then four male passengers and five crewmen – the men only allowed in the boat because they were needed to work it.

One of the men looks around Thia's deck hoping to see his family. He put them in the second boat to depart. A steward from *Titanic*, Frederick Ray – who'd encouraged the family to sail on *Titanic* and thus feels responsible for their safety – helps the man look. He's one of many, frantically searching.

Thia's crew try to take the boats on her lee side, but the next to arrive is forced to unload at a starboard gangway, the others already occupied. The boat carries Léontine Aubart, Benjamin Guggenheim's French mistress. But not Benjamin Guggenheim.

The next boat brings Douglas, the little boy with the toy polar bear. When he's placed in a mail sack the bear falls, forgotten, to the bottom boards. There he remains as the men climb the ladder, the ladies are hauled up in the swing, and a handsome little Pekinese called Sun Yat Sen, named after the first president of the new Republic of China, are all brought safely aboard.

As Elizabeth Shutes is raised she hears the words, 'Careful, fellers; she's a lightweight,' but still she bumps against Thia's hull so much she feels like a bag of meal. Her hands are so cold she can hardly hold the rope, but she's fearful of letting go. *Lord, what a night.* Never has she seen a sky more brilliant, or so many falling stars. And the first wish of all was to stay near *Titanic*. They felt so much safer near the ship. But then, there were so many unfulfilled wishes that night.

When Henry Sleeper Harper, owner of the handsome little Pekinese, climbs through the gangway, he sees his friends the Ogdens nearby and says, as casually as may be, 'Louis, how do you keep yourself looking so young?' This is not the first time he's been on a ship that collided with an iceberg – it happened ten years ago off the Grand Banks of Newfoundland.

Meanwhile, *Titanic* steward Frederick Ray locates the family he was looking for and leads Dr Washington Dodge to the first-class dining saloon where he finds his wife and son wrapped in warm blankets. Ruth is overjoyed to see her husband, and when they find out that Junior – too young to understand – saw his father on deck earlier and thought it would be a great game to hide from Daddy, they are too relieved to be cross. They are lucky in the midst of misfortune. So many people stand at Thia's rails, praying as each boat comes in, only to have their hopes dashed again and again.

The sole lifeboat to have raised her mast and sail is under the command of Officer Harold Lowe. En route to Thia, he sees one of the collapsibles in poor straits and changes course to go and make sure of her. At first, her passengers worry that he wants to transfer people to them but are relieved when he instead offers them a tow. He secures her with his painter and begins anew to Thia, but before long sees another collapsible in even worse plight. She's sinking.

This was one of the last boats to leave *Titanic*. She and a second collapsible washed off the deck as the ship went under. Both were pushed clear of *Titanic* by the surge created from a falling funnel. They were surrounded by hundreds of people in the frigid water, but only about two dozen were able to haul themselves aboard the now-sinking collapsible in the few minutes they had before the cold sapped their strength and mobility. Lowe transfers the survivors to his boat. The second collapsible that washed clear did so upside down, and men balanced atop its hull for hours, up to their knees in water, many succumbing

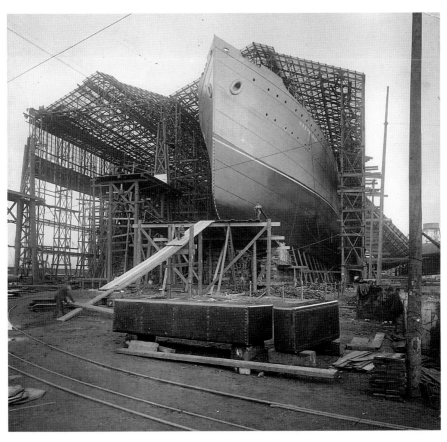

RMS *Carpathia* almost ready for launch at the C. S. Swan & Hunter shipyard, 1902.
(Courtesy of Tyne and Wear Archives and Museums: DS.SWH.4.PH.3.274.1)

RMS *Carpathia*. (Courtesy of The University of Liverpool Library, Cunard Archive, D42/PR1/49)

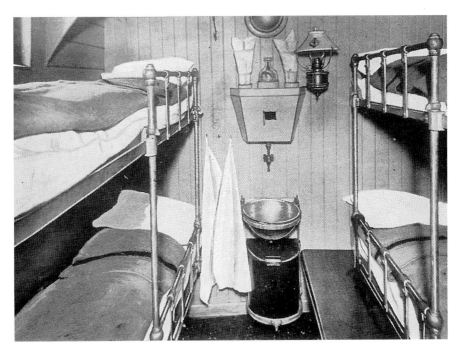

One of *Carpathia*'s third-class four-berth rooms. (Courtesy of The University of Liverpool Library, Cunard Archive, D42/PR1/49)

Carpathia's second cabin dining saloon. (Courtesy of The University of Liverpool Library, Cunard Archive, D42/PR2/1/48/D2)

Sailing and engine department of RMS *Carpathia*. (Courtesy of The University of Liverpool Library. Cunard Archive. D42/PR2/1/48/G1)

Titanic lifeboats approaching *Carpathia*. Boat 14 with its mast raised is towing the other boat. (Courtesy of the United States National Archives and Records Administration, 278336)

One of *Titanic*'s collapsible lifeboats, with canvas sides. (Courtesy of the United States National Archives and Records Administration, 278338)

Titanic survivors on *Carpathia*'s forward deck. (Courtesy of the Library of Congress, LC–USZ62–56453)

Titanic survivors aboard *Carpathia* after being rescued. (Courtesy of the Library of Congress, LC–USZ62–99341)

New York crowds awaiting survivors from *Titanic*. (Courtesy of the Library of Congress, LC-USZ62-26635)

The officers of RMS *Carpathia*. Captain Arthur Rostron seated middle, behind the silver loving cup awarded to him by survivors. (Courtesy of the Library of Congress, LC-DIG-ggbain-10-432)

Titanic's lifeboats at the White Star Line's Pier 59. (Courtesy of John Oxley Library, State Library of Queensland, neg. 179710)

River view of Pier 54 in 1951. An observation platform extends from the pier end into the river. (Courtesy of the New York Public Library, 2040793)

to hypothermia before those remaining were picked up by other lifeboats en route to Thia.

About an hour after *Titanic* sank, Lowe distributed his passengers amongst the other boats, retaining only a small group of volunteers who went with him to search for survivors. Not knowing how quickly the icy water would work, they did not return soon enough and found more dead bodies than anything else. From the sea they pulled Steward Harold Phillimore, who'd climbed on to some floating wreckage; steerage passenger Fang Lang, who'd likewise lashed himself to a door and who at first they'd presumed to be dead, the swells washing over him; and steerage passenger and stonemason Emilio Ilario Giuseppe Portaluppi, who'd clung to an icefloe to stay afloat.

The survivors are taken aboard Thia until all that remains in Lowe's lifeboat is a heavyset man at the stern, his clothes wet. It had required the collective efforts of the men who'd returned with Lowe to pull him into the boat. When they finally succeeded they found him bleeding from the mouth and nose. They took his collar off and loosed his shirt but it made no difference. He died before Thia arrived. Her crew bring his corpse aboard.

When Lowe took the survivors from the sinking collapsible into his boat, he left behind three other corpses. Men who'd succumbed to hypothermia. It was hardhearted, but he was more concerned with saving the living.

'Caroline!' As the collapsible Lowe took into tow is unloaded, one of the ladies is greeted by her cousin and taken to her relieved sisters, uncle and aunt.

'But where is Edith?' Lottie asks Caroline.

'I . . . I don't know.' When she's warm again she tells them the story. 'Some of the men called to us to get into the boat. Three or four seized Edith and started to lift her over the rail, which came to our chests, but she cried out for them to put me into the boat first, as I had children.' Caroline's eyes fill with tears. 'They took her at her word and put her down. They seized hold of me and let me drop into the boat. I called to Edith to follow but I did not hear her answer. Almost at the same time the men in the boat cast it adrift from the steamship. I could hear the *Titanic* crew ordering all on deck to go to the opposite side and take the boat being lowered there. But I had not seen any boat being prepared there and I think the order was given to keep them away from the rail so that they would not leap into our boat and swamp us.

'It does not seem to me there was time to clear away another boat, even if there was one to lower. When our boat pulled away from the side of the *Titanic* she was so far down that the water was running over the forward part of the deck. I saw men plunge into the freezing water. I can still hear their cries ringing in my ears.'

Nothing will efface the memory of those moments.

———

The next boat brings Bruce Ismay, director of the White Star Line. Dr McGee is at the gangway when Mr Ismay climbs on deck. Tall and dark haired, he stands with his back against Thia's bulkhead, dressed in his Romeo slippers, pyjamas and an overcoat, mumbling, 'I'm Ismay . . . I'm Ismay.'

Concerned, Dr McGee approaches. 'Sir, will you not go to the saloon and get some soup, or something to drink.'

'No. I really do not want anything at all.'

The reply is distracted, but the doctor gently persists. 'Do go and get something.'

'No. If you will leave me alone I will be very much happier here.'

Dr McGee can't bring himself to do so. The man is clearly cold and in shock. Then, as though a new thought has occurred, he finally gives the doctor his full attention. 'If you will – get me in some room where I can be quiet, I wish you would.'

All further attempts to coax the man to take some warm liquids fail and the doctor finally concedes. He sees the man to his personal cabin before returning to attend to other survivors.

———

The next boat brings the lady with the music box pig. And so they come. The next so heavily loaded – one of the last to leave *Titanic*, when the danger was by then evident – that when one of the ladies aboard leans against the gunwale her hair trails in the water. The next carries another million-airess, Mrs Margaret Brown, and yet another Pomeranian with his mistress, Mrs Elizabeth Rothschild. The boat is in the charge of Quartermaster Hichens, who had refused to go back and search for survivors despite the protests of Mrs Brown and others. The next brings the Countess of Rothes.

As Ruth Dodge watches the other women, from safe within the shelter of her husband's arms, while holding the hand of her son, their moans of anxiety and disappoint-ment as each boat fails to bring up those they are looking for is awful.

At 8 a.m. eight bells are struck. James Bisset takes over from First Officer Horace Dean as officer of the watch. He's had no rest but is too keyed up to notice any fatigue.

Horace goes to assist with the boats. The next three, having tied up during the night, arrive together. The first carries among its 40 or so occupants stewardess Violet Jessop and first-class passenger Mrs Madeleine Astor. The next, the youngest survivor at nine weeks old, Miss Millvina Dean, with perhaps 50 others. The last of the three boats contains about the same number, and is manned by Second Officer Charles Lightoller.

'Hullo, Lights! What are you doing down there?' Horace calls. There is a hint of levity in the words, but mostly welcome relief.

Charles looks up at the familiar voice to see Horace, the best man at his wedding, peering down at him from Thia's deck. He calls back a reply. For a moment, just a moment, things don't seem so bad.

As these boats are unloaded Arthur sees a small steamer, steel-hulled with four masts, coming out of the icefield towards Thia. Her red house flag and soft pink funnel with a black tip identify her as a Leyland liner. He turns his attention back to the boats but there is a sinking feeling in his gut. He doesn't know the survivor tally yet, but *Titanic* carried over two thousand souls. He didn't bring even half that on board and there are no other boats in sight.

Through it all, Thia's crew sees to the every need and comfort of the survivors. And, as young Robert Vaughan hurries about his stewarding duties, he can't help but notice the absolute beauty of the sunrise.

The absolute beauty.

WAR SERVICE

1918

IN JULY, WHILE THIA WAITS PATIENTLY AT HUSKISSON
Dock, in the Port of Liverpool, for the naval escort that
will see her convoy of merchant ships – some bound for
the Mediterranean, others the Americas – through the
Southwest Approaches, Captain William Prothero visits
his wife and children at their home in town. A proud
Welshman, he nonetheless moved his wife – like Arthur
Rostron, he married a Minnie – to the city on the Mersey
soon after they wed and he began working for Cunard. It
allows him to visit home more frequently. Now, his eldest
son, Gwilym, is almost eighteen.

William and Arthur are like night and day. Where
Arthur is tall, lean, charming and devout, something like
a gentleman sailor, Sailor Bill, as William is known in the

company, is burly and weather-beaten and can hail the pier head from the bridge without using a megaphone. Yet, the thing that unites them unequivocally is the call of the deep blue. Like Arthur, he keenly misses the days of sail and there are few things he enjoys more than putting into port at New York and inviting aboard the salty old skippers that frequent the waterfront, reminiscing about an age that will never return. He misses singing sea shanties while crewing on a big, three-skysail yarder in the China trade, whole-sail set on a moonlit night.

And now, like Arthur, he captains steamers. He's Thia's longest-serving captain, in fact. Though these days she's more of an armed merchant cruiser than ocean liner, courtesy of Cunard's agreement with the British admiralty that allows them to requisition ships during wartime. Her funnel has long since shed its red-black livery and now favours battle grey.

It's been that way almost since Fiume; since Franz and Sophie. On the return voyage, after repatriating the Americans from Naples, they'd travelled dark. Had been forced to paint her funnel in the rain. A wild rumour had washed across her decks that she was about to fall prey to a pack of German warships. But that voyage was blessedly uneventful.

Then she traded Mediterranean adventurers for munitions and troops. She's spent most of the war as a pack mule, hauling horses for the cavalry, aeroplanes for the air force and oil in her double bottom. Against her will she smuggled wartime contraband, the Central Powers desperate for rubber to make tyres for their military transports. On one occasion she carried $25 million in securities from the Bank of England, sent to America as surety against the future purchase of supplies and machines of war. For the last few years it's been Canadian troops conveyed by the thousands, then the Americans when they finally join the cause, many of whom stop and read the small brass plaque at the foot of Thia's main companionway and take heart that the ship carrying them to the Front has passed her own test.

Somewhere during these years, she acquired armament. A 4.7-inch gun that weighs as much as an elephant. But it's no gentle grey beast perched on its haunches on Thia's deck, big ears flapping in the sea breeze. The eighteen-foot rapid-fire barrel can hit a target at 16 500 yards and it has a 210-degree arc of fire. Thia's two gunners are Royal Naval reservists, and she carries 50 shells that each weigh 45 pounds and are packed with explosive lyddite.

The gun caused a furore in New York when she first arrived with it: the largest, at the time, ever brought to the city aboard a merchantman. Its presence, at Thia's back, should bring comfort, but instead it's a constant reminder of the war in which she's inextricably caught. The greatest one the world has ever known, though 'great' is hardly the right word for it.

2006

Even when World War I is over, humanity still won't have learned its lesson. Another great war will come and send to the bottom of the blue thousands more ships and their bells, each one waiting in silent testimony for the men who will one day dive these underwater monoliths.

For them, recovering a bell and identifying a wreck is like returning her to the world. This is why some bells find afterlives in the glass cases of museums. There are those who believe they should all have this fate – that divers who keep bells are little more than vultures.

But consider it from the diver's perspective. The British Museum, for example, has eight million artefacts but only one per cent of them are on display. Like a cargo hold that never sees light, these artefacts are kept in storage. Unless a ship is very important, that is where you will find her bell. Carefully put away so it can be preserved, but not seen. But who is it kept for? And will *they* ever be able to see it?

When it comes to wreck divers, bells are displayed on mantels, tucked away in spare rooms, and even sold on at premium prices. Some are lost forever when a recovery goes wrong and the bell plunges back down, to who can say where.

But the decision to keep or surrender a bell does not lie with the diver who recovers it.

They must declare all salvage – that is to say, any part of the vessel, its cargo or equipment they recover – to the Receiver of Wreck. This office dates to the time of wrecking, when men would murder the crew of any ship wrecked close to shore so they could claim the vessel's cargo. To discourage this kind of criminal salvage, the Receiver rewarded those who assisted in saving the lives of wrecked sailors in peril. The Receiver maintained order and prevented pillaging, and if they had to hurt, maim or kill to do so, the *Merchant Shipping Act 1894* gave them that power.

Today, the Receiver considers the interests of the salvor, owner, archaeologists, museums and other concerned parties interested in the salvage. Legal owners have one year to prove their title claim. At the year's close, unclaimed salvage from outside territorial waters is returned to the finder. If it is inside territorial waters, it becomes property of the Crown. But often, in lieu of a salvage reward, the Receiver grants the finder ownership of the salvage.

This is the case with most of the bells Ric has found. Except the bell of HMT *Kurd*. She and Thia are alike. They were caught in wars not of their making, and both, in their time, daring heroes.

1940

When Whitley Bomber P4966 of Number Ten Squadron takes off on 14 September from an airfield in Leeming, East Yorkshire, its crew's mission is to bomb the invasion barges at the Antwerp Dock in German-occupied Belgium. The Whitley is outbound over the North Sea when its starboard engine fails. The sun has nearly set and its five-man bomber crew are only twenty miles off Spurn Head, but there is no time for pilots Squadron Leader Kenneth

Ferguson and Sergeant Charles Rogers to bring the bomber about and return to land.

They have to ditch.

The statistical chances of surviving a controlled ditching are actually quite reasonable. But in the growing dark? Atop a minefield?

They have no choice.

Had the ocean been calm they would have tried to bring the bomber down with its nose to the wind, counting on that to help it slow without stalling. But the waves are high and they can't chance smashing into one of those walls of water. As they begin the ditch they keep the bomber's wings up. One tip in the water and the plane will slew uncontrollably. And they pray its other engine does not fail.

Miraculously, Ferguson and Rogers land safely atop the swells and the minefield. Alongside the three other crewmen, they clamber from the sinking Whitley into an emergency dinghy. But it hardly matters. They are too far out to sea to make for land and are surrounded by mines.

It is at this moment, when they have no hope of rescue, that they see *Kurd*. The little trawler is being used by the Admiralty as a minesweeper. She's nearby, and when she learns of the downed plane she sets off on a rescue mission.

The Whitley's crew watch her approach with disbelieving eyes. A normal ocean rescue is one thing, but to come through a minefield is something else entirely. It's at least as brave as steaming full ahead through an icefield in the dead of night.

2006

Now, the Whitley Bomber is one more wreck on a seabed littered with the carnage of more than just ships. Amidst the ocean liners and U-boats of Ireland's *Cionn Mhálanna* there is a stretch of Sherman tanks that appears for all the world like the tangled remnants of an undersea battle, skittered about by some goliath. And so is *Kurd*: just one more wreck that went down at the close of a war.

In 1945, two months after peace was declared, *Kurd* was still at work, clearing the water. She dragged a distance sweep that exploded mines by mimicking the sound and magnetism of a ship, and a contact sweep to cut a mine's mooring line so it would rise to the surface, where the crew would use it for target practice. As *Kurd* brought in her sweep wire she snagged a mine. It blew off her stern and she sank in seconds.

When Ric finds *Kurd*'s bell he declares it to the Receiver, who asks him to donate it to the Royal Navy Museum in Portsmouth. He does this willingly, and through the museum he meets one of the old boys, in his eighties, who was on *Kurd* when she sank. He tells Ric the story of how, as he came up the companionway to the deck, she disappeared below him. Sank right under him and took sixteen men with her. It makes the hairs on the back of Ric's neck stand on end and the ghost of that sensation never fades. This is the only time he's met a survivor from one of his wrecks, and it's fair compensation, to his mind, for surrendering *Kurd*'s bell.

THE HARDEST MOMENT

1912

CARLOS HURD IS AWAKENED BY THE SUN SHINING IN HIS face. He's unsure why this is cause for concern until he realises that it has not happened before. His porthole faces south, has done so every day since they left New York. Then he realises that Thia is stationary. Through the porthole he sees icebergs, spectres in the dark transformed into glittering mountains of crystal, and a few miles distant an ice plain from whose midst rise mammoth forts, castles and pyramids of ice, almost as real as though placed there by man. They are stark against the cold blue sky and the deeper blue of the Atlantic.

Thia stands amidst this Arctic wonderland.

Hurriedly pulling on clothes, Carlos leaves the state-room half dressed. He's met by the sound of wailing, deep and prolonged, from the other side of the ship and sees one of Thia's stewardesses leading two bedraggled women, weeping as though their hearts are broken.

'What's happened?' Carlos asks. 'Is something wrong with the ship?'

'We're fine,' the stewardess replies without stopping, 'but the *Titanic* has gone down. We're taking on her passengers.'

Carlos reacts with disbelief, much like every other one of Thia's passengers, even though he can see and hear the evidence. Returning to his room he informs Katherine, who is anxiously waiting, and finishes dressing. But he's not just a passenger; he's also a reporter. Thursday morning's *World* lies on the shelf, and he quickly tears out and pockets the story about *Titanic*'s sailing.

'Where are you going?' Katherine asks as she dresses.

'To find Colin Cooper and propose a collaboration on a story about the sinking.' He tosses the hurriedly formulated idea over his shoulder as he departs. Cooper, an illustrator for the *New York Tribune*, is another of Thia's passengers. They met him on her first day out.

As Carlos searches, he listens carefully to snatches of conversation, including who's still missing, keeping in mind the scions of Edwardian society named in the article in his pocket. There are aid stations in the different dining saloons. The ordinary class restrictions of second cabin are forgotten and he walks amongst first class as easily as though he belongs there.

At the bow the last of the lifeboats is unloading. An awful despair falls over the people on deck, over all of Thia, as they realise there are no more boats to pick up.

Urgency compels Carlos as he searches for Cooper. Elsewhere in the world the Mississippi River is in flood and raging through the South, British coal miners are striking, the Irish home rule bill is pending, and the Republican party is split between Roosevelt and Taft. But happenstance has placed him at the scene of one of the greatest catastrophes in the world. Perhaps ever. The sinking of an unsinkable ship. And he has that peculiar need of a newspaper man, to uncover the story for a world that wants to know. He's sure Cooper must feel the same.

But the other man doesn't.

When Carlos suggests a collaboration, Cooper says he is not interested. *He is on vacation.* The reply leaves Carlos bemused. As if a vacation is a valid reason to ignore the story of the century.

Cooper's reply forces him to re-evaluate his hastily formed plan. He still needs help, so he turns to the one person on whom he can rely. As unlikely as she may be.

'Carlos, I'm not a reporter. I wouldn't know what to do, much less what to say.' Katherine's tone underscores her reluctance.

In the privacy of their cabin Carlos entreats his wife. 'I realise that, but I'm in a predicament. I have to get all the facts from the survivors. The job is too immense to do alone.' He uses logic to press his case. 'I'm only asking you to interview some of the women. They've set aside a special section for women in the library and won't allow any men in there.'

'Carlos, I don't –'

He can read the answer on her face, but he's desperate. '*Please*, Katherine.'

Her reply is a few moments in coming and full of misgivings, but in the end she can't refuse him. 'All right. I'll try.'

———

On the bridge, Arthur surveys the wreckage in the water. There's precious little evidence to mark the tragedy. A deckchair or two, a few lifebelts, a good deal of cork; no more flotsam than one can see on a seashore drifted in by the tide.

The officer he sent to the top of the wheelhouse reports back that he counted 25 icebergs over two hundred feet high and dozens more between fifty and one hundred and fifty feet high. There are too many growlers to count.

Then the pink-funnelled boat arrives. It's the tramp steamer *Californian*. They're too close to use wireless so she and Thia exchange messages by semaphore. Thia conveys the news that *Titanic* has sunk, and that she has rescued passengers from the lifeboats. The detailed exchange takes some time, as only a few words a minute can be conveyed with the red and yellow flags. Then Thia signals: *Think one boat still unaccounted for.* The movement of passengers between lifeboats before they arrived, and from the collapsibles, two of which were abandoned, has Arthur unsure.

While the exchange occurs he orders all spare hands to hoist as many of *Titanic*'s lifeboats as possible. While raising one of them, a wet white mass falls hard to the deck, unseen. Six boats are deposited in the fo'c'sle beside the derricks, and seven in Thia's davits. The rest are set adrift.

With other pressing matters requiring decision, and Bruce Ismay's presence having just been reported to him, Arthur seeks out the doctor's cabin on the shelter deck. The man he sees when he enters looks nothing like the wealthy, charismatic chairman of a prestigious shipping line. This man is fragile, perhaps even broken, as though the toll claimed by the Atlantic night is more than he can bear. But he is who he is, and decorum dictates he be consulted.

'Sir,' Arthur says, after greeting him, 'once we finish boarding the survivors there's the matter of what port to make for.' If Thia continues to the Mediterranean the next place she can disembark survivors is the Azores. But travelling east takes her further out of wireless range and they'd require more food, clean linen, blankets, et cetera, than they have available. It would also mean another ocean passage to remove survivors from the tiny archipelago, and the very idea seems cruel.

That leaves Halifax, Boston or New York.

'Do what you consider best, Captain.' Ismay's tone is passive.

'New York, sir. I consider that to be the best option. Halifax means ice.'

Just the sight of it surrounding Thia has her passengers uneasy, the survivors distraught. Steaming towards New York puts them closer to the wireless land stations and, once there, Thia can re-coal and reprovision. Nor will railroad passage from some other port to New York need be arranged. One less trial for the distressed survivors.

As Arthur looks at *this* distressed survivor, empathy stirs. But he cannot afford consolation right now. 'Don't you think, sir, you had better send a message to New York, telling them about this accident?'

'Yes,' Ismay replies.

After a moment of searching, pen and paper are located, and Arthur watches. It's clear that writing the message is a test of the other man's will.

Ismay hands him the slip. 'Captain, do you think that is all I can tell them?'

Deeply regret advise you Titanic sank this morning after collision iceberg, resulting serious loss life. Full particulars later. Ismay.

'Yes,' Arthur says. What more can they say? What words can adequately convey what happened here? People will try, again and again, without satisfaction. 'One other thing, sir. I believe we should hold a service.' It seems fitting that they do so here, where *Titanic* went down. As though he has no more left to give, Ismay assents.

Arthur leaves the man to his misery. On the bridge, he informs *Californian* of Thia's imminent departure. He wants to be away from the ice while the light and the weather remain favourable. The *Californian*'s captain signals, asking whether he should search for any other boats, and Arthur replies yes. Then he summons Purser Brown and sends him to find one of Thia's passengers. Technically, Cunard regulations forbid passengers on the bridge, but Arthur is more interested in the man's calling than the rules.

Reverend Father Anderson, of the episcopal Order of the Holy Cross, leaves off comforting the survivors to attend the captain. Arthur meets the man as he climbs the bridge ladder and walks him to the port wing. There they stand, a captain in his uniform and a dark-haired young priest in his religious habit, looking out at the polar scene.

'Padre, I've been following the sea all my life,' Arthur says slowly, shaking his head sadly, 'and I have never seen anything like this. I'd like you to do something if you would, please. We are practically over the spot where the *Titanic* sank, so before we leave I'd like to have you go down into the saloon and conduct a service. I have two things in mind. One is thanksgiving for those we have been able to save. The other is a prayer for those who have died.'

'Of course, Captain,' Father Anderson agrees. He does not mention that before Thia's journey was interrupted he was on his way to Naples to recover after a serious illness. One that still saps his strength, making it difficult to perform his duties in even ordinary circumstances. He simply hurries away to prepare.

———

Ten minutes later, Chief Officer Hankinson finds the Reverend Father and leads him to the first-class dining saloon. He offers Arthur's apologies; the captain is needed on the bridge. Despite the hurried preparations, word spreads quickly across Thia, and when the Father enters the saloon it is full of people. A patchwork of crewmen in their uniforms, caps doffed, Thia's passengers in their warmest garments, donned for a morning spent at her rails, and survivors in nightgowns, evening clothes and overcoats, or ill-fitting clothes borrowed from Thia's passengers, sitting huddled together, stunned and weeping.

Father Anderson begins by reading a brief section of the burial service. Now is not the time for sermonising. His words carry up across the crowd of solemn, grieving spectators, to the walls, panelled in ivory and white enamel and gold, up to the stained-glass dome. He offers a prayer for the souls of those who died this day.

As the words wash over the crowd, for the most part, each person thinks of someone who, only hours before, was such a constant fixture in their life they could not imagine that life without them. Now such impossible imaginings are reality.

Even Thia's crew weathers a loss. Young Robert Vaughan listens and remembers the musicians he served in the smoke-room only weeks ago, as the Father reads from Corinthians: 'O Death, where is thy sting?' Roger Bricoux and Theodore Brailey, cellist and pianist, were glad to leave Thia for *Titanic*. 'O grave, where is thy victory?' Glad to leave the lousy food, which isn't even that lousy. And though Robert can't claim a connection of any great magnitude, they were people that he knew. And now they are dead. 'But thanks be to God which giveth us the victory through Our Lord Jesus Christ.'

And words and prayer somehow don't seem enough.

———

Thia cruises slowly about while the service is underway. Arthur wants to be as certain as he can that she has not missed anyone. But all he sees is a single corpse in the water.

The hardest moment comes when Thia turns away. Her rails are lined with people looking out over the polar sea. Widows and sons and daughters whose families have been broken. Some stand sobbing. Some in silence. Blistered hands clutch her rails, welcoming pain that is physical.

She's more cemetery than boat. Weighed down by anguish. The degree of which, words fail. Some eyes scan the water, desperately searching for another lifeboat. Others look with anxious fear, hard learned, at the enormous icefield that is far too close. And the icebergs in their bitter beauty.

When Thia bears south-west it seems a betrayal. Like conceding their loss to an eternal berth, two miles below, with only a metal wreck and dead strangers for comfort. And if they just stand at Thia's rail long enough, things can return to the way they were yesterday.

If only she could make it so. But all she can do is keep them safe and carry them home.

———

Thia's passengers quietly speculate about which of the icebergs is responsible for sinking *Titanic*. The one with two peaks that resembles the towers of a cathedral? Or the huge berg that seems to bear a red scrape down low? No one can be certain. Dr Blackmarr and Louis take more photos as Thia sails south along the ice floe. Other passengers turn their attention from what was for some, frankly, a rather thrilling rescue, to Thia's cargo of abject misery.

The survivors are bruised and some have fractures, earned by jumping from *Titanic* to the lifeboats during loading. Overwhelmed, some women faint; others cry or laugh and can't seem to stop. There are blessedly few exposure-related illnesses, though both Thia's hospital wards are full. Harry, the telegraphist from *Titanic*, has frostbitten feet. Jack Phillips, the senior telegraphist, didn't make it.

Down in the warmth of Thia's rooms, six-year-old Douglas Spedden cries for his lost toy bear, Polar. His parents buy him a small brown bear from Thia's barbershop, but it's not the same. Not far away, a seven-year-old girl cries for the loss of her own teddy bear. Her mother cannot yet bring herself to tell the little girl that her father is also lost.

Tragedy evokes the cream of human kindness, and Thia's passengers dispense it without measure. That their holidays and adventures have been disrupted matters not. Thia's berths are filled to capacity; her passengers – including one honeymooning couple, the Hutchinsons – turn in with their neighbours or other acquaintances to free up one or the other's cabin to survivors. The men, and sometimes the ladies, give them over entirely and sleep on straw mattresses in the saloons and smoking rooms, on the dining tables, or in chairs on deck.

The women collect and distribute as many of their own clothes as they can spare: everything, including undergarments. They sew warm clothes out of Thia's sheets and blankets for those who are without, steerage passengers having lost all their worldly possessions. They make little coats and leggings for the children. There is no great demand for masculine apparel, but one of Thia's male passengers gives away his nice felt slippers and the dozen toothbrushes he carries. The barbershop is raided for ties, collars, hairpins and combs.

The women bathe and feed and care for the children. They assume the roles of nurses, gently coaxing some to stay abed, others to take the air on deck. Thia's own steerage passengers don't receive their first meal of the day until late in the afternoon, but without complaint.

Saloon passengers Nellie and Maurice McKenna give over one of the berths in their cabin to Mrs Ada West and her two young daughters from *Titanic*. The McKennas take the eldest girl, four-year-old Constance, out onto Thia's deck dressed in one of Maurice's shirts. There, the little girl asks him for pencil and paper to write a letter.

'Whom do you wish to write to?' he asks.

'My daddy.'

She's a bright little girl but doesn't seem to understand. Still, he gives her his pencil and some paper.

Daddy, she addresses the letter. *We don't know what is keeping you. We are on this boat. We arrived before you and want you to come here.*

Her little hand quickly tires and she asks Maurice to steady it. He does, helping her write.

'How will you send the letter?' he asks.

She points up to Thia's masts, to the Marconi wires. Finally, she wearies of writing and asks Maurice to look for her father. 'He always wears a white coat, a white waistcoat and a grey hat. Except when he has particular business. Then I always make him wear a black coat.'

She knows he's lost, but not what that means.

Her father is just one of the things lost. One that can't be replaced. Of course, there are lost treasures. Money and jewels, trunks of Parisian haute couture, Blondel's neoclassical *La Circassienne au Bain*, an edition of *The Rubaiyat* whose binding was of gold and contained over a thousand rubies, amethysts, topazes and emeralds, depicting three peacocks, symbolic of Persia, in full plumage. Some of these can't be replaced either, but it's not the same.

The world doesn't know these things, *these people*, are lost. They do not know that *Titanic* has sunk. The first wireless messages to make it to shore are reports that she has struck a berg. Messages she transmitted herself. The papers are full of rumours, and no mention at all of Thia, whose transmitter is too weak to make land and convey news of *Titanic*'s fate.

On deck, one of *Titanic*'s rescued crewmen sees a small pile of wet white fur. 'Hello, there. Fancy seeing you again.' He picks up the familiar mass, squeezes out the water and heads down the stairs into the warm saloon. 'Polar!' Douglas Spedden runs over, gathering the toy bear in his arms, hugging and kissing him.

Rumours spread across Thia that a pig was saved. This seems to the survivors too much, beyond the pale when so many died. But in the way of rumours, it's untrue. Maxixe, the pig, is a music box. The only animals saved from *Titanic* are the little dogs. Whenever Emma Hutchinson, the honeymooner who gave up her cabin, sees those dogs, she has an insane desire to kick them.

‘It's no good,’ Harold Cottam replies, his brow knit over the pile of marconigrams just delivered by a steward, though the survivors have only been aboard a scant hour or two. Their personal messages are to be sent for free and the stewards have been handing out slips all morning. ‘We're out of touch with land stations for two more days and nights.’

The messages in front of him are brief, the words ‘safe’ or ‘missing’ reappearing again and again. But there is not a damn thing he can do with them. Plus, the operator on the *Californian* has been jamming him all morning, chatting about inane rubbish. Other than advising all stations they no longer need to stand by and letting *Baltic*, who'd also been steaming to the rescue, know that she was no longer needed, he can hardly get any messages out. Not that it would do much. Like Thia, none of the ships in range have sets strong enough to relay the messages back to America.

The news is not what Carlos wants to hear. Having just finished interviewing the ruddy-faced young Englishman and hearing of the extraordinary luck that led to him catching *Titanic*'s distress call, and having heard accounts from some of the *Titanic* survivors of the events that led to the astonishing circumstances in which they now find themselves, there is nothing to do but wait. And write the story. Frustrated but determined, Carlos thanks Harold and exits the wireless shack only to pull up short. ‘*Captain.*’

Arthur is equally surprised by the almost-collision. When the man opposite stretches out his hand, he takes it, reflexively.

'I'm Carlos Hurd, Captain.' They shake. 'With the *St Louis Post-Dispatch*.'

Tension grips Arthur.

'My wife and I are aboard your ship on holiday. I'm writing a news report of the disaster to transmit once we're in range of shore.'

There they are. The words Arthur knew were coming before he could get one in edgewise. 'Mr Hurd, these people have undergone a terrible calamity. Most have lost someone they love. They are grieving and distressed and they are in my care. I do not intend for them to be bothered by press men.'

Carlos is surprised at this vigorous opposition. 'Captain, the world will want to know what has happened. *They have a right to know.*'

'I am not concerned with the world. I am concerned with the people on this ship.'

'*Sir.* It is my duty to report on these events, and I intend to.'

Short of confinement, Arthur can't stop the reporter talking to anyone who is willing. 'Probably you will be able to pick up some incidents,' he begins. 'A list of the rescued is to be made up and you can even see the purser about copying it,' he adds. Then his voice becomes resolute. 'But you may positively not use the wireless.'

Then he steps around Carlos into the shack.

A little while earlier, Arthur had given Harold this message for Cunard: *Am proceeding New York unless otherwise ordered, with about 800, after having consulted with Mr. Ismay and considering the circumstances. With so much ice about, consider New York best.* As Cunard is his employer and Thia's owner, Arthur is subject to the company's direction. The message he now sends is the same in essence, but addressed to three parties. The first is Cunard, again, and the second the White Star Line, *Titanic*'s owner.

'The man who was just in here, did he want you to send a telegram?' Arthur hands the slip to Harold as he asks the question.

'Yes, but I told him we are out of range.' Harold looks down at the message: *Titanic struck iceberg sunk Monday 3am 41.46N 50.14W Carpathia picked up many passengers am proceeding New York Rostron.*

The third party the message is directed to is the Associated Press. Arthur knows the world will want news, but the people on shore who are most desperate for that news are those with family and friends aboard *Titanic*. What they will want, more than anything, is to know who survived.

'With the exception of that telegram,' Arthur gestures at the slip, 'do not send any other press messages. Under no circumstances are you to send any news story from that gentleman who was just in here. The wireless is to be used for official messages, transmitting the list of survivor names, when it's compiled, and personal messages from survivors. Do you understand?'

Harold nods. The captain doesn't explain his reasons for this embargo to the young man, but with it firmly in place, he returns to the bridge. Harold sets the slip aside with the captain's earlier message. Until they are in range of a station or a ship that can convey the messages back to land, there is nothing he can do with them.

———

To Carlos, Captain Rostron's edict is a jolt to the jaw. Of course, it's moot until Thia's in range of New York. When she is, every newspaper in the city will besiege her with questions and he can't imagine that her wireless operator will remain impervious to the offers that will come his way. For the time being, Carlos continues interviewing the survivors. He does not bother those who are unwilling to talk; there are more than enough people who find some relief in speaking. But their accounts are fragmentary, often contradictory, and he is left struggling to make sense of it all.

———

When she was still a girl, Katherine was the May Queen. She sang in the Great Festival Hall at the St Louis World's Fair and got into countless questionable escapades with her many siblings and cousins. Courage has never been absent.

But she pauses outside the door with the glass panel that says 'Library' in large gold letters, reserved for first cabin passengers. Katherine's never crossed this threshold. That, coupled with the anxiety she feels about helping Carlos, and she'd rather leave it uncrossed.

Steeling herself, she opens the door and is met by a stark contrast between the room and its occupants. The walls are panelled in a rich, dark timber, the floor is covered in thick Axminster carpets, and gold silk draperies frame the promenade windows. A collection of elegant wooden desks bearing sheafs of Thia's personal stationery gleam in the light of the pendants suspended from the white coffered ceiling. Calf-bound, gilt-edged volumes are sequestered on a low bookcase, atop which sits a glass case containing stones. The wall behind the bookcase is composed of glass tiles that peek out into the alleyway. Amidst all this, reclining on thickly padded easy chairs and lounges dotted about the large room, are women of wealth and refinement. But their usual equanimity is absent.

Faces are carved with grief. Bodies brittle. Evening gowns, night gowns, kimonos and wrappers are as present and as summarily ignored as those fortunate – oh, the breadths and depths of that word – fortunate enough to be clad in everyday steamer-wear. It's a kaleidoscope of ragged butterflies and careworn moths, inhabiting some foreign realm.

Katherine's throat thickens. She blinks several times. Then she steps inside.

Any thoughts of what Carlos wants are summarily forgotten and she sits down beside a woman, roughly her own age, who looks as though a single ripple will overtop the dam. Katherine gently introduces herself and the woman reciprocates. Lily May Futrelle. In the face of sympathy and the offer of genuine comfort, her story comes pouring out.

'I have given up hope.' Lily May's Georgian accent is soft and wretched. 'I have given up hope of him having been picked up by some other ship. I begged Jack to get into one of the lifeboats with me, but he told me there were enough for everyone and he would be rescued later. I clasped him in my arms and begged him to come. "For God's sake, *go*," he fairly screamed at me and tried to push me away. I could see how he suffered. Then one of the ship's officers forced me into a lifeboat. It was one of the last to leave the ship. He was – he was smoking a cigarette on deck with Colonel Astor. I didn't see him again.'

The woman in the white silk evening dress is Dorothy Gibson, a famous silent film actress and the poster girl of popular artist Harrison Fisher. She sits beside her mother. Along with two gentlemen, who Dorothy had insisted enter their boat and in so doing saved their lives, they had been playing bridge in the lounge the night before, violating the strict Sabbath rules of English vessels. They had even persuaded a steward, when he applied to them to turn out the lights, to let them finish their rubber and to bring them some Poland water. Dorothy and her mother suffered no more than material losses.

Katherine sits beside a woman lying on a sofa, cocooned in a blanket, her wet clothing on the floor beside her. The woman, Rhoda Abbott, tells Katherine that she was on the deck of *Titanic* waiting to get into one of the collapsible lifeboats. The men were trying to ready it when the ship's bow suddenly plunged and a rush of dark water swept over the deck, knocking her down. She floundered near the collapsible, which had also been swept from the deck. Rhoda called for help, but the men who'd clambered aboard the half-submerged boat, wet and freezing and intent on their own survival, didn't answer her call. She pulled herself aboard by some feat and waited out the long hours until dawn, the lone woman in a broken boat, while around her men succumbed to hypothermia and fell back into the sea.

Rhoda is the only woman on Thia who did not leave *Titanic* already aboard a lifeboat. What she doesn't tell Katherine, can hardly speak of to anyone, is that her two teenage sons – the eldest, Rossmore, seventeen and too old to be allowed a place in a boat and whom she refused to leave – were swept off the deck with her. She lost her grip on Eugene's hand. Like Lily May, she has no hope they have been picked up by another ship.

———

For hours Thia steams parallel to the pack ice, two or three hundred yards away. Late that afternoon her engines are stopped and Father Anderson is called upon to render service once more. A small group gathers at Thia's gangway, profoundly silent, listening to the sound of steel doors swinging open and a platform being lowered.

Four bodies, sewn up in sail cloth, are laid down and covered with the Union Jack. Amongst them are first-class passenger William Hoyt, third-class passenger David Livshin and Steward Sidney Siebert. The lifeboats brought these men to Thia already dead.

Father Anderson begins to pray. The cloth coffins have been weighted at the feet. When the Father finishes speaking, the flag is lifted and the first body is pushed off the platform. It strikes the water silently. Some of Thia's passengers turn away, unable to watch.

Hours earlier, when Able Seaman William Henry Lyons jumped from *Titanic*'s deck into the icy water he was fortunate, more so than most. One of the lifeboats that recently launched was nearby. When she returned – the only lifeboat to do so immediately – he was hauled aboard with seven other men, all plucked from the sea.

Born in County Cork, William was the son of a publican and the eldest of three handsome Irish lads. His brother Denis is a civil engineer and John is a medical student. By the time the lifeboat reached Thia, William was deeply unconscious. Her crew carried him to the hospital and stripped off his wet clothes, wrapped him in warm blankets and tried to revive him with brandy.

He was the only one of the rescued to die aboard Thia.

One of the bodies strikes flat. The sound of the splash is like a slap to the face. It might be William, but it's impossible to tell from the anonymous sacks.

———

After the funeral Thia resumes course, steaming alongside the immense ice floe, trying to find its end. Trying to find the land of the living. The white wall unsettles her passengers until day edges towards night and they see, to their infinite satisfaction, the last of the icebergs and the field fading astern.

Meanwhile, Harold works the *Olympic*. She left New York on Saturday afternoon, two days after Thia, and has been steaming full speed towards *Titanic*'s coordinates. At 2 p.m. she finally picked up Thia's faint sparks and began hurling questions at her. Harold replied, *Steady on, I can't do everything at once.*

When Harold sends them a summary of events they send a message asking, *Shall I meet you and where?*

The reply comes from Arthur. *Do you think it advisable Titanic's passengers see Olympic?* The sister ship is almost a twin to the lost liner. *Personally I say not.*

Nonetheless, he then consults Ismay, who is in the doctor's care and under opiate. Ismay shudders at the thought and orders that *Olympic* not be seen by Thia, and that no passenger transfer take place.

After Harold uses *Olympic* to relay the captain's messages of that morning to New York, the other ship asks if Thia can forward the names of survivors. Arthur replies, *Captain, chief, first, and sixth officers, and all engineers gone; also doctor; all pursers; one Marconi operator, and chief steward gone. We have second, third, fourth, and fifth officers and one Marconi operator on board.* And then: *Will send names immediately we can. You can understand we are working under considerable difficulty. Everything possible being done for comfort of survivors. Please maintain Stanbi.*

Harold starts to send the names of the first- and second-class survivors. He taps out, *Please excuse sending, but am half asleep.* He never did go to bed, nor has he eaten in 21 hours, so when *Olympic* slips out of range in the early evening, he's free to leave the shack for the dining saloon. *Olympic*, meanwhile, turns her attention to a long night ahead, relaying Thia's news to a world who still doesn't know that *Titanic* has sunk.

———

Carlos corners Harold at table. Having mentally tallied his funds, Carlos quietly offers Harold a bribe. Then he sweetens the pot. 'I can promise *substantially* more from the *New York World* if you can get even a short message through for me.'

The money is more than Harold could make as a wireless operator for a good long time. He wants to accept, but . . . 'I'm sorry, Mr Hurd. I can't. The captain has strictly enjoined me – no message not expressly authorised by him can go.'

Over the evening meal in the second-class dining saloon, surrounded by Thia's passengers – who waited patiently to dine until after the survivors – Carlos tries earnestly to change Harold's mind. But by the time the young man returns to his shack he's made no headway. Impressed at the discipline Arthur maintains, even as it stymies him, Carlos leaves off trying to sway Harold. If money will not work, his efforts are better directed at the captain's sensibilities.

———

A small cough captures Katherine's attention. Moving quickly to the berth, she strokes the chestnut curls buried in her pillow, soothing the sleeping toddler. Every other child brought aboard Thia has been claimed, except this little one and his older brother, who is about four. Around the same ages as two of hers back home.

In hopes he won't catch Lolo's cold, his brother Louis is being cared for in a different cabin, though separating them might not be for the best. They haven't spoken a word. Not even to ask after their father. A widower, he'd handed the boys through a ring of crewmen who'd locked arms around one of the collapsibles, allowing only women and children to pass. Then he'd stepped back, trusting the strangers in the lifeboat to care for his sons.

Now they're all alone.

Thia's passengers have taken to calling them the Titanic Orphans and sharing the care of them, though the New

York heiress Miss Margaret Hays, who speaks the boys' native French and has not suffered a personal loss, has primary responsibility for them at present. In the future . . . well, their future is uncertain.

———

The Monday papers reported that *Titanic* struck an iceberg and, with no other details to convey, the stories they told were pure conjecture. Even as survivors were being brought aboard Thia, they said that *Titanic* was safe, being towed to Halifax by the *Virginian*. That she'd gone down, but all her people were aboard the *Parisian* or *Virginian* or *Californian*. The *New York Times*, by pure luck, were closest when they said she was sinking and the women were put off in lifeboats.

On Tuesday morning, as the papers break the truth to the world, Dr McGee walks through the fog lying heavy across Thia's deck and climbs to the bridge. He finds Arthur still on duty. The captain could hardly have retired even had he the inclination. His cabin is occupied by Mrs Astor, Mrs Thayer and Mrs Widener, all newly wrought widows. His officers' cabins are likewise occupied.

'Captain, I'm pleased to say that there is a clean bill of health amongst the survivors.' The doctor's news is welcome, if surprising. There are minor issues – fractures, bruises and contusions – but on the whole the survivors are physically well. It seems to Arthur that there should be some somatic manifestation of such a terrible experience. Some evidence written on their bodies.

As the survivors' shock ebbs in the wake of a new day, the question of blame arises. Is such a tragedy a vagary of fate? Perhaps. But human nature needs something – *someone* – to hold responsible. The someone at hand is Bruce Ismay. As he is managing director of the White Star Line, there are those aboard Thia who feel that he should have gone down with *Titanic*, who think he pushed her captain to sail at reckless speeds in pursuit of the Blue Riband, the fastest Atlantic crossing. It's not true, but the truth is at the bottom of the Atlantic, and bitter recriminations make their rounds in Thia's overcrowded saloons and alleyways. In fact, for every male passenger who survived the question of cowardice arises. If the order given was that women and children are first, people wonder, how is it that there are male survivors when women and children died? The crew, needed to man the boats, are exempt from this criticism, but the passengers are condemned, if not in speech then in thought, simply for living.

As the day wears on, Thia makes contact with *Minnewaska* and flashes her the names of *Titanic*'s surviving crew members to relay before they pass out of range. The *Minnewaska* operator can tell how tired Harold is by the mistakes in his keying. The poor atmospheric conditions, jamming from other ships and the limited range of Thia's wireless set have all complicated the task of transmitting the list of survivors. As a result, Harold has been unable to begin sending any of their hundreds of personal messages.

Meanwhile, the New York papers, lacking any details of *Titanic*'s sinking other than that an iceberg was involved, and slowly receiving confirmation from one ship after another that they carry no survivors, realise that Thia is at the heart of the story. She soon becomes the focus of the entire world.

———

Half an ocean away, out of contact with that world, Arthur knows nothing of this. He is otherwise occupied. He requests that all *Titanic*'s first-class passengers meet in the large saloon after lunch to select a committee to assist in caring for the rescued. As he steps down from the bridge to attend this meeting he crosses paths with Carlos. The younger man entreats him to change his mind about the wireless, to no avail.

When Arthur reaches the saloon, Frederic Seward, a lawyer and Glee Club member during his college days, who'd been playing cards with Dorothy last night, organ- ises a committee of seven people from those present, himself included, who did not lose any loved ones the day previous.

Chaired by Samuel Goldberg, on his way to America to attend the French Bull Dog Club of America's show, the committee includes Swedish-born Mauritz Björnström- Steffansson, who jumped into a lifeboat from *Titanic*'s deck in the last moments before she was swamped; Tuxedo Hill elite Frederick Spedden, father of the boy with the toy polar bear; and New York lawyer Isaac Frauenthal. There's also George Harder, returning from his three-month-long honeymoon in Europe, and lawyer and tennis star Karl Behr, who boarded *Titanic* to continue his courtship of Miss Helen Monypeny Newsom, a friend of his sister's, now aboard Thia. There is only one female member: Denver heiress, feminist and suffragette Mrs Molly Brown.

On behalf of the survivors, Samuel expresses their heartfelt thanks to God for their deliverance. Further, that it is the unanimous opinion of the company that no words can express their gratitude to Thia's captain, officers and crew for their self-sacrifice and unsparing efforts in the noble work of rescue.

By now these cabin passengers have recovered some of their equanimity and turn their attention to two matters. The first is the steerage passengers. They make plans to collect subscriptions for a general fund and from it resolve to make provisions as far as possible for those left destitute, but also to award a loving cup to Arthur and medals to Thia's crew, with any remaining funds allocated to *Titanic*'s crew.

Frauenthal offers to act as treasurer and Molly to see to the rendering of any necessary immediate assistance. Then a unanimous resolution is read from the women survivors that expresses heartfelt gratitude and unrepayable indebtedness to Thia's officers and men, enlarging upon their tender kindness, chivalry and gallantry, and their self-sacrificing devotion to the rescued.

That afternoon, at the committee's behest, second cabin passenger and teacher Lawrence Beesley accompanies Karl to visit the steerage passengers. They take down the names of all those saved, their nationalities, their addresses if they have them, how much money they possess and whether they have friends in America who can assist them. Meanwhile, response to the subscription appeal is immediate with pledges ranging from $5 up to $250.

After the committee meeting Arthur turns his attention to Harold. The boy hasn't slept in two and a half days, so he sends a message to sickbay and asks if Harry Bride can help. Early that evening, frostbitten feet bandaged, the *Titanic*'s young operator is carried to Thia's shack to assist.

As *Minnewaska* moves out of range, the boys finally establish contact with shore, the station at Sable Island, a crescent sandbar 200 miles south-east of Halifax. The papers, who are issuing special bulletins at the drop of a hat, report the contact and announce that the world can soon expect details of the disaster. But the Marconi station on Sable Island is barely within range of Thia's wireless, the weather conditions are poor, and Harold and Harry continue to be jammed by other ships seeking information about *Titanic*. They can hardly work the station and the expected news is not forthcoming.

The world becomes increasingly anxious about what it perceives as Thia's silence. Most people can do nothing about it, but US President William Howard Taft, concerned about his friend and military aid Major Archibald Butt, has more resources at his disposal than most. President Taft directs the Secretary of the Navy to dispatch scout cruisers USS *Chester* and USS *Salem*. *Chester*, already at sea east of Nantucket Shoal, is directed to intercept Thia. *Salem*, off the Virginian coast, makes for *Nantucket Lightship* to act as a relay between *Chester* and the navy shore stations.

———

Meanwhile, on Thia, Carlos meets Katherine in their cabin to compare notes. He protests the captain's continuing edict concerning the wireless and press messages, having been unable to get the man to reverse his ruling. Katherine's attention is momentarily arrested as she tenders wifely commiseration, before it returns to their room. There's something . . . not quite right. But she can't place her finger on it. The cabin has been tidied, the beds made, but one expects the stewards to attend to these matters.

She begins to tell Carlos some of the stories shared with her, just as she did yesterday, and he writes them down in his notebook. Even in the retelling she feels echoes of sorrows that aren't hers, yet somehow are. But still, the room niggles at her.

'Carlos, does it look to you like –'

'I need more paper.' Carlos's voice unintentionally drowns out Katherine. Before she can finish what she'd been about to say, he nips out to purchase some of Thia's stationery, which bears an inked engraving of her under full steam and beneath, scrollwork that reads *On Board the Cunard RMS 'Carpathia'*. He returns scant minutes later with a look of bemusement and frustration. 'The store won't sell me any paper.'

During his absence Katherine was able to devote her full attention to their room and the question of paper does not presently concern her. 'I think someone has gone through our things.'

'How can you tell?' He looks about, surprised.

'They are out of place. Not how I left them.'

'Is anything missing?'

'No.'

'The stewards are the only ones with access.' They share a look. Suspicion growing but unable to be certain, Carlos escorts Katherine to the library. The room is now littered with straw mattresses packed as closely as sardines. The copious sheafs of stationery that had been available on every writing desk in the room only yesterday are gone. Not used, one of the ladies tells Katherine, but removed.

She reports this to Carlos and they soon find that paper has become scarce all over Thia, at, apparently, her captain's orders.

'I think he had the stewards search our room,' Carlos says.

'Surely not.' Katherine can't countenance the idea. They're hardly engaged in some wrongdoing, for goodness' sake.

But Carlos is certain and, increasingly, she comes to believe the same thing. The couple take precautions. Carlos writes his story on every scrap of paper he can beg from sympathisers, even on toilet paper, tucked into odd corners about Thia, deliberately avoiding her officers as he writes.

When the stewards come to tend their cabin, Katherine makes it a habit to remain in the room. She sits on one of the upholstered chairs and pretends some interest elsewhere, all the while intensely sensitive to the actions of the stewards. The way they straighten the beds, hands slipping under mattresses. The way they tidy the desk, opening drawers to put things away. Edwardian etiquette adroitly at play, they would never ask a lady to stand, and so never know that she is sitting on what it is they have, perhaps, been tasked with finding. Because the Hurds cannot be sure of the sanctity of their cabin when they are not present, during the day Katherine hides Carlos's notes in her corset.

———

Late that night, just before Sable Island passes out of wireless range, Arthur finally gets a message through to Cunard. Thia will arrive in New York by 11 p.m. on Thursday. The poor weather that has all day made transmissions difficult, worsens.

———

Karl Behr is asleep fully clothed on a hard tabletop in the forward smoking room. The committee member is exhausted after a long day interviewing steerage passengers, many of whom speak only foreign languages. He's wrenched awake by a terrific crash. Sure that Thia has struck an iceberg, he rolls off the table and rushes out the door, starting for his sweetheart, Helen. As he hits the deck a flash of lightning almost knocks him down. Then there's another crash.

Relief weakens him, adrenaline draining when he realises that it's only a thunderstorm waging war on the Atlantic. Lightning streaks harpoon the sea and thunder drowns her roar. Ahead, he can see the bridge, rain belting against the wheelhouse glass. There, taking what shelter he can, Arthur rolls in time with the swells that rock Thia's hull, keeping his feet with long years of practice. In their berths, on pallets in the saloons and alleyways, survivors huddle under their covers, drawing them up tight, as if the cloth cocoons can protect them. For the first time since they were raised up Thia's sides, fear edges out grief. Every crash of thunder is a collision with an iceberg, and prayers are whispered, and pillowslips taste like the sea.

———

On Wednesday morning the survivors wake up still afraid. The feeling leaches into Thia's passengers, and the fog is no help. As carefully as Thia carries them, she cannot stem their fear that she too will fail; echoes that won't fade.

Harold's body protests as he wakes, a legacy of falling asleep hunched over his desk. He glances at the clock. Barely three hours of sleep, the first rest he's had, though hardly restorative. He sets to work immediately, seeing who's about, hoping to send some of the hundreds of passenger messages awaiting transmission. With Harry to relieve him they're working watch and watch.

A little after 6 a.m. he picks up the Cunarder *Franconia*. She sailed from Boston on Tuesday morning with a *Globe* reporter who has directions to find out, amongst whatever else he can, the exact number of survivors. Reports have varied between 675 and 868. When the request comes from *Franconia*'s captain, Arthur replies: *Saved total 705.*

Thia then uses *Franconia* as a relay before the other ship is out of range with Sable Island.

Just as Harold finishes sending the first personal message, Dr Blackmarr enters the shack. They exchange pleasantries before the doctor begins to direct the conversation to his purpose. Before he can finish, Carlos enters.

Harold tenses imperceptibly.

Carlos, having heard about *Franconia*, comes straight to the point. 'I need you to send a message for me immediately. It's vitally important.'

'Who is it to?'

'The *New York World*.' Carlos cannot lie about it – not that he would – but one can hardly send a letter without addressing the envelope.

'I'm sorry, Mr Hurd.' Harold really would like to help the man and he can't see anything terribly wrong with it, but the captain has given him specific instructions. 'I can't.'

Marconi officers work for the Marconi Company, not the shipping line of the vessel they serve upon, so there may be some possibility Carlos can persuade Harold to defy Arthur. But sermons about freedom of the press and the people's right to news have no effect. Work for Marconi he may, but the company's rules make Harold utterly subject to the captain.

Carlos has already tried bribing him once and he can hardly be so blatant in front of the doctor, but, 'Truly, I can recompense you generously for your efforts.'

'I'm sorry,' Harold says once more, shaking his head. 'No messages to the press.'

Frustrated, Carlos nods to the doctor as he exits the shack.

His wake is filled with a brief silence. 'Well,' the doctor says, 'he was rather earnest. I'm not certain why you wouldn't take his missive.'

'Captain has ordered no press messages. The wireless is for official messages, sending off the lists of survivors, and their personal messages.'

'Why no press?'

Harold shrugs. 'I don't know. He didn't explain it to me.'

'I see. I was actually hoping to send a message this morning.'

Harold holds out a blank slip. 'That's fine, Doctor. I'll send one for you.'

'Yes, well, you see, I want to send it to the *Chicago Tribune*.'

The slip in Harold's hand wavers. 'Doctor . . .'

'Hear me out.' Having witnessed Carlos's unsuccessful arguments, Dr Blackmarr tries a different tack. 'It's not a press message. Sending it to the *Tribune* is just the most expedient way of letting all of my friends at home know that the Chicagoans aboard this ship are in good condition.'

Indecision splits Harold's face. He likes the doctor. They've become friends and saying no to him is much harder than to Mr Hurd, about whom the captain was explicit.

The doctor presses. 'I'm also prepared to recompense *you* for helping me alleviate the concerns of my friends at home.' He shrouds the bribe in a guise that Harold can justify. 'It's just like those personal messages,' he gestures to the pile. 'They are entitled to know the Chicagoans aboard are safe.'

Safe. One of those words he keeps seeing. 'All right,' Harold capitulates, and hands over the slip.

Dr Blackmarr scribbles his message: *Carpathia picked up seven hundred Titanic, mostly women. Over two thousand lost. Ice berg continuous mass twenty five miles. Chicagoans this ship well.*

If Harold thinks anything of the fact that it's more like a disaster report with the bit about the Chicagoans tacked on at the end, he says nothing. Only messages from survivors are to be sent for free, so Harold counts the words. 'I can't give it to you at press rates.' Such a thing would cost 23 cents, but it's not a press message. 'It'll cost $8.66.'

Dr Blackmarr hands over the money and something extra as promised. Harold writes him a receipt, then turns to the key and begins to tap out the message.

———

As the clicking of the wireless plays out over Thia's stern, a new rumour begins the rounds: that *Titanic* received ice warnings before the collision. As the rumours become a furore the survivors put the question to one of the surviving officers. He confirms that it's true, but when sailing the Atlantic, he tells them, ice in the track is a common hazard, one well known to the crew. The usual practice is to keep a sharp lookout but not to slow the ship. She runs to a schedule, the same as an express train, and cannot slow more than a few knots in uncertain conditions. *Titanic* was not even running at maximum speed.

———

That afternoon, Sir Cosmo Duff-Gordon seeks out Arthur. He tells him that he promised the crew of his lifeboat five pounds each to replenish their kit. Arthur says that this is unnecessary, but Sir Cosmo replies that he promised. He asks one of the crewmen from his boat to gather the others, whereupon he gives them each a cheque for the amount promised. A rumour begins aboard Thia that the money was a bribe, to stop the men returning to collect survivors from the water. This is untrue but it clings, and never goes away.

Dr Blackmarr sees the group, outside the smokeroom, and asks if he can take their picture. Sir Cosmo and Lady Lucy consent. The sailors even go and get their lifebelts for the photo.

When some of the passengers see them coming, clad in the things, they panic, until they learn the reason. Officer Lowe, who manned the lifeboat with the sail, is unimpressed with the production and in no uncertain terms tells the lord and lady what he thinks of them.

———

Later that afternoon Thia comes into range of *Chester* and relays the names of the third-class survivors. It takes hours, as Harold has to send the names several times due to the differences between the Marconi Company's Continental Morse and the American code used by their navy.

As *Chester* relays the names to *Salem*, which in turn sends them to the naval station at Newport, Rhode Island, Thia's operators are forced into silence, unable to compete with the strength of the scout cruisers' signals. Thia soon comes within range of the wireless station along the New England coast, but the Newport station, which in good conditions can raise Panama, cannot contact Thia because of interference from a multitude of other stations and vessels. Despite favourable atmospheric conditions, for perhaps the first time since she turned towards New York, the cacophony of signals flashing between stations results in a hissing fizz that drowns Thia's voice. The Newport station commander eventually asks all stations to clear the air.

Desperate to hear from her now she's in range, the US government and the Marconi Company agree to silence all of their respective stations north of Norfolk, Virginia, to give Thia an uninterrupted field for transmitting. The only exceptions are those stations – Siasconset, Sagaponack and Seagate – needed to relay her messages as she passes in and out of their range. The silence order directs them to only handle traffic from Thia. Never before in history has such effort been made to contact a single ship: the silencing of the entire north-eastern seaboard of the United States, in the hopes that Thia will speak.

Late that night, after the interference from other stations recedes, a transmission is sent from *Chester* to Thia: *The President of the United States is very anxious to know if Major Butt, Mr Millet and Mr Moore are safe.* They are not. *Please inform me at once so that I can transmit to him. Chandler, commanding USS Salem.*

Even with Harry to assist, Harold is exhausted. The former spends most of his time preparing messages for sending, the latter working the apparatus. By now he's taking and sending by rote, scarcely aware of the contents. Simply keying a series of letters, or transcribing them, then setting them aside to be delivered. He misses the import of the message from *Chester*.

Arthur is equally exhausted. He has hardly left the bridge in four days and has had less rest than even Harold. He has his hands full and when he scans the latest messages, none of which he has the luxury of giving his undivided attention other than ascertaining that there are no dangers to Thia – he's concerned about this wretched fog – he notes one that says the president is anxious about survivors. As the message is signed by the commander of the *Chester*, Arthur doesn't realise that it is a direct request for information from the President of the United States.

One that he unintentionally ignores.

Meanwhile, Harold and Harry are besieged by shore traffic from those stations permitted to transmit. They send official messages from the government, Cunard and White Star; messages from relatives; and frantic requests for news from dozens of New York papers, asking for exclusives, narratives by prominent passengers and the full details of the sinking, and promising liberal pay for such. The two young men do the best they can to ignore this cacophony. They work through the night once more, focusing on the most important thing: sending the survivors' messages home.

In the early hours of Thursday morning Harold receives a wireless he cannot ignore. It's from Guglielmo Marconi, the man who invented the apparatus he's currently working, and who owns the company that employs him. *Carpathia*, the message reads, *wire news dispatches immediately to Siasconset or to navy boats; if this impossible ask captain give reason why no news allowed to be transmitted.*

Bound by Arthur's orders, Harold nonetheless runs the message up to the bridge. He'd rather not have to tell Mr Marconi that he ignored his request. But Arthur, as ever, makes no reply.

When dawn comes the papers are as much in the dark as ever about their most pressing questions. How can an iceberg sink a ship? A supposedly unsinkable ship? Why could it not be avoided, since ice is common on the western track at this time of year? Why were so few saved? Why did so many die? Given the lack of news from Thia, the New York morning papers are decided in suggesting that she's complicit in a conspiracy to keep the true details of *Titanic*'s sinking a secret – perhaps at the behest of White Star or Ismay, currently aboard Thia and still occupying Dr McGee's cabin.

None of that is true. Arthur is not following any company policy or requests to withhold information, he is trying to protect the privacy of the survivors. And the only thing Thia is intent on is closing the remaining distance to New York.

As dawn gives way to morning, Thia passes *Nantucket Lightship*. The familiar sight, heralding land, is visible even through the fog and the feeling of relief amongst the passengers is strong. Even so, a stirring of discontent reaches Arthur's ears.

None of the survivors have received replies to their messages. The Harrys are still intent on dispatching the hundreds of them – with great difficulty, because of the poor weather and Thia's old set with its limited range – not on receiving words that do little more than clutter the airwaves at a time when they are not a priority. A rumour starts, as they are wont to aboard Thia these days, that the delay is due to the sending of messages to the press. Something that could not be further from the truth. As sympathetic as he is to the plight of the survivors, Arthur is not about to allow false rumours to flourish. He takes the wireless message from Marconi and posts it to Thia's bulletin board, alongside one of his own:

> NOTICE TO PASSENGERS
> I hereby declare that no press messages at all have been marconied from this ship with the exception of a short one of about twenty words to the Associated Press, sent immediately after the passengers had been picked up, and the passenger messages have been dispatched with all speed possible. The reason for this statement is that it has come to my attention that several passengers are under the impression that the delay in dispatching their private messages is due to the instruments being used for the press.
> *A.H. Rostron, Commander*

Carlos again seeks out Arthur. But the most urgent and respectful appeals fail to convince the man to change his mind, and Carlos, who spent most of the night writing and revising his copy, still has no way to get it ashore.

Neither is he aware of the very many attempts to contact him that have occurred over the last three days. On Monday, the *St Louis Post-Dispatch* sent a wireless asking him to rush through a rescue story, including the experiences of any St Louisans; on Tuesday, the *Dispatch*'s sister paper, the *New York World*, wanted to impress upon Carlos the urgency of getting into wireless communication with them, and the *Dispatch* sent another message asking that he please disregard Associated Press requests and only give the story to the *World*. On Wednesday, the *Dispatch* advised him that a *World* steamer would meet Thia, and that he should have a completed story ready to throw over to them, while *The Sun* tried to tempt him, saying they would pay handsomely for an exclusive when he lands. Of course, he receives none of these messages and can send none of his own.

In any case, the heavy haze continues to interfere with Thia's wireless. Poor weather has clung to her since she left that ice floe in the Atlantic, as wretched upon her return as it was pleasant upon her departure.

It hinders the efforts of two sea tugs dispatched to meet Thia.

The *Boston Globe*, the paper that put the reporter aboard *Franconia*, chartered the *Salutation* out of Connecticut. They installed a wireless set and sent her out, a little after midnight last night. The *Mary F. Scully* left Rhode Island at noon Wednesday, carrying wireless operator Jack Binns, whom the *New York American* hopes to put aboard Thia. Three years earlier he became famous for working the SS *Republic*'s wireless as she sank after colliding with SS *Florida* in fog. The *American*'s idea is to have Binns relieve Harold – by now beyond exhausted – and, it goes without saying, for Binns to transmit exclusives back to the *American*.

But neither tug can find Thia in the thick fog. They are forced to retreat to Ambrose Channel and wait.

On the bridge, Arthur rings the telegraph for dead slow. For hours, they grope past Nantucket Shoals. The nerve-racking noise of the whistle blows every half-minute. It distresses the survivors. All that suspense and agony, that heartbreaking experience, and now the terror of sea fog adds to their suffering. If he could, Arthur would wish it away.

———

The low deep call of Fire Island's lightship answers Thia in the late afternoon, and soon after the fog lifts. As they approach Sandy Hook, Karl Behr steps onto the bridge. He's become familiar with it, and Arthur, over the past several days, his work on the survivors' committee bringing them into contact daily. They converse for a few moments but the captain's mind seems to be occupied, a hint of a frown in his eyes. It's not long before Arthur enlightens him. 'I've been receiving wireless requests from the press asking permission to board when we take on the pilot at Sandy Hook.'

Arthur has staunchly maintained a single position concerning the press, yet the constant entreaties, from Carlos and others, soften his stance . . . 'I am opposed to having survivors interviewed. What is your opinion?' His gaze rests on the younger man.

Karl may not have lost anyone aboard *Titanic* but grief weighs on him nonetheless. And the thought of Helen being exposed to the curiosity of newspapermen is untenable. He returns the captain's stare evenly. '*Carpathia* is no place for newspaper reporters. Not right now.'

Had the younger man sided elsewhere it probably would have made no difference, but his agreement reaffirms Arthur's resolve. Something he will need in the coming hours. As Karl leaves him on the bridge a message arrives from Charles Sumner, Cunard's New York manager, about modified customs and immigrations procedures for Thia's arrival, and a warning. *If any vessel attempts put newspaper men aboard, claiming have authority from me, it is false.* And Arthur begins to wonder, exactly, what awaits Thia at Sandy Hook.

ARTEFACTS

2007

JEFF CORNISH, AN EXPERIENCED DEEP WRECK DIVER AND venture capitalist, spends most of his first descent working to free Thia's remaining brass telegraph head from the rubble and plating, uncertain if he'll succeed. When he finally does, he bags the telegraph, fills the bag with air and releases it. The yellow skin breaks the surface and for a moment the support team in the chase boat think it's a bailout. Their hearts are in their throats until they recognise the lift bag. After wrestling with the telegraph Jeff has a few moments of unease as he tries to find the shot line. It's dark and he's tired.

The men diving Thia don't have much luck filming her. The pressure implodes Jeff's video lights, as well as the housing that protects Carl Spencer's £10 000 high-definition camera. The sometimes diver, sometimes dirt-bike racer, sometimes helicopter pilot is gutted. Edoardo Pavia, meanwhile, whose camera survives, spends his time filming Thia only to discover when he reaches the surface, six hours later, that his camera is not switched on.

Other equipment is crushed by the intense pressure. They're on the depth-threshold, the edge of where things work. Nothing is designed for below 500 feet. Every so often, as they're swimming along, they hear an underwater *boom*. Dive torches, spot lights, video cameras, contents gauges, all become victims of the Boom Club, as they take to calling it.

That night, as they shoot the breeze on *Dancer*, Ric watches while Carl pulls apart his camera to see if it's salvageable. The others mess about trying to resurrect their own failing equipment. Carl's face is grey; one of the youngest men present, right now he looks like he's aged several years. It wasn't a good dive for him, though it's Andrea Bolzoni who is the first limper of the group. Andrea is from Trento, a cold, sweet little city in the northern part of Italy. It's close to the cave systems at Valstagna, which he dives often – though he prefers wrecks. Sometimes the lads shrug off these small signs of bends. Sometimes they can't. They put Andrea on oxygen all night and he's recovered by morning.

They also speculate about what Jeff's telegraph is worth. Thousands of pounds, unquestionably. But how many thousands? The *Titanic* artefacts that sell most often in association with Thia are the medals awarded to her crew. Created by Dieges and Clust Jewellers, Silversmiths and Medaleurs, they were presented in Thia's saloon by the Survivors Committee, during the presentation when Arthur received his loving cup. The officers were in dress uniform. Arthur wore a sword as per his right as a Royal Navy reservist. The others came as they were, trimmers and stokers garbed in coal ash. Fourteen gold medals, 110 silver medals and 108 bronze medals were presented, according to rank. Auction prices are capricious, but today a bronze sells for not less than US$5000. The record for a gold medal set at a Sotheby's auction was US$55 000.

So how much for a bridge telegraph from Thia?

The debate rages, as those not diving the next day put a dent into what must be half the contents of Threshers bottle shop. The liquor loosens lips, the stories start and laughter sounds across the dark water to *Janus*, whose crew is engaged in their own entertainment. Two spots of light on the black Atlantic.

The next day, as Ric finishes his first dive, he begins the long hours of decompression. Meanwhile, news reaches Comex that Jeff has recovered the last bridge telegraph. They ask for it. Politely, of course.

The lads *do not* want to give it up.

But if they fall out with Comex it will be war at sea.

So far, Paul-Henry Nargeolet's team have been nothing but accommodating. The discussion aboard *Dancer* is heated, and Jeff is gutted, but with a week's worth of diving at stake – Comex could make it impossible for them to dive safely – and the memory of what happened the last time they had something that Titanic Inc. wanted, they decide not to fight. Though, they also decide to have a little fun with the competition.

When Comex sends a boat across to *Dancer*, Paul-Henry is in it. Clad in jeans and a denim shirt, hair scruffy in the wind, he clambers aboard. The men with him are in black windbreakers and black baseball caps. They're all wearing scarlet life jackets that set them apart from *Dancer*'s lads. They bring across a case of beer. It's nice of them, but a sorry consolation.

'Before you look at the telegraph, there's something else we found that we thought you might like to see.'

Paul-Henry looks over in interest. Two of the lads bring out an object, carrying it between them. It's metal, painted a dull grey. But it's the shape that catches his eye. It has a curve and a waist, and more than vaguely resembles a bell.

On it, they've scrawled in thick black marker: *Carpathia 1903.*

Paul-Henry bursts out laughing. It's an amusing but provocative reminder, and it goes at least some of the way towards breaking the tension that results from the reason they've come.

The telegraph is resting in a large round plastic tub, submerged in seawater. The men from Comex lay protective foam across the deck, then lift the heavy telegraph from the tub to the foam. They wear white gloves and won't let anyone touch it bare skinned. The lads think it's all a bit precious. They normally just throw stuff in a bucket.

The telegraph is missing its pedestal base. It looks like a rusty wheel rim with a hint of verdigris, encrusted in barnacles. The facing panels that once indicated Thia's speed are broken, the telegraph levers frozen in place like clock hands frozen in time. Paul-Henry takes photographs as they conduct an inspection and make field notes; all the while Jeff stands nearby, watching intently.

The other lads are clustered a little further back, also watching. The way the Comex crew handle the telegraph is in sharp contrast to their own casual approach. As though it's an historical artefact, not a piece of salvaged wreck.

The Comex crew wrap it up to take back to *Janus*. Once there, they'll put it in one of her preservation tanks – which are always covered when the lads are aboard, and about whose contents Comex is very circumspect – to await proper conservation. Their goal is to passivate artefacts and to prevent them from becoming damaged by contact with the air.

———

Down below, Duncan Keates swims through an open section of Thia's hull. A rising wash of tiny bubbles indicates that air is leaking out of one of his emergency tanks. He and Ric are bunk mates, but this is the first time they've dived together. Dunc replaced a mutual friend who bowed out of the expedition because of one of the few things that curtails a diver: his wedding. Dunc was supposed to be a guest at the big day, but Thia's allure was too strong. So Ric and Dunc are 'buddies': each diver descends in a two-man buddy team, but once down they separate and go their own way.

Ric would think twice about going inside a wreck at 100 feet. It's too easy to get trapped or nick a hose, but Dunc is fearless. That or mad. When he emerges, he's carrying several plates in a familiar blue and white. When Team One dived yesterday they recovered some and told Dunc where to find them. Comex allows them to keep the plates, and at the end of the trip they each come away with tangible evidence of being the only men on Earth to have seen Thia in person, after her 90 years at the bottom of the deep blue.

Tim Cashman films her with his *video on a stick*, as the lads call it, though he prefers stick-o-vision. When Carl's video camera joined the Boom Club he lent Tim his filming lights, and Tim spent several hours jury-rigging them to his homemade video housing, a condemned aluminium dive cylinder whose ends he replaced with clear polycarbonate. He's mounted the stick-o-vision to his underwater scooter. It's a testament to home engineering that this is the only camera housing that holds up at depth.

Nor does Helmuth Biechl escape the Boom Club. During his dive his primary light implodes. Ric didn't know him at all before this trip, but he's struck by how precise the German diver is in everything he does. His descent took ten minutes and he stays exploring for seventeen minutes, within a 50-metre circumference of the shot line. On Thia Helmuth sees portholes and china but chooses to leave them as they lie.

Mark Elliott – Eric the Viking – gets a call from his missus before he dives. She tells him she's pregnant. He still dives Thia, but only once.

On Ric's second dive he misses the wreck. So does everyone on Team Two. Comex wanted to move *Janus*, so the lads had to pull up their shot line. When they redeploy it they just miss Thia and end up on the seabed. Normally, they'd clip in and reel off until they find the wreck, but she's so deep they don't have time to search. As Ric ascends he sees one of Comex's rovers filming her and realises they weren't far off. The rover is big, its searchlights cutting through the water. Seems to Ric like somethin' out of *Aliens*.

———

On his third dive Richie Stevenson uses his scooter to circumnavigate Thia. He wants to make sure he sees all of her. His mouthpiece wobbles in the current. His scooter is locked on full tilt and dragging him along when the mouthpiece comes loose, causing the loop to tear free and fly over his head, which leaves him breathing water. As he tries to grab the hose his scooter drags him down to the seabed. To have that happen, at that depth . . . A diver can never know what might go wrong. But they train hard in the expectation that if the worst can happen, it will. Richie recovers his regulator then sorts out his scooter.

This is the story that goes around the dive world. Richie says all that happened is the zip tie came loose and the front loop popped off. That there was no drama and no swallowed water. The truth is probably somewhere in the middle.

———

After the lads have been on site three days, Comex wraps up its expedition and Paul-Henry and his team depart, leaving the lads none the wiser as to what they recovered. After six days of diving and three dives each, only a few of the lads are willing to go again. So they decide to head for home.

They've had a fair go at Thia and recovered plenty of evidence to show for it. Dozens of plates, and after Comex's departure some of the lads brought up portholes. They can't help wishing they'd played the long game and left the telegraph alone, but they couldn't have known when Comex would leave.

From the more than twenty dives conducted by Comex's Super Achille rover, here is what it recovered: portholes, a partial ceramic cup, a silver oval dish, two metal rings, a triple coat hook and a triple coathanger, telegraphs (bases and tops), a soup bowl, a saucer, a brownware teapot and creamer, plates, tiles (one small, one multi-pieced, two blue, two blue and white, one octagonal and red), part of a decorative pot, several cups (including one with the Cunard logo), a drain grill, a hinge, two soap dishes, a deck light, several bottles, a clock, a chamber pot, a flask, binoculars, a table lamp, a 'Boots' jar, an inhaler pot, artillery shell casings, a metal dome, a brown jug, blue-patterned crockery (cups, plates, saucers and bowls), an S-shaped hook, part of a tip basin, a ceramic light fixture, a glass jar and lid, a wine bottle, a carafe, a fragment of flooring, pieces of coal and a Pepsi bottle.

But no bell.

No prizes from the trophy cabinet.

And no stones from The Roman Wall.

RETURN TO NEW YORK

1912

AS THIA COMES ABEAM *AMBROSE LIGHTSHIP* IN THE EARLY evening, she's met by a flotilla. More than fifty vessels wait at the gate of New York, a blockade of sea tugs, including *Salutation* and *Mary F. Scully*, ferry boats, yachts and steam launches. One of the larger tugs contains the mayor and other officials. It blasts a salute from its steam whistle which prompts answering bells, whistles and sirens from every boat in the harbour. The sound cascades across the water and stirs the waiting city.

The small vessels make for Thia like she bears the Messiah. The pilot boat *New Jersey* is amongst them, white hull gleaming. Arthur and his officers stare at the astonishing sight and realise, as one, that Thia is about to be swamped. Arthur rings *all stop* then issues an order without taking his eyes off the swarming boats.

'No one comes aboard except the pilot.'

His officers sound their assent then take their stations for entering port. Second Officer James Bisset remains on the bridge with the captain; the chief officer is to the bow and the first officer to the stern. Third Officer Eric Rees heads to the gangway, to see the pilot aboard.

The sea is rough and choppy with a strong east wind. The *New Jersey* puts a yawl overside and the occupants begin to pull for Thia. By and large the other boats contain reporters and photographers, chartered by the many broadsheets vying for news, carrying huge placards proclaiming their affiliation: *New York Times*, *New York American*, *The Sun*, *New York World*. There are vessels that contain concerned family and friends, and still others bearing those who are merely inquisitive or think it a lark to meet the rescue ship. Tragedy is horrifically compelling and, Arthur finally realises, the world is in utter suspense.

It's like a fleet of small destroyers bombarding a battleship. Magnesium flashes flare, explosions in the night. As Thia halts, boats surge close on the chop, vying for position near her closed gangway doors.

Carlos Hurd waits behind them, near Officer Rees, hoping representatives from the *World*'s tug will be permitted aboard. He doesn't know about the captain's edict but by now he knows the man, and that he may have to throw his story overboard. This afternoon as Thia approached the harbour he took the precaution of wrapping it in a water-proof bundle. A fellow St Louisan and a *Titanic* survivor, Spencer Silverthorne, made him a buoy out of a cigar box filled with champagne bottle corks, and they attached the two together with rope.

The doors are opened but Thia's crew make no move to lower her gangway. When it becomes clear that only the pilot will be allowed to board, bedlam ensues. Reporters shout questions through megaphones up at the passengers lining the deckrails, in a deafening cacophony that drowns itself out. Some call up to Arthur, at first entreating, then badgering, to be allowed aboard. Others call for *Titanic*'s crew to jump overboard, waving fistfuls of cash, or try to entice passengers to answer questions or lower ladders or ropes overside. Thia's officers, alongside her boatswains, seamen and masters-at-arms, line her deck; maintain her sanctity. Her passengers are oddly quiet.

As the yawl approaches, Pilot McLaughlin, a friend of Arthur's, yells up to him on the bridge wing, 'Can these fellows come aboard?' Several reporters are with him. It's not easy for Arthur to refuse a friend so he prevaricates. He cups his hands and sings down, 'I can't hear you.' Quietly, he sends a message to Rees at the gangway doors, and when the ladder is lowered for the pilot there's a rope bent at the bottom.

Rees climbs down and waits, several feet above the choppy water, as the yawl comes alongside. When he steps onto the thwarts he guards the ladder as surely as his captain commanded. 'Stand back.' The officer's voice is hard. 'Pilot only. Captain's orders.'

To hear James tell it, Rees was rushed and punches were thrown. But, as he is strongly built and made stronger by sea service, the reporters earn themselves only bruises. They resort to bribes and even trickery when one man pretends a hysterical fit, complete with frothing mouth, claiming his sister is aboard.

The third officer is having none of it. The pilot begins to climb and with only a brief pause Rees is up after him, while the crew hoist the lower rungs under his heels so that the reporters cannot follow. Their frustrated profanity is lost in the din. All the while, no other boat, including the *World*'s tug, is permitted close enough for Carlos to throw his story. Then the pilot is in, the doors are closed, and his chance is gone.

———

As dusk darkens the sky, the wind begins to blow hard. Thia steams up the Lower Bay pursued by the flotilla. For days, the people aboard her have longed to reach land. Harder and deeper than the usual kind of longing. And now that it is within sight a storm gathers, as though written.

The mail was brought aboard when they stopped for the pilot, and a bundle of letters and telegrams is delivered to Arthur on the bridge in the pelting rain. He tucks it into his pocket and gives Thia his attention. Later, in a lull, he

leaves the pilot and slips down to the chartroom. He with-
draws a single item from the bundle. A cable.

There are only a few words but the name at the bottom
soothes him, lessening the tide of anxiety and responsibility that came in days before and has not yet receded. It's
as though a higher power knew what he needed. He slips
Minnie's message back into his pocket and returns to the
bridge and the storm.

———

Thia slows near the small artificial islands that serve as
New York's quarantine, off the larger Staten Island, to allow
health and immigration officials to board. Arthur looks
about for tugs. He wired White Star asking them to send
some to quarantine as Thia cannot dock with *Titanic*'s lifeboats obstructing the mooring ropes on her foredeck. He
even had the boats lowered halfway to the water in order
to avoid wasting time, but there are no waiting tugs and he
worries about what he will do when it comes time to berth.

The brief slackening in speed allows the fleet to catch
Thia, and Carlos, railside with Silverthorne, battles the dusk
and the thunderheads and the drizzling rain as he searches
for the *World*'s banner. He hears his name through a megaphone, someone calling for him to throw them his story,
but before he can find the source the other boats catch on
and they too begin calling for him: 'Hurd, here we are!
Throw it over here!'

This might be his last opportunity to deliver an exclusive before Thia makes port, when it will be too late, but he can't find the right boat.

With the health officials on board, the usual medical inspections are waived on grounds of compassion and Thia is granted pratique immediately. She resumes passage, getting up speed, when Carlos spies something through the gloom. He narrows his eyes, trying to discern . . . It is! There! Charles Chapin, editor of *The Evening World*, whom he met last week.

The man stands at the bow of a tug, gesticulating wildly and shouting through his megaphone. Carlos and Silverthorne wave back, and Carlos yells, '*Here*. I'm *here*.' Chapin spots him and the *World*'s tug manoeuvres alongside, far below.

Carlos takes the small waterproof package from under his coat, steps onto one of Thia's rails near a stanchion, and slings his story towards Charles Chapin's outstretched arms. The small bundle tethered to its cigar-box buoy sails out from Thia's side, but it's wrenched from the air when the tether snags on the fall of one of *Titanic*'s lifeboats, suspended overside.

Well beyond Carlos's reach.

High above the waiting tug.

All that work. Days of listening to sorrow-tale after sorrow-tale, Katherine too, until the hurt became too familiar; agonising over the right words; battling the captain and every obstacle placed in his way, and now there it is, suspended from a lifeboat as though unsure whether the clamouring world is ready for the truth.

He grips the rails, uncertain.

Then he sees, on the deck below, one of Thia's sailors swing himself out over the railing, over the long fall down to the hard water. The sailor reaches for the tangled package.

Further along the shelter deck one of Thia's officers shouts down at the sailor. Carlos is certain he's ordering the man to confiscate the package, but his words are drowned by the small crowd near Carlos, caught up in the drama. 'Throw it! *Throw it!*' The urgent cries come from the passengers, from Carlos, from Chapin on the megaphone below. The sailor hesitates . . . then, for better or worse, he tosses it down to the *World*'s tug.

———

It's dark by the time Thia enters the Narrows. A week – it's been only a week since last she was here. Oh, but the world has changed. She has changed. If a man called Frank stood on the banks of Brooklyn and looked at the water that lay between him and Staten Island . . . well, you know how it goes. The lightning splits the sky and the promised thunder rolls in from the horizon. In the electric flashes, the pretty verdigris of Liberty is a fractured horror show.

Nothing will ever be the same. No one will ever forget.

The rain falls in a torrent but it can't wash away tragedy. It only flows across the soil, across the city streets, back into the Hudson and on to the deep blue. Fitting then, that the sea is the flowing boneyard.

Thia runs dark except for her side and masthead lights. Flashes of lightning in the north-west accentuate her shadows and her silence, reveal a deck black with passengers. The darkness is an omen, the parade of glimmering tugs following her through the night, a trail of bobbing souls.

A Cunard-chartered tug meets her off Liberty Island. To Arthur's relief, the tugmaster instructs Thia to proceed to White Star's pier, half a mile up from her own, and discharge *Titanic*'s lifeboats. At the Battery ten thousand people line the sea wall as she glides past like a ghost ship. Great crowds gather at other vantage points along the North River.

When Thia comes abeam of the Singer Building one of the news tugs swings close and a reporter from the *New York American* makes a desperate leap towards an open gangway. In the wireless shack Harry receives a message that makes him turn to Harold. 'Listen to this, it's for us: *Arranged for your exclusive story for dollars in four figures. Mr. Marconi agreeing.*'

'*Four figures?*' Harold asks. The two look at each other. They scarce make six or seven pounds a month. After a moment of discussion between them, Harry goes back to sending the survivors' messages.

Thia passes through a forest of shipping on either side of the river. Then pretty pink granite, black in the night. Beyond that, a city that is terribly, heart-brokenly, impressed. Flags are at half-mast on City Hall, on every municipal and borough building, and so many along Wall Street that they obscure Trinity Church. Every celebration and festivity has been abandoned.

The even tenor of New York has been shaken as never before.

She is in mourning. And, in the absence of any definitive news over the past four days, braced for the worst.

Waiting at the docks are more than fifty motor ambulances, like covered wagons with long running boards over rubber-rimmed wooden wheels. Standing just outside the entrance to Pier 54 and thronging into West Street are scores of surgeons and physicians, nurses and white-clad attendants with stretchers and wheelchairs. Every hospital in Manhattan, Brooklyn and the Bronx is represented. Behind the ambulances are wagonloads of coffins, an undertaker, and attachés from the Coroner's Office, uncertain how much death Thia brings.

Hours earlier, a company of mounted and regular police clad in navy coats and covers marched to West Street, to the junction where Fourteenth Street meets the river. There were only a few hundred people about since Thia wasn't expected until near midnight. The officers cordoned off the area in front of the pier for a hundred feet, using ropes dotted with green lights. Beyond this barrier they closed Fourteenth Street back to Tenth Avenue to all traffic except trolley cars and ambulances, diverting vehicles and pedestrians going westward to Fifteenth Street and eastward to Thirteenth Street. But even there, none could pass who did not have business at the Cunard pier.

Now, the lawmen establish a human wall for two blocks to the north, south and east of the docks, along Tenth Avenue between Sixteenth and Eleventh streets. As news rounds Manhattan Island that Thia was sighted off Sandy Hook, the city begins to converge. The Ninth Avenue elevated trains deposit crowds every few moments at the Fourteenth Street Station. Men in bowler hats and Chesterfield overcoats and women in long skirts that brush the wet sidewalk hurry towards the Cunard piers, only to be held back by the police line. The officers allow no one through save those bearing permits from the government or yellow cards from Cunard, which has been besieged with requests.

Those from the highest social echelons arrive in motor-cars. If they have relatives or friends who sailed on *Titanic* they are permitted to park at the pier, in the cordoned-off area. Their numbers grow every minute and by nine o'clock hundreds of automobiles are assembled.

The crowd swells until Thirteenth, Fourteenth and Fifteenth streets are walls of bodies, from the riverfront to Ninth Avenue, held back by officers in glistening rain-coats. A band of Salvation Army folk stand on the kerb at Tenth Avenue singing hymns in the rain. People spill into

the streets from the Broadway theatres, which are virtually abandoned when word arrives of the drama about to
play out at the docks.

Along the North River it seems as though every small
hotel, lodging house and boarding place has thrown open
its doors, eager to offer shelter gratis to survivors in need.
And so too the Municipal Lodging House, various immigration societies, even Gimbels department store. On offer
are over five thousand beds, far in excess of what's needed.
And many other acts of kindness besides . . . Companies
send fleets to serve as proxy ambulances, subscriptions are
collected, theatrical and vaudeville benefits are planned,
as well as a New York Giants exhibition game. Even free
passage west is offered by the Pennsylvania Railroad.
Anything to alleviate the misery.

On the pier itself, around two thousand people amass
in the enclosed terminal. The smaller part of this crowd
comprises a collection of staff, officials, medical personnel,
charity aid workers and a limited number of pressmen who
were able to secure passes. There are more than a hundred
and fifty Cunard and White Star employees stationed along
the pier to hold back the crowd. They form a lane for the
survivors to walk through, until they're well clear of the
gangplank. Fifty members of the women's Relief Committee
for the Steerage Survivors of the *Titanic* wait with baskets
of clothing ready, and from the New York Stock Exchange
there are representatives bearing $20 000 to distribute to
the destitute – half of that from Vincent Astor, who futilely

hopes his father is safe aboard Thia. Like many, he's sent telegrams to the ship hoping for news, but hampered by the same circumstances that impeded Harold and Harry while working to send messages to shore, they never reached Thia.

Further aid comes from members of the Salvation Army, the Red Cross Emergency Relief Committee, and an assemblage of Sisters offering spiritual comfort: those of Mercy, of Charity, of St Francis of the Poor. Also the French Sisters, the Dominican Sisters and the White Franciscans, many of whom speak the languages of steerage. More than a hundred customs officials wait to greet the survivors, near areas they've designated alphabetically by surname. It is behind these sections, behind a placard marking a letter, that the larger part of this crowd waits: the family and friends of *Titanic* passengers, who for days now have scanned unreliable survivor lists and whose desperate hope is all that keeps despair at bay.

Class is forgotten. Labourers rub shoulders with millionaires, the likes of the Pierpont Morgans, Astors and Guggenheims. All that matters now is Thia.

Along the entire length of the pier shed, the ports are opened so those inside can watch the river. At the end of the pier beyond the shed that juts 800 feet out into the river, hundreds wait on the observation terrace. They peer down the black Hudson. It's too dark to see Thia, but still they look. As she passes each local harbour mark – Sandy Hook, the Narrows, Ellis – her progress is reported to the crowds. The two thousand or so on her pier, the tens of thousands held back by the police line, uncaring of the night, the cold, the pouring rain, wait in almost silence. A smile or a laugh would be blasphemy. When word comes that Thia has passed Liberty, unease sweeps the crowd. For better or worse, the waiting is almost over.

Thia steams close to the opposite bank so she will have room to turn into her pier. Her silhouette, eclipsing the electric blaze of the New Jersey shore, betrays her presence. Tension in the crowd redoubles.

Arthur looks at Pier 54. Blazing electric letters atop the two-storey shed spell out 'Cunard'. The light falls over the crowd gathered on the observation platform. As Thia draws close, the thunderclaps finally abate. But, to the crowd's consternation, she doesn't stop. She continues upriver until she reaches the White Star pier then swings about with a degree of cruel leisure.

'Mr Bisset, see to the lowering of the boats,' Arthur orders.

'Aye, Captain.'

James hurries down the ladder to the boat deck and oversees the crew as they lower the boats that hang in Thia's davits. Each one is sent down manned by two of *Titanic*'s rescued crewmen. Then he continues to the foredeck. The boats there are lowered by derrick.

A report reaches Arthur that, despite every precaution, a pressman has boarded Thia. He orders him brought to the bridge. The man arrives escorted by several crewmen, and Arthur asks how he came aboard. The captain is reluctantly impressed to hear that the man, taller and stronger than average, leaped from a tug in a jump that risked his life. Still: 'What do you mean by being on this ship? I made it clear off Sandy Hook that the press was not allowed aboard.'

'Captain Rostron, why have you not given the public the truth of this affair?'

The truth? Over the past several days the wild rumours that flowed across Thia's decks filtered up to him on the bridge. The ridiculous assertions that officers shot themselves; that Ismay is a villain who tried only to save himself – the man is broken, Arthur has seen it; that *Titanic* was attempting to claim the Blue Riband when her top speed was simply not as fast as that of *Mauretania* or *Lusitania*. As far as *Titanic* is concerned, there is no single truth. No absolute. There never can be. As for the public? The only public he is concerned with is aboard Thia.

'Why did you not answer the president's message about Major Archibald Butt?' the pressman asks.

What message from the president?

The pressman takes the captain's silence as a refusal to answer. 'Can I see some of the passengers? I am friends with Mrs Jacques Futrelle. Can I see her?'

'You cannot see any of the passengers.'

The man begins to protest, but Arthur is firm. 'I will not allow the distress of those aboard this boat to be compounded by inquiries from the press. This is why I refused all requests off Sandy Hook. You have willingly contravened this edict and boarded a Cunard vessel without permission. When we reach the pier I will turn you over to Captain Roberts, Cunard's marine superintendent. Until then, you will remain on the bridge. I put you upon your honour not to leave, but if you do, I *will* put you in irons.'

'I want to see Mr Ismay. I want to see him for the American people.'

'You cannot.'

The pressman continues with his questions, frustration mounting. 'Captain Rostron, do you realise that this is the most gigantic tragedy in the history of the sea and the world will not accept your whims in giving it the information it wants?'

Arthur eyes him steadily. 'I realise, sir, that you came aboard this boat in spite of orders from a thousand sources otherwise.'

The man continues to ask questions which Arthur ignores.

It takes twenty minutes to lower the lifeboats, but the wait – more waiting – is excruciating for those on the pier. When it is done, gleams of light from Thia's portholes fall across the dark river. As the boats bob gently on the water their white hulls shift between gleam and shadow, and for a heartbeat the word *Titanic* is visible, then gone again. The silent crowd catches its breath. There's something about those mute witnesses . . . the only pieces that remain of a supposedly unsinkable ship.

A steam launch comes from the White Star pier and takes the boats in tow. Arthur watches them pull away into the pitchy night, and it brings to mind the last occasion upon which they were lowered, from a ship destined never to arrive at this port.

Soon after, James returns to the bridge, and the captain puts him in charge of the reporter with orders to hand him over to the marine superintendent.

As Thia moves slowly towards Pier 54, the northern shed ports are closed so that she can dock, except the two that will accommodate her fore and aft gangplanks. Those people positioned near an open port watch as Thia looms larger in the darkness, and those aboard crowd her New York side as the tugs swing her with the tide into her pier.

At the same time, another message comes through the wireless: *Go to Strand Hotel. 502 West Fourteenth Street, to meet Mr. Marconi.*

When Thia is warped into her dock, the tens of thousands of people in the streets push towards the river until it seems as though they will inundate the thin police line and overflow the dark water. And the thing that marks it all is the silence: heavy hawsers secured without the usual shouting of ship's officers and pier hands, a flood of New York humanity spellbound, and the ship, Thia, always silent, never having said so much.

As the survivors pass onto land Arthur is glad to see them go. The relief, watching from the bridge in the rain, is like being released from confinement. One of duty, yes, and guardianship, but wearying and sorrowful and such that leaves a mark. It seems as though no one could be more grateful than him to see them finally safe, but then he has not waited for days in an agony of not knowing whether those he loves are still alive.

At each gangplank a portable fence marks off some fifty feet of the pier. Waiting within are the one hundred or more customs officials; waiting without, the crowd.

It seems a wretched torment when the first down Thia's gangplank is a hurrying crewman in yellow oilskins. A sigh, like a sob, sweeps the mass.

As for the survivors, landed, social decorum reasserts itself. First is a woman wearing clothes that are a patch-work of contributions from Thia's passengers, eyes red from weeping. Then there's Dr Frauenthal, who fell atop poor Annie Stengel in the lifeboat, and his wife. Then Miss Margaret Hays with Lolo and Louis and the rest of her party, and Charles H. Marshall's nieces. Following them, a steady stream of survivors file down the gang-plank. They're met by an eddy of parties with an interest on Thia, wending their way aboard.

Amongst them are Cunard officials eager to meet with Captain Rostron, and two United States senators accompanied by various authorities, there to serve subpoenas to Bruce Ismay and the *Titanic*'s officers that they should appear before the Senate Inquiry into the sinking that begins tomorrow. Before Thia leaves New York, Arthur will be one of the first witnesses to testify.

In the weeks and months to come, Thia's captain will be hailed as a hero. He'll be honoured and feted wherever she puts into port, and she'll be visited by over 100 000 curious people during her resumed Mediterranean voyage. The survivors will award Arthur a silver loving cup, and present captain, officers and crew with gold, silver and bronze medals according to rank, depicting Thia and the rescue embossed in bas-relief. Arthur will receive thousands of letters of appreciation, and write his own letter of apology to President Taft about the overlooked wireless message. Taft, in return, will present him with a Congressional Gold Medal for his courage and gallantry rescuing the *Titanic* survivors – an act which will follow him always.

While James is escorting the *New York American* reporter, who's twice his size, to Captain Roberts, the man breaks free and charges down the gangway like a bull moose and disappears into the crowd.

Then Guglielmo Marconi boards and makes immediately for the shack on Thia's boat deck. Striding alongside him is Isaac Russell from the *New York Times*. Guglielmo was having dinner at the residence of the American manager of his company not an hour past, when Isaac came seeking a letter granting permission for *Titanic* and Thia's wireless operators to speak to the *Times*. Isaac hadn't expected Guglielmo Marconi himself to be there, and what's more he hadn't expected the man to ask if the *Times* could issue him a pass for the dock – he's concerned about the reports that his operators ignored messages from the President of the United States.

Like other press associations, the *Times* received four passes, but all are in use.

So Isaac decided to lie.

He banked on the fact that the police would not stop the man whose invention was responsible for saving the lives of all those aboard Thia.

And he's right. Recognising him from press photos, the police let Guglielmo through. What's more, they mistake Isaac for a Marconi employee and allow him aboard also.

Guglielmo finds Harry – Harold Bride – alone in the shack, still sending. He's sitting on a high stool, his feet swathed in bandages. On a plate beside him is his untouched dinner. Guglielmo watches for a moment, listening long enough to realise the boy is still keying survivor messages. 'That's hardly worth sending now,' he says gently, and lifts Harry's hand from the key.

The young man is intent on his task and resists. 'The people out there want these messages to go, I must send them – the people waiting by the cabin.'

'Everyone is going ashore,' Guglielmo reassures him. 'You must stop and have your injuries attended to.'

It takes a long moment before recognition comes but there is a picture on the shack wall bearing this man's likeness. 'You're Mr Marconi,' Harry says, and finally takes his finger from the key. He assures Guglielmo that no message from the president was deliberately ignored and then, with gentle urging from Isaac, tells them his story.

———

As Carlos and Katherine Hurd battle the crowd to reach the nearest subway station, intent on making the *World* building, Carlos hears newsboys crying out an extra with his story. The paper went quick to print, before Thia even docked. When the Hurds arrive, Ralph Pulitzer himself rewards Carlos with $1000 in cash and an additional three weeks of leave.

Meanwhile, Harold Cottam, having hastened down the gangplank immediately when Thia docked, waits in the lobby of the Strand Hotel. But Mr Marconi is nowhere to be found. An hour passes. An hour and a half. No one comes from the company. He's unsure what to make of it. Perhaps he has gone to the wrong place? But the wireless message was clear.

The passengers who remain aboard Thia are uncertain what will become of them. Their plans have been forestalled and they are back where they began. But a few minutes after Thia docks, a message is posted saying that she sails at four the following afternoon. It means that she, Arthur and the crew, who have already given so much, cannot yet rest. They must resupply and prepare her for departure – but that is the reality of life as a merchant mariner. When last she was here she had two weeks, now she has eighteen hours. Fortunately, *Saxonia* is at the neighbouring pier and Thia is able to borrow clean linens from her sister.

At the Strand, a reporter from the *New York Times* finds Harold. The *Times*, coincidentally, whose reporters have been instructed to get the story from both *Titanic* and Thia's wireless operators, have set up shop in this hotel, a block from the pier, renting one entire floor and installing four telephones with connections to the *Times*' newsroom. Perhaps realising that they were behind the message telling him to meet Mr Marconi at the Strand, before Harold sells them his story he first seeks permission. It's late in the night when he telephones Mr Marconi's hotel, Holland House, and receives his consent.

All the while, as these events play out, survivors file down Thia's gangplanks.

The vast throng surges against the police cordon. The people on the pier frantically scan the faces of the survivors as they leave Thia's protection and enter the waiting furore. It is not such a terrible thing, to be for a moment in the spotlight of thousands of desperate gazes, if what waits at the end is the comfort and relief of loving arms. Those fortunate few are wrapped in warm blankets and run the gauntlet of pressmen and photographers before they are whisked to waiting automobiles or taxicabs. Even those of steerage class who have no relatives in this new world, and no possessions, are welcomed by the Sisters of Mercy, by the Salvation Army, by kind strangers who offer comfort.

These four days past, scores of women have clung to the hope that some other rescue ship exists. That their husbands are not dead. As they disembark they are met by families who know that Thia is the only ship that carries survivors, but not who is aboard. These reunions are bittersweet. Daughters are returned, but not sons. And they know for certain now that they are widows, not wives.

Every survivor who passes down Thia's gangway is accosted by the desperate inquiries of strangers. *Have you seen my son? my father? my husband? my daughter? my wife? Here is a photograph. Are they aboard, do you know?*

Silence and restraint are the distant past. A cry echoes through the cavernous building and is joined by other voices, until a great wail washes across the mass pressing hard against the fence that holds them back. As the flow of survivors becomes a trickle, as those fortunate ones leave, those waiting continue their vigil in the storm, looking up at Thia.

Until all hope is gone.

WHITE WAKE

1918

CAPTAIN WILLIAM PROTHERO STARES AFTER THE SIX retreating warships: destroyers USS *Stevens*, USS *Ammen* and USS *Shaw*, minesweepers HMS *Snowdrop* and HMS *Sir Bevis*, and patrol gunboat HMS *Kilgobnet*. At the wake that fades quickly, as though they were never there.

His gaze flicks up to the black smoke belching from the funnel of *British Major*, the small tanker sailing alongside Thia, to where it billows across the bright blue sky like a thundercloud.

It must be visible, clear for twenty miles.

Major is struggling to make the ten knots that the rest of the convoy maintains. Years of captaining Thia through the bloodiest, most wretched war in history and he knows well to be concerned. They may as well broadcast their position across the wireless.

William glances at the bridge clock to see if it's time. It's not.

Seventeen ships, including Thia, were in the combined convoy that left Liverpool two days ago. For almost three weeks she had waited patiently at the Huskisson Dock. First, for the other convoy vessels to arrive, then for their naval escort – and there was comfort in that. In a merchant armada protected by heavily armed warships, sailing across the ocean in formation.

In the wake of the military escort that slips towards the horizon, another ten vessels detach, splintering the fleet. Convoy O.E.18, Outbound for Eastern Mediterranean ports, bears south-east, leaving Convoy O.L.24, Outbound from Liverpool, heading west with a contingent of seven.

These ships continue in four columns. *Major* heads the first, then Thia, *Tenasserim* and *City of Bombay*, behind them respectively *Eurylochus*, *Harmodius* and *Elmina*, a mix of mostly passenger and cargo vessels, alongside one small, slow tanker. The columns are six cables apart, the ships that follow two cables behind. Eight bells sound the end of the morning watch. Thia is the largest ship that remains. Her only defence, for herself and those she protects, is her 4.7-inch gun mounted on a special platform on her aft starboard deck.

William looks over at the bridge clock again and then commands the quartermaster to turn Thia starboard.

Across the water, the other convoy ships execute the same manoeuvre at precisely the same time.

Zigzagging, weaving a vessel from her port of origin to her destination, instead of sailing a straight, predictable course, makes it difficult for the German *Unterseeboots* to attack. The U-boats can discern information about a surface vessel, such as her size, distance and speed, by listening to her underwater acoustics. But zigzagging convoys make it difficult for a U-boat to gauge how columns are disposed and the spaces between vessels, forcing her to expose her periscope more often and for lengthier intervals. If she can't predict a vessel's movements she can't judge her own so as not to be hampered at the moment she wants to fire. She might one minute be flanking her quarry, waiting for its centre to cross her sights, and when next she periscopes, find the ship bearing down on her.

The zigzagging is regimented. Precise. Convoys often have scores of ships occupying a dozen square ocean miles, and maintaining formation is critical to avoiding collision. Yet there's a beauty about it too, like watching the synchronised movements of a school of fish, flicking their tails as one in some new direction.

2007

It happens while the lads are diving a big old steamer near the Scillies, an archipelago off the coast of Cornwall. The reefs and rocky offshores here are notoriously treacherous, so the area has plenty of wrecks to explore. They decide to stop and dive some before returning to Plymouth.

It probably isn't the wisest thing they've ever done. After going deep, it takes a while to recover. That's why the lads dived Thia in two teams on alternate days: one day of diving, one of recovery, repeat. So after Ric's third deep descent within the space of six days, the next day should have been spent firmly aboard *Dancer.*

But after 550 feet of water, 390 feet seems shallow.

Sod it. I'll be all right.

When they deploy the shot line it lands just off the wreck, to the stern. Ric swims hard to get to the bow. He knows better. Never work hard at depth, it increases blood flow, which increases gas uptake. But they don't know her name so they're looking for her bell. When he arrives at the bridge he finds a telegraph, works it free and sends it up. But nothing to identify her.

Finally, Ric swims back to the shot line and does about four hours of decompression.

When he's back on the surface it's a lovely calm day. The sun is shining and he feels great. He's been on board about half an hour and is below deck sorting his gear, packing it into his bags, when *Dancer* starts rocking. And *rocking.*

Must have hit the wake of another ship.

But it doesn't stop. Arms out for balance, unsteadily he climbs topside. As soon as he reaches the deck he knows something is wrong. The sea is flat like glass. It's Ric who's rocking. Then the world starts to spin.

He knows straight away: it's an inner-ear bend. His symptoms are classic. Jeff recognises them as well. He was diving with someone recently who had the same thing happen.

Ric's had mild cases of the bends, the usual pain in his elbows and knees caused by gas bubbles forming in the body during decompression. He's even had a skin bend, a red rash on his shoulder where the gas was caught in fatty tissues. But nothing like this. This time the bubble is in his inner ear. It affects his balance. Sends his senses all 'round the twist.

The first line of treatment is pure oxygen, so Jeff helps him sit then gets him a cylinder with a regulator. Ric closes his eyes, leans forward, braces his arms on his knees and breathes deep. The longer the bubble remains in his inner ear the more damage it will do. It blocks the artery and stops blood flow. Inner-ear bends can permanently screw up a man's balance, and with Ric being a fireman, if he can't walk in a straight line he'll lose his job. Might even lose his hearing.

'How are you feeling? Any better?' Jeff asks after a couple of minutes.

Ric takes the reg out of his mouth and is sick all over Jeff's trainers.

The oxygen is not working.

The lads have a quick consult but there's no question, really. 'Ric, we're gonna put you in the chamber,' Jeff says, worry in his voice. They're concerned, far more than they let on. Ric's afraid too.

A hose blew off the hyperbaric chamber when they tested it during the outward voyage. If that happens with Ric inside, it'll be like being blown back to the surface – instant decompression. He could trade a single bubble in his inner ear for a bloodstream full of them. Then he'd be in a lot more trouble. That would kill him.

1918

William Prothero's strong Welsh voice gives the order to bear to port. And so it continues, zigzagging across the deep blue.

For the majority of the war, ships have been most in danger when en route eastward, because of Germany's blockade of Britain and their desire to keep the Americans neutral. An effort that failed when they declared unrestricted submarine warfare on any ships in the war zone. The resulting American losses ended their neutrality.

Since then, the eastward voyages, when Thia is laden with American troops and cargo, are comparatively safe. The convoys are large and well protected, escorted the entire way by warships. Now the danger lies in returning to America. When berths and holds are empty, protecting tonnage becomes less of a priority and naval escorts only see convoys clear of the danger zone around the Southwest Approaches, where the U-boats hunt.

None of the ships in Thia's convoy warrant protection. Thia bears no cargo. Her crew complement is 228, but the dangers of serving in the merchant marine during wartime are simply part of their lot. She carries a scant 57 passengers. Only the very brave venture far from home during war times.

In the dining saloons Thia's passengers finish their breakfasts of oatmeal porridge and milk, stewed fruit, bacon and eggs, toast and preserves. The roster is exclusively male in steerage and comprises mostly cattlemen and a few tradesmen. Her cabin passengers are primarily middle-aged bourgeois: men with professions and women who keep homes.

Catherine Law, Rosie Smets and Annie Dennison are the only young ladies in cabin class. It's natural for them to gravitate to each other – and that their interest might be captured by the group of American naval signalmen: Orion French, William Jones, Steve Barron, Ross Stewart and Hugh Halsey, the eldest twenty-two. Returning home, they're members of the armed escort that saw Thia over to England. Young, handsome soldiers are enough to set any girl's heart aflutter, much less three teenagers adrift in enforced proximity with limited diversions. They're more than enough to instigate covert glances and shy smiles.

Amongst the passengers are British Expeditionary Forces Captain Claude Stibbard and Lieutenant Allen Coryn, Royal Air Force Lieutenant Ernest Sliter and Royal Naval Reserve Lieutenant Francis Perry. Over cups of tea and coffee they discuss the retreating warships, the implications of a smaller convoy and the latest war news.

The Spring Offensive began four months ago, when the Central Powers realised that they would be unable to win the war once American troops and resources were fully deployed. Along the Somme they broke through Allied lines to push the British Expeditionary Force back, in the strongest advance by either side since the war began. In the space of five hours the enemy fired a million artillery shells at Allied soldiers and fifteen days later half a million men were dead. But the victory is hollow. While Allied forces can be replenished from American troops, the German losses are irreplaceable. In the intervening months the offensive continued with the Battle of the Lys and the Third Battle of the Aisne, and hundreds of thousands more dead. But the world can sense Germany's desperation, the strengthening tide of the Allies, and they know, *they know*, that the Great War will soon be over.

Promenading on Thia's deck, Mrs Sadie Reuben enjoys the sea air and the glorious summer day. A few other passengers mill about, conversing.

On the aft deck, Gunner George Skinner is on watch when he sees . . . 'Here she comes!' The urgent shout rings across the deck to the bridge.

William follows the gunner's voice like an arrow, aport 300 yards. A shadow under the swell cuts a swift channel through the deep blue, its white wake rapidly closing with Thia.

2007

Ric's so ill that he's willing to risk the chamber. The lads help him downstairs to where it nestles into *Dancer*'s bow. The large, white, horizontal cylinder is several metres long with an entry hatch on its stern end. There's a panel of gauges that measure air pressure, oxygen and depth. Yellow pipes and hoses fitted with red valves run from the gauges through the thick metal shell, regulating the internal atmosphere.

The lads help Ric inside the chamber. Helmuth goes in with him since he's the only one who's not had a beer – and alcohol contributes to dehydration, which increases susceptibility to decompression sickness. The space is small and would feel entirely claustrophobic if not for the small portholes that provide a visible connection with the outside world.

Edoardo sticks strips of white duct tape down the side of the chamber, overlapping them until there are two columns, each wider and longer than a sheet of paper. In black marker he begins a treatment log. *Entry @ 8.10.* They set the depth at 40 feet and flood the chamber with oxygen. As though someone's flicked a switch, and technically speaking they have, colour floods back into Ric's pale face. The vertigo and nausea dissipate almost instantly.

And the hose stays put.

The lads' relief is immense and every moment their confidence grows. They buckle a wristwatch around one of the yellow pipes so they can log accurate times. Ten minutes later Edoardo passes water through the airlock and Ric drinks 100 millilitres. It's essential that he avoids dehydration. Fifteen minutes later he has an air break, a precaution to prevent oxygen toxicity that develops with prolonged breathing of pure oxygen at pressure. An excess of the gas within body tissues causes cell damage to the central nervous system, lungs and eyes, and can be fatal.

And so a cycle of oxygen, cut with air breaks and water consumption, begins.

At 9.10, an empty bottle is placed inside the airlock. A few minutes later Ric sets it carefully to the side, as there's no lid.

On the log Edoardo writes: *Pee ok*. Difficulty urinating is an indicator of decompression sickness so this is a good sign.

But not everything is going quite so well. On the bridge, all of *Dancer*'s electrics have gone down. The crew don't know why. No one tells Ric; they just navigate using dead reckoning.

At 10.35 Edoardo writes: *Ascent start*. Then, at the top of the second duct-tape column: *30ft reached*. Ric feels fantastic. He has from the moment the chamber went under pressure and now it's simply a case of waiting out the deco schedule. It's a bit boring, but he's not complaining. The alternative was much worse.

In a little while, one of the lads comes down and tells them that *Dancer* just cruised within three feet of a metal post. When Ric hears this they have to tell him about the failed electrics. Even as he's thinking *bloomin' hell, we're too close to the reef*, there's an almighty crash and *Dancer* shudders violently. The bottle of pee goes flying all over the chamber.

Ship wide, men rush out on deck. Ric is stuck in the chamber, the last place anyone wants to be during a collision. What if they have to abandon ship?

The news comes down that *Dancer*'s struck rocks. Looking out the chamber portholes, Ric watches the lads running back and forth, checking the bow, the hull, trying to work out whether she's sinking. Ric can't help it. Despite the worry, he nearly kills himself laughing. They look like keystone cops, running frantically in every direction and colliding, unsure of what they're supposed to do or how to do it.

While he's paddling around in his own pee.

But through it all they're aware of one of the basic tenets of patient care: reassure the casualty. So even as they're checking to see if *Dancer*'s sinking, and Ric can *see* them checking, *knows* what they're doing, whenever one of them passes the chamber he calls out, all overstated pacification, 'It's all right, Ric.' Then, another will scurry by in the opposite direction and say, 'No need to worry. Everything's oh-kay.'

Even as Ric's laughing at the irony, he's thinking one thing: *Uh-oh.*

1918

'Hard-a-starboard,' William orders. 'Port engine full astern.'

But it's too late.

The torpedo hits Thia's side and detonates. A plume of water shoots up towards the bridge and she shudders hard from the impact, bleeding black smoke. A moment later a second torpedo explodes her engine room.

Passengers scream and scramble for cover while the soldiers run for the deck and scan the deep blue, searching for the threat. On the bridge the officers, and aft the gunners, do the same. There are no enemy vessels in sight. The attack is from a U-boat and as long as she remains submerged, Thia's gun is useless.

'Full stop,' William orders.

Below, Third Engineer William Greenoway and Boilermaker William Davis, badly burned in the explosion, stop both engines then struggle to close the watertight doors. There are men down, but they can't stop to help them.

'Damage report,' William barks. 'Send a distress call. Sound the general alarm. All hands to boat stations.'

Thia's bell rings rapidly, the urgent toll washing across the deck. Sailors and passengers respond, mustering at their assigned boats quickly but calmly, just as they practised out from Liverpool. There is no time to gather any belongings. The report comes to William: Thia's engines are wrecked, as is the whistle gear and all electrical gear. Two lifeboats are damaged. The force of the explosion knocked out her wireless.

'Signal *Tenasserim* to call for help. Send up rockets.'

The other convoy ships have already begun to scatter, but one of the officers raises *Tenasserim* with the flags and she sends out a distress call over wireless, reporting that Thia's been torpedoed and giving her numbers: 49.30 N, 10.43 W.

As soon as the way is off, William gives the order to lower the boats. As passengers and crew are descending one of the ladders, its lashings give way and they fall into the water. Most are wearing lifebelts. But one of the crewmen is not, and he also can't swim, so he panics. St Elmo Jones, a young West Indian able seaman, jumps overboard and goes to his aid.

Meanwhile, an officer fires the first rocket, hoping to attract the attention of any nearby patrol boats.

Both torpedoes struck Thia portside dead amidships. The first below the bridge between the stokehold and No. 4 hold; the second, the engine room. The little tanker *Major* was out of formation, running a cable behind where she should have been, leaving an open path to Thia. With water flooding in, Thia lists to port then settles. Somehow she manages to keep her keel from listing further, as if she knows it's this, and only this, that allows the crew to safely lower the laden boats into the heavy swell.

Most of the passengers and crew get away safely, and one of the boats stops to collect the people in the water.

But Thia's doctor, William Core, has been attending to the badly scalded engineers. There's hardly anyone left aboard. The doctor enlists Chief Steward Ernest Pimbley, and he in turn two assistant cooks – all he can find – to get the wounded men into a lifeboat. One is scalded beyond recognition. The other unconscious.

The doctor boards with them; then Pimbley and the cooks, who are little more than boys, struggle with the painters, trying to lower the huge lifeboat. It's a task that none of them are trained for and which normally requires far more manpower. But extraordinary situations call out the best in men and somehow they manage.

Then they clamber down the ladder, step onto the thwarts and take the tiller and oars. It's the eleventh and final boat to launch. William, his first three ranking officers and the two gunners remain aboard Thia. The gunners man their post in case the sub appears. The officers continue to send up daylight stars.

William destroys and scuttles all confidential documents and code books. As he works, Thia begins to settle rapidly, sinking deeper at her head. Uncertain how much longer she can hold out, he signals one of the boats to come alongside, and the six men scramble down the ladder.

Then they abandon her.

Once, small white hulls pulled for her like she was salvation. Now, salvation lies elsewhere.

The passengers and crew wait in the boats, defenceless, afraid that at any moment the sub will surface. Commanded by Kapitänleutnant Wilhelm Werner, SM *U-55* has little regard for life. Last July she torpedoed the cargo steamer *Belgian Prince* and took the crew from their lifeboats onto her deck. Their lifebelts were removed. Their lifeboats sunk. Then the Kapitänleutnant ordered *U-55* to dive.

All but three of the men drowned.

Not all U-boat captains are monsters, but the people in Thia's lifeboats are right to be afraid. As they wait, they see the remainder of the convoy disappear over the horizon. There can be no help from that quarter.

The doctor attends to his patients, soaking the engineers' burns in oil, but there is nothing he can do about the salt water that washes in and soaks their bandages and the agony it inflicts.

William gathers the boats in formation and distributes his officers amongst them, ensuring all are evenly loaded and manned. And then he waits. Most U-boats come for the captain.

In the distance he sees two periscopes off Thia's starboard bow. They disappear quickly.

For an hour or more, the sense that something must happen, and soon, grows – in both the U-boat crew and the 280 souls in the small white boats. For Werner, it's a decision about whether to expend another torpedo. When they exhaust their supply they'll have to return to port, so he hopes the wounds they've already inflicted are mortal.

But Thia remains stubbornly afloat. It seems she will not go gentle. And every elapsing minute increases the danger for *U-55*. The attack came not long after the naval escort's departure, so help is not far away. There may even be patrol boats that are closer and already en route. The time the Germans have to finish her is limited.

Finally, the hulking black behemoth surfaces on Thia's port side, 40 yards away, low in the water. She fires. It wasn't so long ago when, very near here, Carpathius of Hy-Brasil came into the world. But Carpathius died when he was still a babe.

The torpedo impacts Thia's hull behind the engine room and there's a tremendous explosion. Water plumes up from the concussive force then floods in, rushing through her alleyways and bulkheads towards her bow. Not even the strongest will to live could save her now.

She fills rapidly as the U-boat circles.

Her bow plunges like a falling tree and crumples as it hits the ocean floor, sending up a sandstorm. Then her stern too, Red Ensign fluttering, slides below the surface.

She's one more war mule, dead at the hands of men.

Not to be seen again for almost one hundred years.

2007

Word comes to Ric in the chamber that all is well. There's been no damage to *Dancer* from her encounter with the reef. But, with the electrics still out, instead of proceeding into the treacherous Scillies the lads decide to return to the mainland. A couple of close calls are more than enough.

After three and a half hours Ric reaches surface pressure and it's safe for him to emerge, no worse for wear. It's a relief. He could have paid a high price for diving Thia. But he's glad for having done it. He's never dived a wreck like her, with her history, at that depth, and the challenge of being so far off shore. And this time he has proof, too many witnesses to be denied, and a memento, a blue-and-white plate with Cunard's rampant lion.

But no bell.

The object that NUMA's rovers filmed when they discovered Thia remains a mystery. Was it her bell? Most seem convinced of it; Ric is. An argument can be made that the marine concretions are wrong, more akin to a steel or iron object, since the bronze shell casings Comex recovered had no such growth. Still, there are documentaries and books about Thia's discovery that all identify it as her bell. Whether they're right or wrong, the fact remains she has one.

But where is it? Still on the seabed? Lying somewhere off her main mast? Secreted away in some private collection?

Sometime after Ric gets home, he opens up the back of his rebreather and is torn between laughing and cursing. There, stuck on the inside, carefully removed from the side of the hyperbaric chamber, are the sheets of duct tape with the log of his recompression treatment. The lads are taking the mickey out of him.

He could rip it off but he doesn't. He leaves it where it is, and every wreck he dives, it goes with him. Like she goes with him. Eventually the black marker fades and the tape wrinkles and peels at the edges, like lingering memories that become soft with time.

1918

The U-boat searches the deep blue where Thia sank. The young American signalmen in one of the lifeboats think they see *U-55* claim something from the water, perhaps Thia's Red Ensign. Then she turns to the small white boats. There are three men in her conning tower. She has two six-inch guns, one forward and one aft.

William watches her approach, on black wings. There are terrified women and children in the lifeboats, innocent passengers, and a crew for whom he is responsible. And there is nothing he can do to protect them. Only hope that her commander is merciful.

Then there's a distant boom and a shell whistles overhead. The water erupts where it falls short of its target. William looks behind even as another shot is fired and sees a ship on the horizon. The second shell almost hits the U-boat and the ship continues to engage, protecting the lifeboats from afar. *U-55* dives.

Within a few minutes William recognises the fast-approaching sloop as HMS *Snowdrop*, the minesweeper that formed part of their armed escort. She and *U-55* are matched in size. Then periscopes appear on the surface and *Snowdrop* resumes firing. She steams full speed past the lifeboats to where the U-boat submerged and begins to drop depth charges, in widening circles. She hunts relentlessly for an hour or more, and only when she's certain it's safe, certain the enemy has retreated, does she return to collect the survivors.

Her captain asks William to bring Thia's boats alongside, one at a time. The moderate swell proves a challenge, but eventually all her survivors are brought safely aboard. *Snowdrop*'s built for a complement of fourscore. With 280 survivors there is barely standing room.

William takes muster of Thia's crew. Five of her men are missing. They never made it to her boats, either killed by the torpedoes or drowned in the flooded engine rooms. Stokers Charles Hughes and James Murphy. Trimmers Edward David Hamilton, Frank O'Neill and Reginald Alfred Peters. All from Liverpool. The youngest not yet twenty.

They're down there with Thia. With her medals and her bell and her stones from Wallsend. Decaying in the deep blue. All that's left above are eleven small boats with white hulls and her name at their bow.

Left to scatter on the waves and drift away, forgotten.

TIMELINE

15 MAY 1900

SS *Carinthia* sinks off Haiti. This event prompts Cunard to build RMS *Carpathia*.

C. 1900

Charles H. Marshall advises Cunard on potential ship names: *Mauretania*, *Lusitania* and *Carpathia*.

10 SEPTEMBER 1901

Carpathia's keel is laid down at C.S. Swan & Hunter shipyard.

MARCH 1903

The end of The Roman Wall is discovered in the shipyard. Several stones are subsequently placed aboard *Carpathia*.

22 APRIL 1903

Carpathia undergoes her sea trials.

5–14 MAY 1903

Carpathia completes her maiden voyage from Liverpool, England, to Boston, USA. 'Carpathius' is born en route.

28 APRIL 1909

American Consul William Henry Bishop flees Palermo and the Black Hand aboard *Carpathia*.

18 JANUARY 1912

Captain Arthur Rostron assumes command of *Carpathia*.

MARCH 1912

The Black Hand symbol appears on *Carpathia*'s bulkheads during the prior voyage before she rescues the *Titanic* survivors.

11 APRIL 1912

Carpathia departs New York for the Mediterranean. RMS *Titanic* departs Queenstown for New York.

14 APRIL 1912

Titanic strikes an iceberg at 11.40 p.m.

15 APRIL 1912

Carpathia receives *Titanic*'s distress call and immediately responds at 12.35 a.m.

15 APRIL 1912

Titanic sinks at 2.20 a.m.

15 APRIL 1912

Carpathia reaches *Titanic*'s position at 4.00 a.m. They see the first lifeboat at 4.05 a.m. All lifeboats are picked up by 8.30 a.m. *Carpathia* departs for New York at 8.50 a.m.

18 APRIL 1912

Carpathia arrives in New York. The survivors disembark at Pier 54 at 9.35 p.m.

8 JANUARY 1913

Captain William Prothero assumes command of *Carpathia*.

28 JUNE 1914

Austrian Archduke Franz Ferdinand is assassinated and World War I soon begins.

3 AUGUST 1914

Carpathia flees Fiume in the Austro-Hungarian Empire one day before Britain enters the war.

6 AUGUST 1914

Carpathia seeks shelter at Malta from the enemy fleet.

18 AUGUST 1914

Carpathia departs Naples carrying American refugees home.

15 JULY 1918

Carpathia departs Liverpool leading a convoy of merchant ships accompanied by a naval escort.

17 JULY 1918

The naval escort departs at 8.15 a.m. *Carpathia* is torpedoed by SM *U-55* at 9.13 a.m. She sinks just before 11.00 a.m. HMS *Snowdrop* arrives around 11.45 a.m.

SEPTEMBER 1999

NUMA mounts its first expedition to locate *Carpathia*. They find MV *Isis* which is publicly misidentified as *Carpathia*.

MAY 2000

NUMA mounts its second expedition to find *Carpathia*. They find a mystery wreck but cannot identify it due to a faulty ROV.

SEPTEMBER 2000

NUMA mounts its third expedition and identifies the mystery wreck as *Carpathia*.

SEPTEMBER 2000

The Northern Gas Team dive HMS *Dasher* as preparation for diving *Carpathia*.

MAY 2001

RMS Titanic Inc. acquire ownership and salvage rights to *Carpathia*.

21–25 AUGUST 2001

The first dive expedition to *Carpathia* takes place.

28 FEBRUARY 2007

RMS Titanic Inc. sell all rights concerning *Carpathia* to Seaventures Ltd., but license the right to recover and exhibit the wreck's artefacts.

16 AUGUST – 3 SEPTEMBER 2007

Comex survey and recover artefacts from *Carpathia* using ROVs on behalf of RMS Titanic Inc.

26 AUGUST – 9 SEPTEMBER 2007

The second and larger dive expedition to *Carpathia* takes place.

GLOSSARY

Abeam – Opposite the middle of a vessel.

Aft – Towards or near the stern.

Alleyway – Corridor or passageway.

Amidships – The centre of a ship, midway between the ends.

Aport – On or towards port.

Astern – Towards the rear of a ship. Also, going backwards.

Beam ends – A ship listing close to 90 degrees, in danger of capsizing.

Bent – Knotted. To bend a rope is to tie it to something else.

Boat deck – The deck where the lifeboats are located.

Boatswain – (Bosun) Crewman in charge of the deck crew.

Boiler – A large metal chamber with furnaces that converts water to steam.

Bow – The front of a ship.

Bridge deck – The deck from where a vessel is navigated.

Bridge wing – A walkway extending from both sides of the bridge the ship's width or beyond, for improved viewing.

Bulkhead – Vertical walls within the hull that provide strength and form watertight compartments.

Bulwark – The raised walls along the sides of a vessel above the deck.

Cable – A unit of measurement that is one-tenth of a nautical mile.

Capstan – A rotating vertical cylinder used to pull in cables and anchors.

Companionway – A ladder or staircase.

Davits – A pair of curved cranes that use pulleys to raise and lower lifeboats.

Dead reckoning – An imprecise system of navigating or calculating a ship's position based on its previous position, estimated speed, time travelled and course.

Deckhouse – A small enclosed structure on a deck, usually surrounded by exposed deck (see superstructure).

Derrick – A crane with an arm that moves horizontally and vertically, for loading cargo.

Eight bells – The ringing of a ship's bell signifies the progress of a watch. Eight bells (strikes) indicates the end of a watch.

Fall(s) – The ropes used to raise and lower a ship's lifeboats.

Fireman – See stoker.

Fo'c'sle – The forward part of the ship, near the bow (forecastle).

Gangway – Doors set into a ship's hull used for boarding and disembarking. Also, plank or ramp used for the same (gangplank).

Growler – A small iceberg, with very little protruding above water.

Gudgeon – A socket attached to a ship in which the spine of the rudder turns.

Gunwale – The top edge of a boat's side.

Keel – The bottommost, central spine running the length of a ship.

Lee – The sheltered side of the ship away from the wind.

Main deck – The principal deck of a vessel. (Often the highest deck in the hull, but in *Carpathia*'s case this was the upper deck.)

Master-at-arms – Crewman responsible for enforcing discipline.

Merchantman – A trading ship.

Painter – A rope used to tie up small boats.

Point(s) – (Compass point) A direction that corresponds to a compass mark, where the compass has been divided into 32 points. For example, three points off the port bow.

Port – The left side of the ship when looking forward.

Pratique – Allows a ship with a clean bill of health to proceed to a port.

Purser – Officer responsible for provisions and finances.

Quadruple expansion reciprocating engine – An engine that uses four pistons which are powered by the expansion of steam as it cools.

Quartermaster – A seaman who acts as helmsman.

Rebreather – A closed-circuit breathing device that purifies and recycles exhaled gases.

Rhib – (R.H.I.B.) Rigid-hulled inflatable boat.

RMS – (Royal Mail Ship) Ships that carried mail for the British government.

ROV – (R.O.V. or rover) Remote operating vehicle, for underwater use.

Saloon – a public room on a ship, often reserved for specific classes. Saloon passengers refers to first- and second-class passengers.

Screws – Propellers.

Scupper – An opening in the ship's side so water can escape from the deck.

Semaphore – A system of visual signalling that uses arms and flags to convey messages.

Shelter deck – A deck exposed to the weather, that shelters the upmost deck enclosed in the hull.

Stack – Smokestack or funnel.

Stanchion – An upright support post.

Starboard – The right side of the ship when looking forward.

Steerage – Third-class passengers. (Derives from them being housed near the steering gear.)

Stem – The prow of a ship, where the hull meets.

Stern – The rear of a ship.

Stoker – Person who feeds and tends the boilers' furnaces on a steamship.

Superstructure – The structure on a ship built above the hull and exposed deck. (More significant than a deckhouse.)

Tender – A boat that transports passengers to and from larger ships moored offshore.

Thwart – A seat spanning a boat, like that where a rower sits.

Track – (North Atlantic tracks) Trans-Atlantic shipping routes with eastbound and westbound lanes.

Tramp steamer – A vessel without a fixed route that will take cargo to any port.

Trim – A ship that is properly balanced.

Trimix – A mixture of nitrogen, helium and oxygen used for technical diving.

Trimmer – Person who transports coal from the bunkers to the furnaces. (Derives from their mining the coal evenly so the ship remains trim.)

Twin screw – A ship with two propellers.

Upper deck – Highest continuous deck inside the hull (see main deck).

Viz – Visibility.

Watch – Aboard ship each day is usually divided into six watches, four-hour periods when a designated part of the crew is on duty.

Well deck – Part of an open deck that is lower than the deck fore and aft of it.

Winch – Device used for hauling or lifting where a rope or chain wraps around a rotating drum.

Windjammer – A ship with sails.

Yard – A long beam (spar) centred on a mast from which sails are suspended.

ACKNOWLEDGEMENTS

WHILE WRITING THIS BOOK, I RECEIVED HELP AND SUPPORT from many people, most of whom could not know what heart I took from their interest and kind words. I cannot name them all, but equally there are some I owe thanks.

First, my parents, who so patiently endured the long hours I devoted to this work, often at the expense of all else; my brother, always interested in my progress; and my sister, my most trusted sounding board.

For the better part of a decade, Dr Ross Watkins has been my teacher and friend. It was his enthusiasm for this topic, which I hesitatingly mentioned – aware, but not really, of the immense amount of research that would be needed to do it justice – that solidified my decision to write Thia's story. This work is infinitely better for his contributions.

Dr Gary Crew, because he always knew that it was as much about *Titanic* as it was Thia, even when it took me a little longer to see things this clearly. He has an uncanny ability to cut to the heart of matters when I try to over-complicate them, and to find what's weak so I can make it strong.

Then there's Ric Waring, who so generously and with a great deal of honesty shared his *Carpathia* dive story with a stranger. Ric never asked to be written about, and I thank him for allowing it. I wish I could have done justice to the stories of all the men who dived *Carpathia* and who allowed me to include some of their experiences: Richie Stevenson, Helmuth Biechl, Tim Cashman (whose video footage was a great help), Jeff Cornish, Duncan Keates, Bruce Dunton, Mark Elliott, Edoardo Pavia, Zaid Al-obaidi, Andrea Bolzoni, and the late Carl Spencer.

I'm very grateful to Paul-Henry Nargeolet who helped me fill in critical gaps concerning RMS Titanic Inc. and Comex's survey and salvage of *Carpathia*, and who furnished the list of recovered artefacts that I had long sought. James Delgado kindly let me make copies of the ROV footage filmed by NUMA when they uncovered the wreck, which is held at Simon Fraser University's Bennett Library in Vancouver. Special thanks to the library and to Tony Power from the Special Collections and Rare Books unit for overseeing the transfer of these VHS tapes into a digital format that I could access, a feat that would have been impossible without their help.

I thank Ken Smith, who wrote the first book about *Carpathia*, for meeting with me in Newcastle and explaining a few key concepts about a ship of her time and design to a landlubber, and for putting me in touch with Ian Rae who worked in the Naval Architects department of Swan Hunter for 30 years; Ian, for answering my questions and sending me all his research materials concerning *Carpathia*; and Roger Pickenpaugh, who wrote a comprehensive biography on *Carpathia* that at times was my bible.

Tad Fitch, for sending me the affidavits made by William Prothero and other witnesses when *Carpathia* was sunk; Michael Pocock, who went to great lengths to solicit a translated copy of SM *U-55*'s log entries from a contact on my behalf; Bill Willard, for providing insights into the Bluelight expedition; and the late Edward D. Walker (Ted), for allowing me to use his beautiful painting *Carpathia to the Rescue*, which often drew my gaze as I wrote and which now graces the front cover. I'm very grateful for the exceptional generosity Ted showed me.

Special thanks to Curator Nigel Wood, for opening the West End Local History Museum and Heritage Centre especially for me and allowing me free rein. He and his wife also took me to visit Sir Arthur Rostron's grave and his former home 'Holmecroft'. It was raining, and they insisted that I stand under the umbrella. Then, for sending me the society's last copy of Brian Ticehurst's hard-to-find *Titanic's Rescuers*.

This research was funded by an Australian Government Research Training Program Scholarship and the University of the Sunshine Coast, including six weeks of fieldwork in the United Kingdom. Thanks to the university research staff who guided me through paperwork and funding applications, in particular Michelle Tucker and Kelisha Lyndon; the university's librarians who fulfilled my endless document delivery and interlibrary loan requests; and the members of the university's humanities student group, in particular Nina Gartrell, who were all doing their own postgraduate research and *just understood*.

Thanks to Holland America and Captain James Russell-Dunford, who allowed me aboard the bridge of the MS *Volendam* when I was trying to understand what it was like to operate a large ocean liner. There is no substitute for standing there and looking out at the bow and the blue horizon. Officer Samuel Hawkins for being my tour guide and explaining how things worked and why they were necessary.

Thanks to the captain and chief engineer of TSS *Earnslaw*, who allowed me into the engine room of the only coal-fired passenger steamship still operating in the southern hemisphere, and for explaining the operation of expansion engines; archaeologist Alex Croom and Roman scholar Mike Bishop for their assistance uncovering information about the Branch Wall stones placed aboard *Carpathia*; Zoe Walters, the archivist who sets the bar high for all others; and Sean and Eileen McGuinness, who so kindly put me up in Belfast, chauffeured me around and gave me a little taste of Ireland.

Finally, I am very grateful to my wonderful editors Sophie Hamley and Karen Ward for their invaluable guidance and considerable enthusiasm for this book. From the beautiful cover to the map to the index, everything is as I had hoped it would be, when I let myself imagine. Thank you.

ENDNOTES

FREQUENTLY REFERRED TO ARCHIVES, PEOPLE AND sources are abbreviated, as below.

ARCHIVES

CA, SJL – Cunard Archives, Sydney Jones Library, University of
    Liverpool
MMM – Merseyside Maritime Museum
NA – National Archives, UK
T&W – Tyne and Wear Archives, Newcastle

PEOPLE

AR – Arthur Rostron
RW – Richard (Ric) Waring

SOURCES

AI – The US Senate Inquiry [American Inquiry] into the sinking of
    Titanic (www.titanicinquiry.org)
ANTR – *A Night to Remember* by Walter Lord, St Martin's
    Griffin, 2005 [1955]

BI – The British Wreck Commissioner's Inquiry [British Inquiry] into the sinking of *Titanic* (www.titanicinquiry.org)

Carp. – *Carpathia: A Biography of the Titanic's Rescue Ship* by Roger Pickenpaugh, Otter Bay Books, 2011

C&T – *The Carpathia and the Titanic: Rescue at Sea* by George Behe, Lulu.com, 2011 (a compilation of primary source documents)

CC – *Captain of the Carpathia* by Eric Clements, Bloomsbury Publishing, 2016

ET – Encyclopaedia Titanica (www.encyclopedia-titanica.org)

NYT – *The New York Times*

PSAN – *Proceedings of the Society of Antiquities of Newcastle Upon Tyne*

RTSC – 'The Rescue of the *Titanic* Survivors by the *Carpathia*, April 15, 1912' by Arthur Rostron in *Scribner's Magazine* 53, 1913

RWI – Richard Waring Interviews

Specifications – *No. 274 Specifications of a Steel Twin Screw Steamer to be built by C.S. Swan & Hunter, Ltd., Wallsend-on-Tyne, for the Cunard Steamship Co., Ltd., Liverpool* at T&W (DS.SWH.4.5.2.274.1)

T&L – *Tramps and Ladies: My Early Years in Steamers* by James Bisset, Criterion Books, 1959

TH – *Titanic Hero* by Arthur Rostron, Amberley Publishing, 2011 (originally published as *Home from the Sea* in 1931)

TM – *Titanic Man: Carlos F. Hurd* by John and Vera Gillespie, Amereon House, 1996

TOSN – *The Other Side of the Night* by Daniel Allen Butler, Casemate, 2009

TTC – *The Titanic Commutator* produced by the Titanic Historical Society

PREFACE

To write the preface, I relied on details gleaned from visits to the Titanic Belfast museum (for shipbuilding processes) and Segedunum Roman Fort in Newcastle, England. Information about Segedunum, Wallsend, Hadrian's Wall and the Branch Wall is drawn from: W.S. Corder, 'Wallsend, Segedunum', *PSAN* 3, no. 1 (1905); *J. Collingwood Bruce's Handbook to the Roman Wall* by J. Collingwood Bruce and David Breeze, Society of Antiquaries of Newcastle upon Tyne, 2006 [1863]; *The Roman Wall* by J. Collingwood Bruce, JR Smith, 1851;

A History of Northumberland by Madeleine Hope Dodds, Andrew Reid and Company Limited, 1930; *An Archaeological Map of Hadrian's Wall* published by English Heritage, 2014; *Segedunum: Roman Fort, Baths and Museum* by W. Griffiths, P. Bidwell and G. Woodward, Tyne and Wear Museums, 2008; W.B. Griffiths, 'Note: A reinstated section of the Branch Wall at Wallsend', *The Arbeia Journal* 4 (1995); *Swan Hunter: The Pride and the Tears* by Ian Rae and Ken Smith, Tyne Bridge, 2001; *History of the Parish of Wallsend* by William Richardson, City of Newcastle upon Tyne, 1998 [1923]; *Itinerarium Septentrionale* by Alexander Gordon, printed for the author, 1726; 'Plan of Segedunum in Terms of Modern Wallsend', *PSAN* 5 (1913); and the following archival documents and photographs at T&W: shipyard plans (DS.SWH.2.4.1.2); Branch Wall marker photograph (DS.SWH.5.3.2.4.3); and excavated Branch Wall photograph (DS. SWH.5.3.2.4.2). Sources that support the stones' presence aboard *Carpathia* include: *Hadrian's Wall* by Jessie Mothersole, John Lane The Bodley Head Limited, 1924; Mike Bishop's blog entry, 'Wall Mile 0', *Per Lineam Valli* available at https://perlineamvalli.wordpress. com/2012/05/29/wall-mile-0/; a photograph of *Carpathia*'s library held at T&W (DS.SWH.4.PH.3.274.5); and 'The Cunard Line's Boston Service: The New Steamer, Carpathia', *The Liverpool Journal of Commerce* (27 April 1903).

THE BOAT RIDE

To reconstruct the boat ride I relied on RWI and the short film *Carpathia 2007 Diving Expedition* produced by Tim Cashman (provided by RW). A sample is available at https://www.youtube. com/watch?v=C6-pSYdPraM. Personal details about RW came from RWI and 'Fireman leads first divers to reach Titanic rescue ship', *Manchester Evening News* (17 September 2007). Note: The Northern Gas Team comprises Ric Waring, Richie Stevenson, Mark Elliott and Tim Cashman.

NEW YORK

Information about RMS *Olympic* comes from: T&L; and an International Mercantile Marine Line advertisement in *The Sun* (11 April 1912). Details about New York, the Hudson River, the Chelsea Piers and the Statue of Liberty are derived from 'Our Ocean Gateway', *The Sun* (3 April 1910); still image 'Great ocean liners at the docks, Hoboken, N.J.', published by The Keystone View Company, available at NYPL Digital Collection; 'Answers about the Statue of Liberty', *New York Times* (1 July 2009); and photographs: 'West Street Story: 1912' at www.shorpy.com; and 'Chelsea Piers' at www.nyc-architecture.com. Biographical information about AR comes from: TH; *Carpathia;* and CC. The number of *Carpathia*'s passengers comes from: TOSN. Biographical information about the Ogdens comes from: '*Titanic* Disaster, Ogden Family Travel Album Containing 30 Photographs Taken from the RMS Carpathia During the Rescue, April 15, 1912, Plus' (sic) at www.rarebookhub.com. Details about *Carpathia*'s interior are included in her *Specifications* at T&W (DS. SWH.4.5.2.274.1). Information about AR's encounter with the sea serpent is located in: TH (the phrase 'turning its head for all the world as a bird will on a lawn between its pecks' is a quote from this source, pg. 31); Senan Moloney, 'Rostron's Monster', ET; *Shadows in the Sea* by Harold W. McCormick, Chilton Book Company, 1963; *In the Wake of the Sea Serpents* by Bernard Heuvelmans, Rupert Hart-Davis, 1968 (includes AR's sketch); and 'On the Track of a Monster', *The Times* (9 December 1933) (the paragraph that begins: 'In the wake of the contemptuous incredulity . . .' is a paraphrase from this article). The line that reads 'a thousand souls in her care' paraphrases James Bisset in T&L, p. 283.

BELLS

Details about *Janus II* and the RMS Titanic Inc. and Comex expedition come from the brochure 'Janus: Oceanographic survey and sub-sea intervention vessel'; the articles '90 years after it sank Janus brings artefacts of the Carpathia back to the surface' and 'Interview with a specialist: Paul-Henri (sic) Nargeolet' in *Comex Magazine* 2 (2008), all available on the Comex website at http://www.comex.fr/; press release 'RMS Titanic Inc. to conduct first research and recovery expedition to RMS *Carpathia*', PR Newswire (14 August 2007); and personal correspondence with Paul-Henry Nargeolet. The scenes aboard *Ocean Dancer* and *Janus II* are reconstructed from details provided in RWI and a PowerPoint presentation about the dive provided by RW. Biographical information about Paul-Henry Nargeolet comes from: Monte Burke, 'Meet the Titanic's greatest explorer (No, it isn't James Cameron)', *Forbes* (30 March 2012). For information about the diver-bell relationship and RW's bells I draw on: RWI; and Leigh Bishop, 'Bell boys', *Diver* (February 2014). Note: The silver loving cup presented to AR by the survivors was not aboard *Carpathia* when she sank (as the *Dancer* and *Janus* teams believed). During this period it was on loan from the Rostron family to the MMM.

MAURETANIA, LUSITANIA, CARPATHIA

The italicised text is the entirety of a letter sent by Charles H. Marshall to the Commodore of the Cunard line: CA, SJL (D42/S9/5/2). Marshall was the passenger whose nieces were rescued by *Titanic* while he was aboard *Carpathia*. As near as I can date it, the letter is circa 1900–1902, as all the names were subsequently used for ships built over the next several years, with *Carpathia* first, named on 9 January 1902: see T&W (D42.B1.5). The *Encyclopaedia Britannica* (1910) and *Encyclopaedia Americana* (1835) were also consulted.

A VIOLENT SIROCCO

AR biographical information comes from: TH; and CC. Details about the Hurds' cabin is derived from *Specifications*. Details about the Hurds' voyage comes from: TM; and Katherine Hurd's letters in C&T. The experiences of Steward Robert Vaughan are derived from his account in C&T. Information about the Black Hand, Petrosino and Consul Bishop comes from: T&L; 'A Word on the Carbonari', *NYT* (11 February 1879); 'Is the Black Hand a Myth or a Terrible Reality?', *NYT* (3 March 1907); 'Petrosino Slain Assassins Gone', *NYT* (14 March 1909); 'Why Petrosino's Slayers Will Escape', *NYT* (13 May 1909); *Big Town, Big Time: A New York Epic: 1898-1998* edited by Jay Maeder, Daily News, 1998; *Joe Petrosino* by Arrigo Petacco, Mondadori, 2010; *Italian Americans in Law Enforcement* by Anne T. Ramano, Xlibris Corporation, 2010; *The Mafia at Apalachin, 1957* by Michael Newton, McFarland Incorporated Publishers, 2012; Mary Elizabeth Brown, 'Joseph Petrosino (1860–1909): International criminal conspiracies' in *The Making of Modern Immigration: An Encyclopedia of People and Ideas* edited by Patrick Hayes, ABC-CLIO, 2012; and Consul Bishop's (28 April) 1909 diary at Yale University Library (William Henry Bishop Papers: MS 83/3/19/89-90).

HUNTING

The information in this chapter is sourced from film footage (used with permission) including: 'Clive NUMA and the Carpathia' and 'Clive Cussler and James Delgado Discussing the Search for Carpathia' on Shipwreck Central TV on YouTube; and episode 'The Search for

Carpathia' in *The Sea Hunters* television series. Additional sources include: *Adventures of a Sea Hunter* by James Delgado, Douglas and McIntyre, 2009; *The Sea Hunters II: Diving the World's Most Famous Shipwrecks* by Clive Cussler and Craig Dirgo, Arrow Books, 2003; and personal correspondence with John Kearney from the Baltimore Diving and Watersport Centre.

VIRGIN WRECKS

The information in this chapter is derived from: RWI; Richie Stevenson, 'Team Spirit – Diving the Dasher' *990 UK Diving in Depth* 2, no. 6 (2000); Mark Reeve, 'The Deepest Cold Water Wreck Dive', *990 UK Diving in Depth* 2, no. 6 (2000); Richie Stevenson, 'Carpathia: A Dive to Remember', *990 UK Diving in Depth* 3, no. 3 (2001); Ric Waring, 'In deep on the Dasher', *Diver* (August 2001); *The Secrets of HMS Dasher* by John and Noreen Steele, Argyll, 2004; and *Aircraft-Carrying Ships of the Royal Navy* by Maurice Cocker, History Press Limited, 2008.

MULE SHIP

The Hurds' experiences are detailed in Katherine Hurd's letter to her sister Francis Lee dated 13 April 1912 held in the Frances Hurd Stadler *Titanic* Collection at the Missouri History Museum. The breakfast fare is derived from *Carpathia* menu cards available on Google images. The service led by AR is described in Katherine Hurd's letter to her sister Emily in C&T. Details of *Carpathia*'s wireless machine, and Dr Blackmarr's experiences the evening prior to the disaster, are in 'Frank Blackmarr', C&T. Biographical information pertaining to Dr Blackmarr is derived from: Craig Stringer, 'RMS Carpathia: Out of the dark of the dawn', *ET*. The account of the wireless contacts and messages are derived from: T&L; *Titanic Calling: Wireless Communications During the Great Disaster* edited by Michael Hughes and Katherine Bosworth, Bodleian Library, 2012; the *Carpathia*'s procès-verbal (wireless operator's log), available in the Marconi Archives at the Bodleian Library, University of Oxford and online at www.marconicalling.co.uk; 'Ice Messages Received' in BI; and Harold Cottam's testimony, AI. Harold Cottam's account of the evening is in 'Harold Cottam', C&T. For details on the friendship between Harold Bride and Harold Cottam see: Aurora Brynn, 'Harold Bride' at http://web.archive.org/web/20050511111920/http://www.geocities.com/College-Park/Library/7958/bride.html. Sources relating to the ship's inspection:

Carp.; TOSN; *Carpathia* general arrangement and deck plans at MMM (B/CUN/8/1903.1/1/1-4) (B/CUN/8/1903.1/2/1-5); photographs of *Carpathia*'s builders model which is located at Segedunum Roman Fort museum. The smoke room is described in: *Carp.*; and 'The Cunard Lines Boston Service / The New Steamer, Carpathia', *The Liverpool Journal of Commerce* (27 April 1903). Information about marine boilers: John Riley, 'Marine engines and boilers', at www.environment.nsw.gov.au. Information pertaining to mules and donkeys is derived from: *The Natural Superiority of Mules* by John Hauer, Skyhorse Publishing Company, 2013; *Animals in the Military* by John M. Kistler, ABC-CLIO, 2011; 'Donkeys' at http://www.mountvernon.org. For sources relating to *Carinthia* see: *Cargo Liners: An Illustrated History* by Ambrose Greenway, Seaforth Publishing, 2012; 'Carinthia Made a Speedy Trip', *Boston Evening Transcript* (27 December 1899); 'On the Way to South Africa Vessel Went Ashore at Full Speed Off The Hayti Coast', *St. Louis Post-Dispatch* (19 May 1900); 'Mule Herders Complain', *NYT* (29 June 1900); 'Wrecked Seamen Arrive', *Rockland County Journal* (30 June 1900); and '(No. 6072.) "CARINTHIA" (S.S.)' in the Board of Trade Wreck Reports held by Southampton City Council Libraries. The phrase 'city in miniature while at sea' is a quote from AR cited in CC, pg. 165. Charles Marshall's nieces: 'Mrs Caroline Lane Brown', 'Mrs Charlotte Appleton' and 'Mrs Malvina Helen Cornell' at ET; the marconigram sent from Charlotte Appleton to Charles Marshall is part of John Siggins' private collection of *Titanic* memorabilia. Note that during this period Haiti was referred to as Hayti, however I have used the modern spelling to avoid confusion.

WHAT'S THAT LYING IN THE SAND?

This chapter is constructed from *The Sea Hunters II: Diving the World's Most Famous Shipwreck*s by Clive Cussler and Craig Dirgo, Arrow Books, 2003; *Adventures of a Sea Hunter* by James Delgado, Douglas and McIntyre, 2009; and *Carpathia* ROV tapes in the James Delgado Fonds, Special Collections and Rare Books, Simon Fraser University Library, (MsC 123: 51.7-14 and 52.1).

THE BEGINNING OF THE END

Information concerning WWI is generally available and so not listed here. Note that during this period Serbia was referred to as Servia, however I have used the modern spelling to avoid confusion.

Information about Franz and Sophie: *The Assassination of the Archduke* by Greg King and Sue Woolmans, Macmillan, 2013. *Carpathia*'s positions are derived from Cunard's *Sailings and Arrivals: Atlantic Steamers (1878–1920)* (D42/AC18/1) at CA, SJL; and *Carpathia*'s Official Log Book (BT 100/310) at NA (the deaths aboard are also recorded in this source). Black Hand and Carbonari: 'Immigrants Form Blackmail Band', *New York Herald* (6 April 1903); and 'Ysobel Finished for New Year Debut', *NYT* (21 November 1910). Whitehead Torpedo: *The History of the Submarine from the Beginning Until WWI* by Farnham Bishop, Salzwasser-Verlag, 2010 [1916]. Events at Fiume and Malta: see log book above; letter from Belle K. Fitzgerald, *Mexico Missouri Message* (10 September 1914); Maud R. Starr, 'My Pilgrimage', *New Smyrna Daily News* (16 October 1914); 'Enthusiasm in Malta', *Gloucestershire Echo* (7 August 1914); 'Monte Carlo Moratorium', *NYT* (3 September 1914); 'Former Herald Reporter War Refugee', *The Washington Herald* (13 September 1914); 'Rochdalian with the Fleet', *Rochdale Observer* (17 October 1914); 'Three Refugees Ships Arrive with More Tales of Hardships', *NYT* (25 August 1914); 'Refugees Sing as Ship Docks', *The Boston Globe* (3 September 1914); 'Italians Generous to all Americans', *The Evening Star* (9 September 1914); 'Carpathia Arrives 30 Days from Austria', *The Evening World* (2 September 1914); '1,000 Home From Europe; Few Sail', *New York Tribune* (3 September 1914); and 'Famous Rescue Ship Returns Refugees', *Indianapolis Star* (3 September 1914). Note that some news reports give conflicting details and I have done my best to determine which details are correct, for example the number of ships in the Anglo-French Fleet. Additionally, while I have written *Carpathia* as escaping Fiume, in line with several accounts, there is a brief article in the *Wall Street Journal* ('Trans-Atlantic Ship News', 4 September 1914) that says *Carpathia* was ordered out of port, but I could locate no other supporting evidence.

THE BEGINNING OF THE STORY

These scenes are recreated from memory and a journal I kept while abroad. Also, RWI.

THE FIRST EXPEDITION

Details in this chapter are derived from: RWI; Richie Stevenson, 'Carpathia: A Dive to Remember', *990 UK Diving in Depth* 3, no. 3 (2001); Tim Cashman, 'RMS Carpathia 2007 Dive Expedition',

Dive Pacific iss. 104 (2008); Maggie Lee and Rachel Shields, '*Titanic* Rescue Ship Yields Up its Treasures', *The Independent* (16 September 2007); *Shipwrecks of the Cunard Line* by Sam Warwick and Mike Roussel, The History Press, 2012; articles in *Comex Magazine* noted in 'Bells' endnotes; *Specifications*; and personal correspondence with Bruce Dunton.

CQD OM

Various accounts of that night are given in: TH; RTSC; T&L; Harold Cottam's and AR's testimony, AI; 'Captain Rostron's handwritten account of the disaster' on ET; Frank Blackmarr, William Collopy, Harold Cottam, Cecil R. Francis, Arpad Lengyel and Arthur Rostron in C&T; and ANTR. Crew names: 'Carpathia Passengers and Crew' on ET. *Carpathia*'s position at the time of the distress call was calculated by: Samuel Halpern, '12:35 A.M. Apparent Time Carpathia' at www.glts.org and Dave Gittins, 'The Rescue by the SS Carpathia: Carpathia's Navigation' in *Report into the Loss of the SS Titanic: A Centennial Reappraisal* by Samuel Halpern et al., The History Press, 2016. Sentence beginning: 'Spotting an iceberg ...' paraphrases AR's testimony, BI.

THE MAIDEN VOYAGE

Details in this chapter are derived from witness accounts collated in C&T. These include: Mrs Charles M. Hutchison (quoted directly in the opening paragraph), Robert Vaughan, Unknown Steward, Unknown Crewman (steward #1), Mrs Louis Mansfield Ogden, Arpad Lengyel, Ernest St Clair, Howard Chapin, Mrs Charles F. Crain, P.M. Albert Hogue and May Birkhead. Information is also derived from: TH; ANTR; TOSN; RTSC; T&L; AR's testimony in BI and AI. To describe the operations of a coal-fired steamship I toured the engine room of TSS *Earnslaw* at Lake Wakatipu in New Zealand. The presence of the northern lights is noted in: Laurence Beesley, 'The Loss of the SS Titanic: Its story and its lessons' in *The Story of the Titanic, as Told by Its Survivors* edited by Jack Winocour, Dover Publications Inc., 1960; and *Great Tales from British History: On the Eve of the Titanic Disaster* by W. B. Bartlett, Amberley Publishing, 2014. Although in this chapter I write that the pressure gauge aboard *Carpathia* was covered over with an engineer's cap, I could not locate the origin of this information. It may simply be rumour; however, as the report persists I have included it, but remain unsure as to its truth. See: 'Clive Cussler speaks on the SOS from Titanic to Carpathia' on Shipwreck Central TV on YouTube. Information about *Carpathia*'s trial trip and maiden voyage comes from: Philip A. Maughan, 'Maiden Voyage of the RMS Carpathia', *The Mid-Tyne Link* at T&W (DS.SWH/5/4/5/SH274/1); 'The North Pier', *Shields Daily Gazette* (12 June 1903); Swan & Hunter Sea Trials Notebook no. 3 at T&W (DS.SWH/4/4/3/2); and *Specifications*. Information about Carpathius comes from: *Carpathia*; 'Carpathia Brings a Healthy-Looking Set of Immigrants on Maiden Voyage', *Boston Journal* (15 May 1903); *Carpathia*'s Official Log Book (BT 100/150) at NA (includes the name of the doctor and the coordinates where the birth occurred); and the birth and death records of John Kelley which are available in 'Massachusetts Births and Christenings, 1639–1915' (https://familysearch.org/ark:/61903/1:1:F46S-QSC) and 'Massachusetts Deaths and Burials, 1795–1910' (https://familysearch.org/ark:/61903/1:1:FHWB-B2H). These records are transcribed on familysearch.org. The transcriptions contain errors in ship name (SS *Norporttna* instead of *Carpathia*) and spelling of father's name and surname (Michard instead of Richard, Kelly instead of Kelley) however I have viewed the originals which correctly detail the baby's birth at sea on *Carpathia*, and his death record notes his first name. Information about Hy-Brasil is derived from: *Hy Brasil: The Metamorphosis of an Island: From Cartographic Error to Celtic Elysium* by Barbara Freitag, Rodopi, 2013; *The Frozen Echo* by Kirsten A. Seaver, Stanford University Press, 1996; *In Northern Mists* by Fridtjof Nansen, Fredick A. Stokes Company, 1911; and *Mysterious Celtic Mythology in American Folklore* by Bob Curran, Pelican Publishing Company, 2010.

SALVOR-IN-POSSESSION

Details in this chapter are derived from: RWI; Tim Cashman, 'RMS Carpathia 2007 Dive Expedition', *Dive Pacific* iss. 104 (2008); and, in particular, for pp. 156–60 of this chapter, the following sources were referred to: 'Titanic Rescue Ship to be Filmed', BBC News (10 July 2004) at http://news.bbc.co.uk/2/hi/uk_news/northern_ireland/3882701.stm; Jeff Testerman, 'A "Titanic" Tale Behind Bodies', *Tampa Bay Times* (15 August 2005) at https://web.archive.org/web/20160304100432/http://www.sptimes.com/2005/08/15/Tampabay/A__Titanic__tale_behi.shtml; Andrew Norfolk and Roger Beam, 'Secret Voyage to take Titanic Treasures', *The Times* (1 May 2004); Marc Davis, 'Titanic Artefacts may have been Plundered', *The Virginian-Pilot* (23 March 2003) at https://web.archive.org/

web/20030407175253/https:/pilotonline.com/news/nw0323tit.html; Mike Lee, 'Plundering the Titanic', ABC News (30 October 2006) at http://abcnews.go.com/International/story?id=2615999&page=1; press release 'Inside Out: Plundering the Titanic' (30 October 2006) at http://www.bbc.co.uk/pressoffice/pressreleases/stories/2006/10_october/30/titanic.shtml; D'Addario v. Geller, 04-1687 (4th Cir. 2005) at www.courtlistener.com https://www.courtlistener.com/opinion/1015543/daddario-v-geller/; RMS Titanic Inc. Annual Report 2002 at https://www.sec.gov/Archives/edgar/data/796764/000104488502000053/form10k.txt; RMS Titanic Inc. Annual Report 2003 at https://doc.morningstar.com/Document/22b0113e4514b9bc.msdoc/original?clientid=globaldocuments&key=52dbc583e1012395; RMS Titanic Inc. Annual Report 2007 at https://www.sec.gov/Archives/edgar/data/796764/000095015207004290/l26114ae10vk.htm; RMS Titanic Inc. Annual Report 2009 at https://www.sec.gov/Archives/edgar/data/796764/000095012309018710/l36885ae10vkza.htm; RMS Titanic Inc. Current Report 31 October 2002 at https://www.sec.gov/Archives/edgar/data/796764/000104488502000081/form8k.txt; RMS Titanic Inc. Current Report 19 November 2002 at https://www.sec.gov/Archives/edgar/data/796764/000104488502000083/form8k.txt; RMS Titanic Inc. Preliminary Proxy Statement 17 January 2003 at https://www.sec.gov/Archives/edgar/data/796764/000104488503000003/schedule14a.txt; US Securities and Exchange Commission Litigation Release No. 18943/October 26, 2004, SEC v. Arnold Geller, et al. at https://www.sec.gov/litigation/litreleases/lr18943.htm; D'Addario v. Geller Settlement Agreement at https://www.sec.gov/Archives/edgar/data/796764/000079676406000023/ex10-25.txt; Seaventures Ltd vs. RMS Titanic Inc., 2014-CA-000917-O, (9th Cir. Orange County) at www.myorangeclerk.com; Seaventures Ltd. corporation details at https://www5.sos.state.oh.us/ords/f?p=100:7:::NO:7:P7_CHARTER_NUM:1680752 Original Filing Date: 02/27/2007; Elizabeth Varner, 'R.M.S. Titanic: Underwater Cultural Heritage's Sacrifice', *Journal of Business Law*, (June 2012) at https://ssrn.com/abstract=2132068; and personal correspondence with Bill Willard. Note: In 2009, Arnie Geller ceased all connection with RMS Titanic Inc. other than as shareholder and the company has since operated under a new board of directors. In 2011, RMS Titanic Inc. were awarded title to the *Titanic* artefacts, with a number of stipulations including that the artefacts can only be sold as a collection, and must remain available for public display, research and education.

THE RESCUE

In this chapter I draw directly on the images and words used to describe events by the passengers and witnesses aboard *Carpathia*. I paraphrase them and sometimes quote brief phrases, for example 'like a snake'. These have been edited and integrated, respecting the source information and this work's narrative voice. It would be difficult to note individual instances, what phrases were used and if/how they were edited, so I will simply include a source list. From C&T: Mrs Charles F. Crain, P. M. Albert Hogue, Arpad Lengyel, Mrs Tim H. Hardgrove, Mrs Charles M. Hutchison, Charles Hutchison, Frank Blackmarr, Maurice McKenna, Cecil R. Francis, Carlos Hurd, May Birkhead, Arthur Rostron and Robert Vaughan ('The absolute beauty'). Sir Cosmo Duff-Gordon's and AR's testimony in BI; Frederick D. Ray's, Harold Lowe's, Bruce Ismay's and Joseph Boxhall's testimony in AI; Mr Emilio Ilario Giuseppe Portaluppi, Mr Henry Sleeper Harper, Miss Elisabeth Walton Allen, Mrs Mahala Douglas (née Dutton) on ET; 'Ismay in Command Says Mrs. Appleton', *Brooklyn Daily Eagle* (19 April 1912); 'Mrs. C. E. H. Stengel', *Newark Evening News* (24 January 1956); 'Dr Dodge's Wife tells story of Titanic Wreck', *San Francisco Bulletin* (30 April 1912); 'Milford man was on Titanic', *The Milford Cabinet* (April 1912); 'Girl Went Down to Save Another', *Boston Daily Globe* (21 April 1912) (Caroline Brown's dialogue is adapted from this article); CC; RTSC; T&L; TH; TOSN; ANTR; *Her Name, Titanic* by Charles R. Pellegrino, McGraw-Hill Publishing Company, 1988; *The Truth about Titanic* by Col. Archibald Gracie, Jazzybee Verlag, 2012 [1913]; *Finding Dorothy: A Biography of Dorothy Gibson* by Randy Bryan Bigham, Lulu Press Inc., 2014; *Polar: The Titanic Bear* by Daisy Corning Stone Spedden and Laurie McGaw, Madison Press Books, 2002; and *Unsinkable: The full story of the RMS Titanic* by Daniel Allen Butler, Stackpole Books, 1998. Much attention has been given to *Titanic*'s lifeboat launch sequence but less to the lifeboats' arrival at *Carpathia*. George Behe has estimated their arrival times in 'The Recovery of Titanic's Lifeboats' in *Report into the Loss of the SS Titanic: A Centennial Reappraisal* by Samuel Halpern et al, The History Press, 2016, but Behe cautions that witness statements and evidence is often contradictory so they can only be approximations (the estimated number of survivors in each lifeboat is also in this book). I use the order of arrival detailed by journalist George Jacub (which varies slightly from Behe's) in 'The order Titanic's lifeboats reached the *Carpathia*. Maybe' at www.titanicsecrets.blogspot.com.au as Jacub explains the process by how he arrived at this order.

Note: At the British inquiry, Arthur Rostron reported that *Carpathia* reached a speed of 17.5 knots while steaming to *Titanic*'s position, an incredible feat for a ship built to steam at only 14 knots. Rostron calculated his speed based on the premise that he was 58 miles from *Titanic* and it took 3 hours and 25 minutes to reach the lifeboats. With *Titanic*'s wreck now discovered, we know that her reported position at the time of the disaster was incorrect and that *Carpathia* steamed less than the 58 miles Rostron supposed. While it is impossible to know what speed *Carpathia* attained, 15 or perhaps 16 knots is far more likely than the legendary 17.5 knots. For these reasons, I have not attributed a specific speed to *Carpathia*'s rescue mission – though without question, she went faster than she had ever gone before. See: Dave Gittins, 'Carpathia's Navigation' in *Report into the Loss of the SS Titanic: A Centennial Reappraisal* by Samuel Halpern et al, The History Press, 2016.

WAR SERVICE

Information in this chapter derived from: *Carpathia*; 'Captain Prothero is Retired at 60', *NYT* (26 May 1931); 'Refugees Sing as Ship Docks', *Boston Globe* (3 September 1914); 'Big Gun Mounted by the Carpathia', *New York Herald* (2 September 1916); 'Trade Division Records: Defensively Armed Merchant Vessels' at NA (ADM 137.2829); Oliver Gliech, 'Rubber', *International Encyclopedia of the First World War* at http://encyclopedia.1914-1918-online.net. HMT *Kurd* and Whitley Bomber: RWI; *Straight & True* by Peter Coupland, Leo Cooper, 1997; *The Other Few* by Larry Donnelly, Red Kite, 2004; and Ted Godding, 'My First Ship HMT Kurd' at http://www.harry-tates.org.uk/veteranstales8.htm.

THE HARDEST MOMENT

The same process described in 'The Rescue' is used in this chapter. Sources from C&T include: Howard Chapin, Wallace Bradford, Carlos Hurd, Arthur Rostron, Mrs Charles M. Hutchison, Robert Vaughan, Frank Blackmarr, John Cargill, Philip Mauro, Arpad Lengyel, Empsie [Emma Hutchinson], May Birkhead, Mrs Tim H. Hardgrove, Maurice McKenna, Chauncey Parsons, and Unknown Steward. Other sources include: *Carpathia*; TM; RTSC; CC; T&L; Joseph Ismay, Harold Bride, Harold Cottam, Guglielmo Marconi and AR's testimony in

AI; Sir Cosmo Duff-Gordon's testimony in BI; Master Edmond Roger Navratil, Mr Frederic Kimber Seward, Mr Samuel L. Goldenberg, Mr Mauritz Hokan Björnström-Steffansson, Mr Isaac Gerald Frauenthal, Mr Karl Howell Behr, Mrs Margaret Brown (Molly Brown) (née Tobin) at ET; 'Messages sent to and from Carpathia' available in the Marconi Archives at the Bodleian Library, University of Oxford and online at www.marconicalling.co.uk; *Carpathia*; *Polar: The Titanic Bear* by Daisy Corning Stone Spedden and Laurie McGaw, Madison Press Books, 2002; Laurence Beesley, 'The Loss of the SS Titanic: Its story and its lessons' in *The Story of the Titanic, as Told by Its Survivors* edited by Jack Winocour, Dover Publications Inc., 1960; Tad Fitch and Bill Wormstedt, 'An account of the saving of those on board' in *Report into the Loss of the SS Titanic: A Centennial Reappraisal* by Samuel Halpern et al., The History Press, 2016; *Finding Dorothy: A Biography of Dorothy Gibson* by Randy Bryan Bigham, Lulu Press Inc., 2014; *On a Sea of Glass: The Life and Loss of the RMS Titanic* by Tad Fitch, J. Kent Layton and Bill Wormstedt, Amberley, Publishing, 2013; extract from 'Roaming Around' by Alec Bagot contributed by John Godl at www.titanichistoricalsociety.org; *The Maiden Voyage* by Geoffrey Marcus, Unwin Paperbacks, 1988 [1969]; *Lost Voices from the Titanic* by Nick Barratt, Arrow Books, 2010; *Titanic: A Night Remembered* by Stephanie Barczewski, Continuum International Publishing Group, 2011; Nicola Greeley-Smith, 'No Light on the Mystery Hiding the Identity of Two Waifs of the Sea', *Evening World* (22 April 1912); Frances Hurd Stadler, 'Every Newspaperman's Dream', *TTC* 17 no. 3 (Nov. 1993 – Jan. 1994); 'Futrelle Met Death Like Hero Says Wife', *Worcester Telegram* (20 April 1912); 'Carpathia Off Sable Island', *Boston Daily Globe* (17 April 1912); 'Globe Man Finds Only 705 Saved', *Boston Daily Globe* (18 April 1912); 'First Chicago Message From Carpathia and its Sender', *Chicago Tribune* (18 April 1912); 'Tragedy Summed up by English Survivor', *NYT* (21 April 1912); 'Carpathia here tonight with Titanic's Survivors' *NYT* (18 April 1912); 'Marconi Co Asked "American" in "Name of Humanity" to Put its Man on Board Carpathia', *New York American* (19 April 1912); 'Her Husband went down with the Titanic', *Liberty Magazine* (23 April 1932); 'Dr Dodge's Wife Tells Story of Titanic Wreck', *San Francisco Bulletin* (30 April 1912); 'Sumptuous Rubaiyat lost on Titanic', *Iran Times* (22 January 2010); and Cunard Company rule book at CA, SJL (D42/GM22/4/4).

Note: The father of the Titanic Orphans was not a widower, but had kidnapped his sons from their mother (with whom they were later reunited); however, the world was not aware of this at the time of the events. Also, though Rostron wired that *Carpathia* had picked up 705 survivors, the British Inquiry found the correct number of survivors to be 711, and the figure most often accepted today is 712. Also, there is significant controversy surrounding SS *Californian*, which was the closest ship to *Titanic* and saw her distress rockets, but did not render aid. This controversy is not mentioned at the point where *Californian* appears in this chapter because it did not emerge until later, during the US Senate Inquiry into the sinking. Finally, the article Carlos Hurd wrote about the disaster while aboard *Carpathia* mentions the women who were in *Carpathia*'s library as though he interviewed them, but Katherine helped him and reported the stories women told her to him, so if the library was off limits to men then it stands to reason that Katherine most likely conducted these interviews.

ARTEFACTS

This chapter is constructed from: RWI; Maggie Lee and Rachel Shields, '*Titanic* Rescue Ship Yields Up its Treasures', *The Independent* (16 September 2007); Tim Cashman, 'RMS Carpathia 2007 Dive Expedition', *Dive Pacific* iss. 104 (2008); 'Carl Spencer Eurotek Co-Founder' obituary at www.eurotek.uk.com/carlspencer.htm (access using the Internet Archive); 'The Titanic Inquiry: The Presentation to Carpathia Heroes', *Cork Free Press* (10 June 1912); *Comex Magazine* (see 'Bells' endnotes); and personal correspondence with Paul-Henry Nargeolet.

RETURN TO NEW YORK

Details in this chapter are derived from: CC; TH; TM; T&L; TOSN; RTSC; Harold Cottam's, Guglielmo Marconi's and AR's testimony in AI; *The Sinking of the Titanic* edited by Logan Marshall, Tales End Press, 2012 [1912]; *The Titanic: End of A Dream* by Wyn Craig Wade, Penguin Books, 1986; *Pilot Lore: From Sail to Steam* published by United New York and New Jersey Sandy Hook Pilots Benevolent Associations, 1922; *The Ambulance: A History* by Ryan Corbett Bell, McFarland & Company Inc., 2009; *Titanic Style* by Grace Evans, Skyhorse Publishing, 2012; *The Maiden Voyage* by Geoffrey Marcus, Unwin Paperbacks, 1988 [1969]; Carlos Hurd, Arpad Lengyel and Mary Fabian in C&T; 'Waiting for Carpathia', *Boston Globe* (19 April 1912); '"My Hands were Tied" says Carpathia's Captain as to News Suppression', *New York American* (19 April 1912); 'St Louisan Tells of Tragic Scenes at Titanic's Grave', *St Louis Post-Dispatch* (21 April 1912); Frances Hurd Stadler, 'Every Newspaperman's Dream', *TTC*

17 no. 3 (Nov. 1993 – Jan. 1994); 'Rescue Ship Arrives—Thousands Gather at the Pier', *NYT* (19 April 1912); 'A Passage into History: Lawrence Stoudenmire's account of the rescue', *TTC* (Summer 1979); 'Crowd on Pier Frantic to Reach Survivors', *New York Tribune* (19 April 1912); 'City's Arms Flung out to Survivors', *NYT* (18 April 1912); 'Cheers for Carpathia as she Departs', *Evening Star* (20 April 1912); 'Women to Care for Steerage Survivors', *NYT* (18 April 1912); 'Cardinal Farley directed first aid to the survivors', *The Evening World* (20 April 1912); 'Meets Carpathia', *Oak Leaves* (27 April 1912); 'New Chelsea Piers Open To-morrow', *NYT* (20 Feb 1910); 'Iceberg tore into the Titanic's Side – Carpathia lands 705 Rescued – 1,475 Dead', *The Sun* (19 April 1912); 'Crowd's Early Arrival Kept Police Hustling', *The Sun* (19 April 1912); 'Crowd on Pier Frantic to Reach Survivors', *The Sun* (19 April 1912); 'Baby Girl Saved From Sea', *The Greenville Journal* (April 25, 1912); Kenneth L. Cannon II, 'Isaac Russell's remarkable interview with Harold Bride, sole surviving wireless operator from the Titanic', *Utah Historical Quarterly* 81, no. 4 (2013); and *Charles Chapin's Story Written in Sing Sing Prison* by Charles Chapin, G.P. Putnam's Sons, 1920. Sentence containing 'fleet of small destroyers bombarding a battleship' paraphrases a reporter cited in *Carpathia*, pg. 99.

WHITE WAKE

This chapter is constructed from: RWI; 'Under Pressure: An amateur dive team makes a historic visit to RMS Carpathia', *Scuba Diving* (January 2008); *Carpathia*; records for convoy O.L.24 in 'Convoys: OL21 – OL41' at NA (ADM 137/2618); files for SS *Carpathia* (box 1468) and *British Major* (box 1464) in 'RG 45: Naval Records Collection and Library, Entry 520 Subject File, 1911–1927' at US National Archives and Records Administration (includes witness affidavits); *Carpathia*'s Crew Agreement (BT 100/310) at NA; Outwards passenger list 1890–1960 at NA (BT 27/886); *Remarks on Submarine Tactics Against Convoys* by Navy Department Office of Naval Intelligence (1917) at www.history.navy.mil; Paul E. Fontenoy, 'Convoy System' in *World War I: Encyclopedia* vol.1 edited by Spencer Tucker, ABC-CLIO, 2005; *A Million Ocean Miles* by Sir Edgar T. Britten, Hutchinson & Co., 1936; 'Captain Prothero is Retired at 60', *NYT* (26 May 1931); 'Launch of Prince Liner', *Whitby Gazette* (17 January 1913); 'The Carpathia Torpedoed', *The Times* (20 July 1918); William Prothero, 'Sinking of the Carpathia', *TTC* 22, no.1 (1998); 'Tells of Carpathia Sinking', *NYT* (7 August 1918); 'Cunarder Sunk', *The Fife Free Press*

(27 July 1918); 'Carpathia Cut in Half', *NYT* (21 July 1918); personal correspondence with Paul-Henry Nargeolet; Michael W. Pocock, 'Daily Event for July 31, 2008' at www.MaritimeQuest.com; and *U-55* Kriegstagebuch (log book) 17 July 1918 supplied by Michael Pocock. The comparison between a school of fish and a zigzagging convoy is paraphrased from: *The Victory at Sea* by Burton J. Hendrick and William Sowden Sims, Doubleday, Page and Company, 1920.

INDEX

Carpathia Dive Expedition 2007. (Courtesy of Ric Waring, front left)

Ocean Dancer, the dive expedition boat. (Courtesy of Ric Waring)